# Therapy American Style

# Therapy American Style:

## Person Power through Self Help

**Kenneth B. Matheny**
**and**
**Richard J. Riordan**

Nelson-Hall nh Chicago

Library of Congress Cataloging in Publication Data

Matheny, Kenneth B.
    Therapy American style.

        Bibliography: p.
        Includes index.
        1. Success.  2.  Personality changes.
    3.  Psychotherapy.  I.  Riordan, Richard J.,
    joint author.  II.  Title.
    BF637.S8M33        158'.1        79-4283
    ISBN O-88229-417-2

Manufactured in the United States of America

        10   9   8   7   6   5   4   3   2   1

# Contents

# Preface

While a person experiences a buoyant sense of involvement and freedom when one is truly in charge of one's life, one often feels detached and constricted when one's life is managed by others—however benign the dictatorship. There is an inherent need within all of us to run our own lives, to influence our own destinies. Henley, perhaps, was expressing this need when he wrote, "I am the master of my fate; I am the captain of my soul." The same need must have prompted the writer of a popular song to exuberantly declare, "I did it *my* way!"

Perhaps a significant amount of societal unrest stems from the beginning stages of a revolution for self-respect, for self-importance, for self-control. People feel best when they *share* control, especially in regard to decisions affecting their own lives.

People can do a great deal more for themselves than they realize. This is especially true when it comes to mental health and psychological growth. While this book is not meant to debunk or disparage the significant contribution of professionally trained therapists to the recovery of seriously disturbed persons, the authors do maintain that many people can successfully "treat" themselves for much of the warping that results from the chronic stress of life.

This book is divided into four parts. In part I, the groundwork is laid for self-treatment by discussing issues related to self-designed change and the crippling nature of a sense of personal helplessness. Part II presents approaches to the strengthening of one's motivation to change. Part III contains available techniques for improving the functioning aspects of the body, as well as the more promising methods for coping with one's emotional life. Part IV is a series of techniques for influencing the behavior of others.

The authors have done considerable screening in selecting the approaches, methods, and techniques presented here. They felt it was better to employ their judgment in order to reduce the size of the book rather than to offer the reader a potpourri of unscreened techniques. The authors believe that each of these prescriptions has proven useful to others. No *one* treatment, however, seems to work equally well for everyone. Therefore, the reader is invited to select the technique or techniques that appear most consistent with his lifestyle from among the alternatives offered.

Don't expect miracles. It took a long time to forge present traits and habits, and even with concentrated effort, *change will come slowly.* Still, few feelings are more rewarding than the sense of Person Power that can and often does result from successful attempts at self-designed change and growth.

# Part I
# Taking Charge

One of the most telling things about people is the degree to which they are willing to direct their own lives. It is easier and less threatening to lean on others. The confidence to direct one's own therapy and personal growth comes late to many. They lack confidence in their judgment. They feel they are not bright enough, skillful enough, or experienced enough to treat themselves, and so they depend on the experts.

While there are occasions when one must depend on professional assistance, nevertheless, most people are perfectly capable of doing most things for themselves. Dependent behavior breeds a childlike dependency. The more one leans on others, the less powerful one feels. In this volume the authors hope to contribute to the reader's sense of Person Power by making him aware of the psychotechnology of self-control.

In chapter 1, which is entitled "Self-Administered Therapy," the tendency to depend on others, the relationship between self-acceptance and the desire to improve, a model for changing behavior, and the criteria used in selecting the many techniques and approaches explained in this volume are discussed.

In chapter 2, "The Sense of Helplessness," the debilitating effects of growing helplessness, the beliefs that

1

contribute to it, and the natural tendency to avoid the anxiety that results from taking responsibility for oneself are discussed.

In part I the authors attempt to create a mind-set to encourage the reader to feel more hopeful about making changes in his life. There are few things in life as rewarding as feeling in control. This feeling is sadly lacking in many lives, and life for these people is far less invigorating and real as a result. Life does not have to be this way, and these chapters seek to raise the reader's hopes for greater self-management.

# 1. Self-Administered Therapy

*Be a lamp unto your own feet; do not seek outside
yourself.*

Buddha

*The Kingdom of Heaven is not "lo here" nor "lo
there"; it is within.*

Jesus

The practice of psychotherapy has a questionable batting
average. Shortly after people stopped locking the emotionally disturbed away from public view, they began
referring them to a cadre of psychoanalysts who probed,
analyzed, and interpreted. Therapy consisted largely of
a trip into the client's foggy past to resurrect unfortunate experiences with parents, siblings, and peers. Freud
reigned, and tedious analyses of the patients' *id, ego,*
and *superego* were thought to yield insights regarding
one's complexes.

Many mental health workers became impatient with
the mysticism that surrounded this approach. The
Freudian prescription was time-consuming and expensive, and its results were questionable. One researcher
(Eysenck, 1965) contended that time itself heals just as
effectively as this therapy.

Other approaches, such as existentialism and behaviorism, challenged the iron grasp of Freudianism upon mental health theory and practice. The skimpy research comparing various psychotherapeutic approaches has so far failed to declare a victor—all seem to have their strengths and weaknesses, which also vary depending on the client. The confusion has led some to believe that they might do just as well for themselves, that they might become their own therapists.

### Independence-Interdependence Dilemma

The human condition involves *inter*dependence. Yet, child-rearing methods in Western cultures view *inde*pendence as a sign of maturity. Independence is fostered even though, of necessity, many persons rely on each other for many of their basic needs. Communal living requires people to respect the rights of others while trying to meet their personal needs. Indeed, much of the process of growing up is concerned with developing an appreciation for interdependence. But herein lies the dilemma: how to produce confident, independent persons who can function maximally in an increasingly interdependent culture.

As the world has grown more complex, people have created a baffling web of technologies and systems to support the increasingly esoteric demands of humans. Ivan Illich (1971) cites the cancerous growth of professionalism as one such trend. As soon as people begin to feel powerless in the face of a social or technological problem, they seek out specialists with the expertise to relieve these feelings. They respond to the slightest feeling of helplessness with a quickness to seek help from others instead of a determined search for latent resources within themselves. The authors hope to substitute this tendency to lean on others with a program of self-control.

### Doing-Being Dilemma

One book on growth groups (Lewis and Streitfeld, 1970) stated, "You don't have to be sick to get better."

Most people are sensitive to the slightest implication that they contain some weakness or flaw. They spend a great amount of time and energy trying to project an image that appears favorably in the eyes of others. It is natural that people frequently ignore areas of their lives where the potential for increased effectiveness is greatest. There is room in everyone's life for personal growth. One does not have to be seriously disturbed in order to use psychotechnology for personal improvement.

How can one continue to strive for improvement, knowing that one will never reach perfection, and yet accept oneself as one is? For self-acceptance is the first requirement for good mental health. The belief that one *should* be perfect leads to discontent with oneself and others. Prather (1970) said, "My day has become a fraction happier ever since I realized that nothing is exactly the way I would like it to be. This is simply the way life is—and there goes one battle I don't have to fight anymore."

Most persons are troubled by the conflicting inclinations to improve their lives on the one hand and to celebrate them on the other. At times one is inclined to follow the early Greeks in their worship of *arete,* or excellence, or the Hindus in their endless search for perfection. At other times one becomes weary at the mere thought of such seemingly neurotic striving and concludes that life is for celebrating, not for changing.

This is the dilemma between doing and being. Claude Levi-Strauss (1969), the French anthropologist, refers to some modern cultures as "hot" and to others as "cool." The temperament of the hot cultures is choleric, active, and consuming, while the temperament of the cool cultures is relaxed, passive, and celebratory. This concept is clearly represented in the themes of two pieces of modern literature—Bach's *Jonathan Livingston Seagull* (1970) and Kavanaugh's *Celebrate the Sun* (1973). Bach's seagull and Kavanaugh's pelican share with the reader their competing views of the purpose of life.

The seagull was bent on defying conventional standards of acceptable performance in his pursuit of death-defying feats and perfect speed. All his waking hours were devoted to straining his muscles to climb higher and higher, to dive faster and faster, and to soar with blinding speed. While others were content to perch on the rocks and lazily spear the fish along the shoreline, Jonathan Livingston Seagull was devotedly struggling to improve his aeronautical skills.

Kavanaugh's pelican, Harry Langendorf Pelican, had spent his youth in quest of excellence and leadership and had taught his offspring likewise. His son challenged him to a contest to see who could dive the swiftest. The son's wings proved too feeble to lift him out of the dive, and he plunged to his death upon the ocean's surface. The pelican grieved over the tragedy, reacted against his earlier perfectionism, and subsequently began to accept life with its imperfections.

By examining passages from each of the two books, one is able to see more clearly their competing value systems.

JONATHAN: As seagulls it took us a hundred years to get the idea that our purpose for living is to find perfection and show it forth.

HARRY: It is not important to be perfect pelicans. We want to be happy pelicans. To always strive is never to be satisfied. We can celebrate the sun.

JONATHAN: I just want to know what I can do in the air and what I can't, that's all. The gull sees farthest who who flies highest.

HARRY: I only fly as high as I want to. I enjoy being here together. We have sad times and good times, tragedy and joy; whatever it is, we will have made it so.

JONATHAN: Why is it so hard to convince a gull that his life is free and that he can prove it for himself if he'd just spend time practicing?

HARRY: I want to know my friends, to enjoy them. And I want to enjoy myself.

JONATHAN:  You didn't die, did you? In death you manage to change your level of consciousness rather abruptly.

HARRY:  I will miss you. I love you so. Maybe that's what death is—missing someone.

JONATHAN:  Heaven is being perfect. You will begin to touch heaven in the moment that you touch perfect speed. Perfection doesn't have limits.

HARRY:  I have enjoyed my life, flying along the shore, sitting quietly on the rocks, feeling the wind lift me into the air, tasting the fresh fish, seeing the sun every day—and loving you, loving you so much.

The values of both Jonathan and Harry have appeal. Like Jonathan one is at times drawn to the perfect—to the ultimate in self development—and senses a gnawing discontent with any incompleteness. But like Harry one at other times finds peace in accepting less demanding views of oneself. Each position has its assets and its liabilities. The drive for perfection, like the search for the Holy Grail, can be exhilarating, but it can also create an insatiable thirst capable of driving one mad. Self-acceptance suggests a less feverish, less militant approach to life, but it may also lead to a kind of narcissistic smugness.

Archibald MacLeish (1968) wrote that modern Americans believe that whatever can be done should be done. This worship of change for change's sake is likely to bend the human condition all out of shape. Often, it is more sensible to accept oneself than to seek to change oneself. The Indian mystic, Krishnamurti (1964), suggested that efforts to change are often counterproductive.

... forget the ideal, and be aware of what you are. Do not pursue what *should* be, but understand what *is*. The understanding of what you actually are is far more important than the pursuit of what you *should* be. Why? Because in understanding what you are there begins a spontaneous process of transformation,

whereas in becoming what you think you *should* be
there is no change at all (p. 197).

Most crucial is a sense of personal control. Choosing
*not* to change may indicate as much self-control
as choosing to change. Yet, while most people would benefit from greater self-acceptance, most people also have
traits and habits that they want badly to change, but do
not know how. Furthermore, the kind of self-acceptance
that comes from feelings of helplessness and resignation
is far less satisfying than self-acceptance that comes from
a reappraisal of the trait in question or an estimate of the
cost of making the change.

Most people also have a deep-seated need to direct their
lives. Self-direction, in the richest sense of the concept,
is made up of a number of abilities: the ability to sense
the effects of situations upon behavior; to expand the
repertoire of alternatives; to focus attention on replacement behaviors that can be converted into habits; to anticipate beforehand the price one must pay for changing;
to muster energy to follow through on difficult commit-
ments; and to respond appropriately to a wide array of
interpersonal settings. The authors will try to contribute
to the reader's sense of self-direction in the following
chapters by assisting in the development of many of
these crucial abilities.

The journey into self-improvement is often lonely.
When the knights in King Arthur's court were setting
out in search of the Holy Grail, one commented that it
"would be a shame to go together." It is precisely because
one must go it alone, because one must fall back on one's
own resources of will, that success in self-improvement
is particularly rewarding. The Beechers (1966:12) suggested: "Life is like driving in the face of on-coming
traffic. . . . We must develop full trust in our own inherent capacities and not flee in panic from the scene."

Changing behavior is often a difficult process, and
perhaps this is why at some level one is always ambiva-

lent about attempting it. As indicated in figure 1–1, the
process involved in behavioral change requires awareness, choice, and practice. One must become aware of
what one is doing and of situations that prompt and reward behavior. One must consciously choose alternative
behavior and seriously commit oneself to practice it repeatedly. In time these replacement behaviors will become habits themselves, and one will no longer need to
work at it. William James likened the forming of a new
habit to the winding of string on a ball. The more string
one winds without dropping it, the better. If one drops

**Figure 1–1. Recycling behavior.** (Used with permission of Richard
Rank, Ph.D., who first shared this idea in personal communication.)

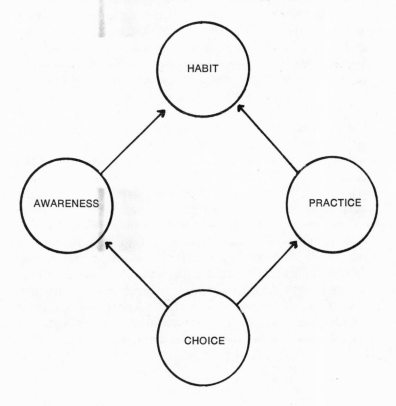

the string, and it rolls, one must spend time in rewinding. Like winding string, behaviors must be practiced again and again to make them habitual.

There is much to this apparently simple process, and throughout this book specific strategies to foster awareness, choice, and practice, as well as motivational obstacles to such efforts, will be discussed. The authors have accumulated a wide assortment of self-help techniques to assist in the private struggle to change. They used three criteria in selecting these techniques. Each technique chosen:

1. Requires little or no professional assistance.
2. Is free or inexpensive.
3. Is free of potential harm to the user.

The approaches suggested in this book are not meant to constitute a philosophy of life that can be drawn together and identified by any existing label. The authors acknowledge that strange paradox of life that bestows success in direct proportion to the intensity of a person's belief that a particular concept is *the* theory, *the* religion, *the* philosophy, or *the* way to mental or physical health. Since no one lifestyle is superior to all others, the responsibility for the shaping of a lifestyle falls to the individual himself. The authors' deep commitment to the preservation of individual differences has directed their efforts to help people to become aware of the options open to them in the area of self-help.

The reader should not expect magical cures in the following pages. The authors have yet to stumble on any such tonic. Growth is a dividend yielded by the investment of energy and self. Perhaps no other key is as crucial as is the old-fashioned idea of involvement. And perhaps there is no sounder contribution to one's mental health than the kind of authorship over one's own life that dispels a sense of personal helplessness.

# 2. The Sense of Helplessness

*If one man conquers in a battle a thousand times a thousand men, and if another conquers himself, he is the greatest of conquerers.*

Buddha

*Helplessness leads to panic, and panic to depression.*

Martin E. P. Seligman

It is a curious thing that many persons demonstrate great competence and confidence in assuming the most ambitious undertakings in their physical and social environments and yet feel helpless about changing personal habits. While one views most obstacles to plans as interesting challenges to personal resources, one views obstacles to personal change as impossible barriers. The buoyant confidence that one normally experiences is missing, and in its place is a depressing sense of resignation. One feels as though one is facing an immense task with hopelessly inadequate resources. One feels that one has tried to overcome before and has discovered that nothing really helps.

Why the astounding difference? Why does a person who is normally aggressive in attacking goals display the most abject depression regarding the chances of breaking harmful habits such as overeating, excessive drinking,

11

procrastinating, or being overly critical? One's seeming helplessness in attacking personal habits is related to certain beliefs that one holds, nonfunctional beliefs that suggest that certain forces hold us in their ironclad grip. This fatalism leads to a pervasive sense of helplessness.

Helplessness comes from not feeling in control, from believing one lacks responses appropriate to a situation, from not being able to predict an outcome. When one meets painful situations and believes that one has the personal resources to deal effectively with them, one experiences *concern*. When one meets these same situations and feels helpless, one experiences *anxiety*. In a provocative article entitled, "Why People Don't Change" (1975: 169), Bakker concluded, "Anxiety is the most conservative force in human existence, with hope as its most powerful counterbalance." Anxiety freezes one into present and often self-defeating behaviors, while hope beckons one to try the new and the better. Dubois wrote, "The important thing is this: to be able at any moment to sacrifice what we are for what we could become." In The *Psychology of Hope,* however, Stotland (1969) concluded that one's willingness to try new things is directly related to the perceived probability of success. Hope is the perceived probability of success, and without it anxiety locks one into neurotic, unsuccessful (but familiar) behavioral patterns.

Bem (1972) sugggested that self-concepts are derived from what one sees oneself doing. There is a circular relationship, however, between self-concepts and actions. For example, a person who believes that he is unable to change is unlikely to engage in activities that would be inconsistent with his presently conceived self. Since acting differently is one of the more efficient ways of changing one's self-concept, one cuts off the likelihood of changing by the belief that one is unable to do so. Once one defines oneself in certain ways consistent with one's beliefs, one seeks situations that are consistent with self-definition, and those situations reconfirm the definition. If one defines oneself as a born loser who is unable to change unfortunate behavioral patterns, one is likely to perpetuate this hurtful self-name-calling by one's unwillingness to try seriously to change. Belief in powerful forces that supposedly control behavior also inhibits the desire to change. One feels helpless, and this helplessness ultimately leads to inactivity and depression.

The build-up of helplessness has a predictable effect on activity levels and feeling tones. Figure 2-1 depicts these relationships.

**Figure 2–1.   The effects of helplessness.**

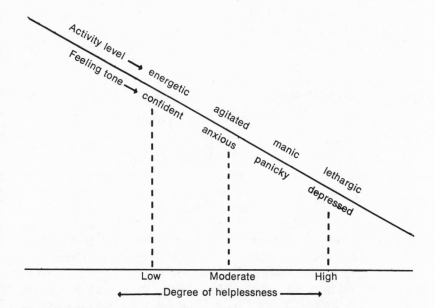

When one confronts difficulties and experiences little or no helplessness, one's activity level is energetic and one's feeling tone, confident. Moderate degrees of helplessness lead to agitated activity and an anxious feeling tone. Further helplessness at first increases the agitation and anxiety, but then abruptly leads to lethargy and depres-

sion. When one crosses the sensitive point where the
maniacal behavior turns into lethargy, and the panicky
feeling into depression, one has usually created a private
reality so far removed from normality that one is clas-
sified as mentally ill. This private reality allows one to
give up the struggle to make all the pieces of one's life
fit together. While this unreal adjustment hardly quali-
fies as idyllic, nevertheless it seems less punishing than
the mania and panic that often precede it. Perhaps it is
for this reason that some mental patients seem ambivalent about getting well. Perhaps they sense that getting
better means moving back through the anxiety and agitation characteristic of the earlier stages of helplessness.

Helplessness, then, springs from the conviction that
forces over which we have no control determine our behavior. These forces may be seen as some kind of internal
intrapsychical power that derives from the cumulative
effects of past conditioning or from current physical and
social pressures.

## The Enemy Within

Since one is sometimes mystified by the nature of certain problems, one is often tempted to believe that they
originate from an unrecognized internal source. There
are, in fact, views within religion and psychiatry to
foster this belief. The Calvinist concept of original sin
and the modern Freudian concept of the unconscious both
suggest that the biggest barrier to personal development
is within. In reference to the influence of original sin
upon his behavior, St. Paul concluded, "I do not understand my own actions, for I do not do what I want, but
I do the very thing I hate (Romans 7:15, Revised Standard Version)." Freud suggested that behavior is overly
determined by unconscious drives. He used the metaphor
of an iceberg to make his point. The conscious was
likened to the small tip of an iceberg, while the unconscious was represented by its huge submerged base. Accordingly, the actual causes of one's actions are said to

be deeply submerged in the unconscious base of the iceberg. In both cases humans are portrayed as puppets with strings pulled by some inner puppeteer. It helps little that the puppeteer is some unfathomable power within us, since it is a power that eludes our will.

Behavior is undoubtedly influenced to some degree by desires and impulses that we have not clearly sensed. Few persons would suggest that they are always perfectly aware of the reasons for their behavior. Still, the case for unconscious factors seems overdone. Most persons are reasonably well in touch with the motives for their actions and are capable of behaving differently. The role of the unconscious does appear to be considerably more influential in the behavior of seriously disturbed persons than in healthy persons. Anxiety-arousing impulses and painful memories may be relegated to the unconscious when one has given up hope of successfully coping with them, but this model of unconscious determination of behavior hardly fits the functioning of the normal person. Most persons are much more aware of what they are doing, and, consequently, they are more responsible for their behavior. They are creatures of habit, and habits are not broken easily, although they will give way to well-designed, persistent efforts to change them.

## The Tyranny of the Past

In Homer's writings, Odysseus says, "I am part of all that I have met." This was Homer's way of emphasizing the important influence of past experience in shaping one. Odysseus bore the imprint of former battles, of far-flung travels, and of multiple loves. Like Odysseus, all persons carry the imprint of past experiences. Relationships within the family, formal schooling, work experiences, and chance acquaintances all have influence.

Even emotional responses to events and objects within the environment are shaped in some Pavlovian manner through past experiences. Associating an emotionally neutral experience with another that naturally evokes strong emotion will in time invest the neutral experience with the ability to evoke the same strong response. Such associations form the basis for prejudiced thinking. The targets of racial prejudice are presented in association with pejorative terms and negative emotional expressions often enough until they become odious.

Once one has become aware of such emotional conditioning, one is ready to experiment with new and favorable associations with the target of the prejudice. One can come to realize that feelings are not necessarily the best guide to behavior, since they merely reflect earlier emotional conditioning that may be either functional or nonfunctional.

Aside from this rather reflexive emotional behavior, past experience with persons and events provides a set of beliefs, expectations, and assumptions through which experiences are viewed. One sees the world not as it is, but from one's own special view. This also means that people are creatures of judgment. They seldom have an experience without evaluating it, and the basis for this evaluation comes from the quality of past experience. These beliefs and expectations serve as glasses—not always rose-tinted—that color experiences bright, ominous, good, or bad.

Once one becomes aware of these restricting beliefs and expectations, one can challenge them. One can become open to present experiences and revise this kind of reflexive thinking to make it conform more closely to reality. Persons are slaves to such archaic thinking *only if they fail to permit it to surface so it can be challenged.*

The authors have attempted to cite ways in which the past influences present behavior. It is possible, however, to emphasize the importance of past experiences to such an extent that one becomes convinced that personal change is impossible. For example, one can come to believe that bad homes, bad parents, or bad love experiences have condemned one to live out his days in helpless enslavement to these influences. Yet such a view does not conform with the facts, since awareness can lead to choice, and choice to the practice of replacement behaviors, and practice to habit.

## Environmental Influences

One's sense of personal helplessness is often aggravated by *overestimating* the controlling influence of pressures in the environment. There is no denying that people are influenced by the responses of others, but it is hardly accurate to say that they are controlled by them.

Some behavioral scientists are fond of saying that behavior is governed by its consequences; that is to say, that persons tend to repeat those behaviors that are followed by rewarding consequences and to drop those that are followed by punishing ones. In an NBC Special Report, entitled *The Blue Collar Trap*, a worker at the Ford Pinto factory complained that he was being paid too well. He felt the pay for his labor was so great that he could not afford to quit despite his total distaste for the work. He saw himself as a gigolo whose body was bought with a handsome wage. He felt he was hooked on the rewarding consequences of his distasteful work.

There are two ways of looking at these consequences. They may be seen as shaping behavior, or the behavior may be their cause. Both views are accurate. One is modified by one's environment, but one also modifies it. The factory worker was encouraged to continue his distasteful work in order to earn his wage, but he caused his wage to be paid precisely because he did his work. In the ultimate sense, he chose to continue his work. People often choose their own conditioners. They may complain that persons with whom they eat lunch influence them to eat too much, but they have chosen their company. A student may protest that he would study more if his crowd were not so socially minded, and yet he chooses to run with them. A woman may complain that it is almost impossible to keep from losing her temper when she plays bridge with a certain man, yet she chooses to continue to play with this person.

It is often possible to anticipate the nature of the influences coming from a situation and to choose a more desirable situation in its place. This may involve selecting different friends, a different occupation, a different school, or even a different spouse. Sometimes, one may choose to maintain these associations because they contribute significantly to one's happiness in some other way. In this case one is still free to choose one's attitudes toward these conditioners. No one can hurt another unless he is allowed to. One is free to attach great or little significance to the barbs of others. Conversely, one can often see through the manipulative praise of others and refuse to be swayed from a position based upon one's best judgment.

One may feel helpless if one fails to see that one's behavior is causing the consequence. If what happens appears to be the result of luck, fate, or chance, rather than the natural result of one's behavior, then feelings of helplessness and confusion may result. When this happens, one does not feel responsible for one's condition, and one approaches one's environment fearfully, seeing oneself as a pawn in the hands of some unfathomable, unpredictable force.

Most of the time, though, a logical connection exists between what happens and the behavior that precedes an event. It is true that some persons have been subjected to very bad parenting, in which rewards and punishments were handed out on a whimsical, capricious basis. They were punished at times for the same actions for which they were earlier or later rewarded. Children coming out of such an environment feel that nothing they do will make any difference. The effects of this kind of conditioning is best seen in an experiment by Seligman and Maier (1967), who subjected a group of dogs to erratically administered mild shock. At first these dogs responded normally by defecating, urinating, barking, and straining against their harnesses. They soon discovered that nothing they did influenced the shocks, and thereafter, they stopped these futile efforts and passively accepted their fate. In a second experimental setting, where half the floor was subject to electrical discharges and the other half was not, these same dogs failed to escape their punishment even though their harnesses had been removed. The external harnesses had been replaced with an equally binding internal harness. They had learned a sense of helplessness by coming to believe that there was no relationship between response and outcome, between behavior and the events that follow it.

In much the same way, many persons have developed a helplessness syndrome that influences how they view the world. It is important to understand that helplessness comes not from the experiences one has had, but from what one comes to believe about those experiences. One carries these beliefs, and they are just as binding as the dogs' harnesses. Therapists generally agree that the most commonly held fettering beliefs are the following:

1. *It is terrible when people become angry with us.* A child who has suffered an older person's anger may have preserved this lesson long after it has ceased to be functional. He now becomes frightened when others get angry at him, and he goes to great lengths to keep them from getting angry or to placate them when they do. Consequently, one is seldom true to oneself, since one measures one's views by the reception they get from others. One has not yet learned that it is impossible to be genuine and still have everyone happy with one at all times. In fact, a good guideline is that approximately one-half of one's friends and acquaintances will disagree with one's opinions on any subject.

2. *One should feel guilty about past mistakes.* Persons spend considerable time rehearsing their past mistakes. While it is obvious that they can do nothing about them, nevertheless, they persist in angry or sorrowful complaints of their foolishness or evil intentions. Perhaps

they believe that self-criticism will deter others from attacking them for their errors. Unfortunately, this focusing on past mistakes robs them of the energy for present pursuits and renders them overly cautious.

3. *One should anticipate all the potential danger of the future.* All situations should be approached fearfully. One should lack confidence in one's resources, be afraid to have a future and try to put it in the past by anticipating it so fully that it will merely seem like a *deja vu* experience when it arrives. One should not trust oneself to live openly and spontaneously; one should always assume a conservative stance to insure against any situation for which one is unprepared. Such overcautiousness, however, destroys the rhythm of spontaneous living.

4. *Each of us should be competent in all aspects of his life.* People exaggerate the importance of making mistakes, of being less than perfect. They lack the courage to be imperfect. Perfectionism is brittle. It leaves one humorless and overly intense. It inhibits one from experimenting with new behaviors and new tastes and limits one to those tasks wherein one is assured of demonstrating competence.

These beliefs create a defensiveness, a cautiousness, a fearfulness about behavior that is just as binding as any external harness. In holding these beliefs, one becomes a mere shadow of the person one could be if risk-taking were greater. The authors will have far more to say about such beliefs in chapter 9.

Seldom are human beings subjected to conditions as extreme as those to which the dogs in the Seligman and Maier study were subjected. Occasionally human beings find themselves subjected to inhumane conditions, but even then they are free to determine their reactions to such conditions. Victor Frankl was interred in a Nazi concentration camp and lived to write about it:

> We who lived in concentration camps can remember
> the men who walked through the huts comforting

others, giving away their last piece of bread. They may have been few in number, but they offer sufficient proof that everything can be taken from a man but one thing: the last of the human freedoms—to choose one's attitude in any given set of circumstances, to choose one's own way (1970, p. 12).

Seldom is an outcome of any event totally independent of our behavior. Nevertheless, one's sense of helplessness is usually predicated upon this assumption. Once one has perceived the connection between behavior and its consequences, then one can change the consequences by changing the behavior. If one does not like the consequences, one may change them by behaving differently. But people are responsible for what happens to them because they are free to change their own behavior.

Quite often the most important consequences influencing behavior are inside human heads and not part of the external environment. Since most behaviors are goal-directed, actions are seldom random. Persons often reward or punish themselves for actions that either aid or hinder them in pursuing personal goals, and these self-endorsing or self-criticizing thoughts are often more influential than those stemming from outside sources. These powerful self-rewards and punishments can be changed with effort.

In summary, while the physical and social environments are important influences upon behavior, these influences are often countered or abetted by what is frequently a more important source of influence—one's goal-directed internal environment. One is influenced by the external environment, but people influence it in turn, and are capable of modifying its influence further by the attitudes that they adopt toward it.

### Running from Responsibility

The Danish philosopher Kierkegaard once said, "Anxiety is the price of freedom." Feeling free and responsible makes people nervous. Growing and changing often involve giving up familiar sources of nourishment in search of new resources in much the same way that an infant must give up the placenta to experience the atmosphere. When one senses the need for change, and yet allows feelings of helplessness to immobilize one, the result is personal stagnation and self-contempt.

Personal change is often forged on a crucible of suffering. When one says, "I can't change," often one means, "I won't change." Growth is frequently painful, and people conveniently adopt sets of personal beliefs that excuse them from trying.

William James wrote, "Compared with what we ought to be, we are only half awake. Our fires are dampened, our drafts are checked. We are making use of only a small part of our mental and physical resources." It is not enough to lament the erosion of a sense of personal control. One must and can do something about it.

If one is to begin to take responsibility for what one is and for what happens to one, then one must give up a lot of favorite villains—mysterious internal forces such as the unconscious, traumatic past experiences, poor parents, the expectations of significant others, and family responsibilities. What these forces can do is insignificant when compared with what people do to themselves by maintaining crippling personal beliefs. Like a broken leg, the cause of the break is unimportant; the important thing is to repair it. The same is true for emotional problems. In *Mrs. Warren's Profession,* by George Bernard Shaw, one of the characters says:

> People are always blaming their circumstances for what they are. I don't believe in circumstances. The people who get on in this world are the people who get up and look for the circumstances they want, and if they can't find them, make them.

This book contains many starting places for the person who wishes to take charge of his life. The authors invite the reader to select as a target for change some personal behavior he or she has long wished to learn, unlearn, or modify. They further invite the reader to examine the strategies suggested in the following chapters to discover ones that appear appropriate for his or her problem.

This book is written in the belief that striving is more satisfying than achieving, that people are most happy when they feel they are improving in some way that seems important. They do not have to change in an all-or-nothing fashion. Gradual improvement in some small sphere can be exhilarating and can furnish the motivation for further improvement. Perhaps the most significant result of self-engineered change is the thrillling sense of control over oneself. For many the new frontier is internal, and conquests there are the most rewarding of all.

# Part II
# The Desire to Change

Behavior is often embarrassingly inconsistent with stated resolutions. One says, "I've simply got to lose weight," but one's behavior says, "It's not really that important."

Therapists often find that clients are ambivalent about changing. They want to change, but resist the inconvenience or suffering that is involved. They often want to change, but not enough to pay the price. While their resolve is sincere enough at the moment they express it, it is often too weak to keep them going when they fall on hard times.

The authors hope in this chapter somehow to deepen the motivation for personal growth; this is the focus of part II.

Chapter 3 contains suggestions of ways to influence one's thoughts and images so they can reinforce rather than defeat a plan for growth. Chapter 4 contains ways to engineer the environment to facilitate the resolve for growth. And chapter 6 concerns the use of literature as a motivating force in change.

If you find yourself saying, "I really do want to change; I just wish I wanted to more than I do," then perhaps you will derive some benefit from the methods and techniques presented in part II.

# 3. Creative Use of Imagination

*Only in man's imagination does every truth find an effective and undeniable existence. Imagination, not invention, is the supreme master of art as of life.*
                                    Joseph Conrad

*There are no days in life so memorable as those which vibrated to some stroke of the imagination.*
                                    Ralph Waldo Emerson

Much behavior is triggered by dominant thoughts and images about oneself. These self-images serve as prophecies that one earnestly sets out to fulfill. One continues to shape one's behavior until it becomes a reasonable facsimile of these mental images. They serve as templates or dies against which behavior is constantly compared. The effort to conform to these images is not totally conscious; indeed, it is quite likely that many of these mental guides are unconscious lifescripts. In a sense all people are actors practicing to portray faithfully these lifescripts. Some of these scripts are for losers; others, for winners. Losers, winners, heroes, villains—whatever the role, much behavior seems calculated to fulfill the prescribed script.

Once one is aware of these subconscious scripts, it seems likely that one can strengthen one's motivation by

110027

the creative use of the imagination. Changing one's
estimates of what is possible—learning to see oneself as
capable—can perhaps lead to a build-up of energy with
which to effect personal change.

## Sharpening the Picture

Carefully defined goals are more attractive than are
ambiguous ones. When the picture of a goal is fuzzy,
when the signposts are out-of-focus, it is difficult to
maintain a sense of direction and momentum. A clear
mental picture of one's destination and any landmarks
en route can greatly increase the resolve to persist in the
face of the pain that is part of personal growth. In animal psychology there is a phenomenon called goal gradient. Researchers have noted that animals increase their
striving for a goal when it comes more clearly in sight.
Racing greyhounds, for example, are egged on when a
rabbit is close to them. For humans this sometimes trans-
lates: the sharper the picture of a goal, the greater its
magnetism. Consequently, time spent in defining the
exact nature of the behavior desired is a step toward improving one's motivation.

Too often persons tend to resist the work involved in
clearly defining their goals and settle instead for ambiguous statements. When the goal is fuzzy, it is both difficult to find the starting gate and to measure progress
en route. For example, one may decide to improve one's
social relationships. Yet, such a vague statement offers
little in the way of practical guidance. This general expression of a goal must be translated into a more specific
statement that says what improved social relationships
means on a personal basis. Is one referring to a need to
be more or less assertive with others? To become more
spontaneous and less guarded when in the company
of others? To develop the skill and courage to express
appreciation and affection for others? To become more
comfortable in groups? Any or all of these may be in-

volved in a general goal implied in improved social relationships.

In refining a goal statement, be as specific as possible. If by improved social relationships, one hopes to increase one's comfort in the presence of others, then one should begin to think primarily about an index of comfort in groups. The goal can be made even more specific. Is one referring to comfort experienced as a spectator or as a participant? What kind of group settings are meant? What kind of participation is unsettling? This dogged pursuit of a more meaningful goal statement may result in the translation of an expression as general as "improved social relationships" to one as specific as "less anxiety experienced while presenting views to fellow workers at the office." Although it is not easy to arrive at so detailed a form, the specific nature of the second goal statement is helpful in suggesting a strategy for attacking the problem and in measuring progress. It is indeed difficult to continue a journey when one is uncertain where one is going or whether one is closer to, or farther from, the goal than when one began.

As a rule of thumb, do not settle for a goal statement that does not suggest immediate steps for its accomplishment, along with a reasonably clear basis for measuring progress. Anything less is totally destructive to motivation for change.

## Anticipating Success

Infrahuman species lack the well-developed associative areas of man's new brain (cerebrum), and, consequently, they are unable to project themselves in time and space. The well-developed human nervous system is endowed with this dubious advantage; it is dubious because the same associative network that enables people to project themselves in time and space also enables them to worry.

This superior endowment also enables them to objectify themselves, to hold in their minds images or pictures of themselves. Much behavior is consistent with these self-images. It is still a matter of dispute among psychologists as to whether these self-images merely represent an abstracted representation of existing behavior, or whether, once established, they assume independent existences and serve to produce consistency in behavior. Some schools of psychology, namely, the self-theorists or phenomenologists, stress the determinative function of the self-image. The authors tend to agree with them; they feel that once the self-image emerges, it appears to be a major source of influence upon behavior.

Changes in the self-image are reflected in one's behavior. An effort to alter self-image has served as the focus of treatment for many therapists. It is well represented in the academic literature by Rogers (1951) and Kelly (1955), among others, and in the popular literature by Maltz (1960) and others.

How does one come to see oneself differently? And how does one accept new images of oneself so completely that they affect one's behavior? Some therapists believe that such images cannot be changed by a frontal attack. They believe that the self-image is the product of interaction with significant others, that one accepts a view of oneself that one sees reflected in the eyes of others. Self-image thus represents a perception of the way others see us. According to this view, one must have help from others to change a self-image. Therapy consists of a corrective emotional experience wherein one comes to accept troublesome aspects of oneself more fully. Since one prizes the opinion of the therapist, his positive response to the disclosure of these troublesome behaviors serves as a direct rebuttal to what one previously perceived to be the negative responses of others; in due time the self-image is altered in a more realistic direction.

### Frontal Attacks on the Self-Image

Other therapists maintain that a frontal attack on self-image is most effective. They argue as follows: if we change the words we use to describe ourselves to ourselves, and if we practice holding different pictures of ourselves, then we can, in time, effectively improve self-image. The trick, these therapists say, is to perceive oneself as already having made the change.

Maltz's theory, called psychocybernetics, advocates direct attack upon inadequate self-images. His theory comes from "cybernetics," a Greek word meaning "steersmanship," and "psyche," another Greek word meaning "mind." The title fits Maltz's position well since his views stress the purposiveness of human nature. Humans are not divided into two warring minds—the conscious and the unconscious. Rather, they are of one mind, which is responsible for goal setting; this mind has a servant responsible for furnishing the means and muscles for accomplishing goals. This servant is what others have called the Unconscious. Maltz calls it the Automatic Mechanism.

The Automatic Mechanism does not have a mind of its own. It is the willing servant of the conscious mind; it is a slave that seeks quietly and covertly to carry out the will of the mind. It works like a servomechanism, an automatic guidance system. It may be programmed by the mind for success or failure. If it is fed information to the effect that one is unworthy, inferior, undeserving, or incapable, then it will guide one's behaviors accordingly. Conversely, if one feeds it information based on a positive self-image, it will order up behavior compatible with such an image. Thus, one creates oneself out of the goals and images one feeds into one's Automatic Mechanism. If one feeds it success goals, it will function as a Success Mechanism; if one feeds it negative goals, it will function as a Failure Mechanism.

The trick then is to achieve a self-image that is positive and enhancing. But the self-image is a product of experiences. Is one not, therefore, condemned to live out one's days enslaved by a self-image that reflects one's past experiences? The answer lies in a deeper understanding of the manner in which the human nervous system functions. It cannot tell the difference between real and synthetic experiences. Experiences that are imagined are as much the cement and bricks of a self-image as those that are real.

It is, after all, not actual experiences that affect one, but rather one's interpretation of these experiences. The Greek philosopher Epictetus said, "Men are disturbed not by the things that happen, but by their opinion of the things that happen." Several centuries later William James concluded, "Since you make them [facts] evil or good by your own thoughts about them, it is the ruling of your thoughts which proves to be your principal concern."

One never knows exactly what are the facts in any situation. Indeed, in any one day, there are facts that can justify either a pessimistic or an optimistic view of oneself. The good perceptions are as genuine as are the evil ones. One's perceptions are not a matter of intellectual honesty or dishonesty; they are merely a matter of what one chooses to focus upon. Focus upon the negative, and one turns one's Automatic Mechanism into a Failure Mechanism; focus upon the positive, and one turns it into a Success Mechanism. Further, if one is unhappy with one's mental images, then one can change them by creatively picturing oneself differently and by acting as if this new picture is an accurate representation.

Getting a clear fix on the nature of a solution takes one a long way toward successful problem-solving. The first order of the day in self-change strategies, then, is to fashion a clear mental picture of oneself as one would be if one had already changed. The second order is steadfastly to hold such an image in one's mind. Attention is either a powerful ally or a powerful enemy. If it focuses upon failure, then failure it is likely to be; if it focuses upon success, then one is much more likely to be successful. How can one, then, constantly attend to successful

self-images if one is programmed to think of oneself as
a failure?

The attention span of the human mind is brief. It tends
to jump rapidly from one thing to another. For this
reason, one is able to center attention for a longer time
upon successful self-images if one embellishes them with
vivid details. If one is attempting to lose weight, for
example, one must mentally picture oneself as slim and
trim. One might imagine one's svelte figure as it might
appear nude before a full-length mirror. One might focus
upon a midsection taut with well-developed muscles and
totally devoid of the usual doughnut of fat. Perhaps one
can imagine the envious response of friends and acquaintances, who admiringly notice one's willowy form
on the beach or at the community pool. Not only can one
*see* the slender form, but one can *feel* the extra surge of
energy freed by the loss of excessive, ugly fat. One feels
oneself effortlessly getting up out of a deep-cushioned
chair and sprightfully walking off. Perhaps one focuses
attention on how one's clothes will look when one is slim.
Perhaps one sees oneself entering the office of a local
seamstress and proudly requesting that the seams be
taken in several inches, or perhaps one decides that one's
new image will now allow one to choose more modern
styles—or perhaps one is now entitled to consider re-
placing the old wardrobe with one containing some of the
styles one has admired on others.

If one's goal is to become more comfortable in the view
one presents to colleagues, then once again one must engage one's creative imagination to paint in vivid detail
a picture of oneself as one confidently expresses oneself
at work. One senses the calm mental state that can expel
the usually feverish condition of fear and anxiety. One
hears oneself speaking slowly and articulately in a voice
that is rhythmical and firm. One is poised and content
to express one's views without necessarily persuading
others to them. There is no trace in one's voice of the

used-car salesman's pitch. One recognizes that it is not overly important that others agree, or that one agree with them, for that matter. But one senses that what one has to say will be of interest to others. One sees oneself accurately expressing views, and one sees others looking at one another and nodding agreement or indicating an interest in one's opinions.

It is important to spend time creating and rehearsing one's goals. One must have these mental experiences repeatedly, and having them means experiencing them in detail. If one is having difficulty with the creation of such themes or mental pictures, one can ask for the assistance of trusted companions, who can often add considerably to versions of one's imagined goals. They can dip into their own experiences and greatly embellish the pictures. One can also prod the imagination with models furnished by acquaintances, films, or books. By selecting the sources upon which one wishes to focus, one modifies one's self-image, and by modifying one's self-image, one modifies behavior.

These products of creative imagination furnish guidelines for new roles to be acted out. Again, one begins to *act as if* these new self-images are real. The new role or lifescript may seem artificial and unnatural at first, and one may even feel hypocritical. One may even conclude that one is acting out of character—that this new behavior is false. Indeed, the new behavior is at first unnatural; indeed, it is unreal, and indeed, *this is precisely why one is performing the behavior.* After all, one has decided that one wants to change, and changing involves changing behavior. For a while these new behaviors will seem artificial, but remember that present habits that now feel so natural were also learned. One is not born with habits. Undoubtedly, present habits felt just as unnatural when one was first experimenting with them as these new behaviors now feel. If one persists in role-playing long enough, one will find that the new behaviors eventually become habits, and it will no longer be necessary to play a role.

Since one has little understanding of the extensive amount of time it takes to master present roles, one is apt to become impatient while trying out new roles. One hesitatingly begins to practice a new lifescript and soon despairs of the possibility that one will ever be able to "act that way." One's efforts are foredoomed to failure because the lack of faith precludes one from being able to play the roles with abandonment. Such feelings can persist in the face of very slow change.

Self-change is a slow process—even when the formula for change is exquisitely appropriate. Maltz suggested that it usually takes about twenty-one days to effect any perceptible change in a self-image. He reminds us that it takes about twenty-one days for patients of plastic surgery to get used to their new faces, about the same amount of time for the phantom limb to disappear from the mind of an amputee, and about the same time for a new house to seem comfortable.

One must go on practicing a new image for some time without seeing the results. This is parallel to a concept in physics called critical mass; physicists point out that energy must often amass over a period of time before it perceptibly changes form. For example, one can heat water for quite a while before it changes into steam. Its temperature may reach 100 degrees, 150 degrees, or even 200 degrees without any visible evidence that change is occurring. Only after water reaches critical mass does is miraculously change its form from liquid to gas. The process of self-change is very much the same. Early efforts often seem unrewarding; one seems to be using a frightful lot of energy and willpower for no perceptible reward. Approaching critical mass is not very reinforcing. Motivation is greatly strengthened, however, when one begins to reach critical mass.

If one persists in the tedious work of self-change, then

one must come to believe in the importance of the repetitive efforts involved in approaching critical mass. One must continue to practice the role, to imagine oneself as one would like to be, even when behavior stubbornly refuses to go along.

A new self-image must be a reasonable facsimile of one's present self. It must roughly correspond to reality. One could imagine oneself able to fly without wings, or as Jesus Christ or Napoleon Bonaparte, but such images have an obvious air of unreality. An image must be a reasonable facimile of a self one honestly believes one can become.

Early efforts to change an image often employ a process behaviorial psychologists call shaping. Shaping refers to efforts to reward improvement. One does not expect full-blown, perfect performance—one only expects a reasonable approximation of it. Once one has approached this level of performance, one can raise the bar of the hurdle a bit higher. Any attempt at self-change involves rounds of approximations, tedious effort, and self-endorsement.

### Autosuggestive Techniques

Autosuggestive techniques have been used informally for centuries and formally for many decades to increase human motivation. The techniques are related to hypnosis; indeed, the practice of autosuggestion is sometimes called autohypnosis. Autohypnosis requires a trancelike state, however, and autosuggestion does not. Such a difference, if it exists at all, is clearly a quantitative rather than qualitative matter, since both require a highly relaxed, unstimulated state.

Throughout the ages in many cultures the practice of hypnotically related states has occurred. There were the sleep temples in Greece and Egypt, where patients received from priests some form of hypnosis to induce sleep for the treatment of physical ailments. Trance induction is frequently brought on in primitive cultures through drums, dancing, and chanting.

The eighteenth-century Frenchman, Anton Mesmer, combined the use of trancelike states with his metaphysical views of astrology to form a unique treatment for physical problems. He believed that the human body was analogous to a magnet, with the top and bottom halves emitting opposite attractions. He thought diseases were caused by an imbalance in the magnetic poles of the body and could be cured by restoring the magnetic balance. His method was to pass magnetic rods over the bodies of patients until they were persuaded that the previously interrupted universal flow of magnetism was restored to its natural rhythm. Mesmer had begun to recognize the significance of suggestion and persuasion in the therapeutic process.

An Englishman, James Braid, coined the term "hypnosis" from the Greek word for sleep, *hypnos*. He dropped the metaphysical trappings of Mesmer's system and induced trances via eye fixations. The applications of hynosis spread rapidly to the medical field. The center of the use of hypnosis in medicine moved to the Nancy Clinic in France, where Freud was to become interested in the technique under the mentorship of Charcot.

A French druggist, Emile Coué, also studied at the Nancy Clinic. He later abandoned the use of the trance and began the practice of "waking suggestion"—autosuggestion. He is said to have discovered this to be more effective than drugs. The flavor of his method can be savored in the following excerpt from his manual (1923):

> Therefore, every time you have a pain, physical or otherwise, you will go quietly to your room ... sit down and shut your eyes, pass your hand lightly across your forehead if it is mental distress, or upon the part that hurts, if it is pain in any part of the body, and

repeat the words: "It is going, it is going," etc. very
rapidly, even at the risk of babbling. . . .The essential
idea is to say: "It is going, it is going" so quickly that
it is impossible for a thought of contrary nature to
force itself between the words. We thus actually think
it is going, and as all ideas that we fix upon the mind
become a reality to us, the pain, physical or mental,
vanishes.

Coué abandoned the trance induction entirely, insisting
that all suggestion is in reality nothing but autosuggestion.

The British Medical Association officially endorsed
hypnosis in 1955 and the American Medical Association
followed in 1958. The method is used primarily by psychiatrists in an effort to integrate psychodynamic
material more effectively. Specific hypnotic techniques
have been developed for age regression, scene visualiza-
tion, imagery activity, fantasy evocation, hypnography,
and other modifications of perception functions.

The current trend is toward an emphasis on a person's
conscious cooperation and away from an inactive and
passive posture. In this sense, Coué's preference for waking suggestion appears to have gained support. Barber
(1973), a leading researcher in hypnosis, has concluded,
as did Coué, that the trance is not necessary to hypnosis,
that hypnosis is a matter of conscious expectancy.
Jerome Frank, in *Persuasion and Healing* (1975),
pointed out that the faith healer, witch doctor, shaman,
medicine man, and psychotherapist alike all manage to
help a demoralized patient by raising his expectations.

If, then, the conscious expectancy can be manipulated
by persuasion and suggestion, behavior appropriate to
the expectancy will follow. Practioners of autosuggestion maintain that such persuasion and suggestion can
come from oneself—that one can engineer one's own behavior through this technique.

The Russian psychologist, Platonov (1967), maintains
that there is a close connection between mental activity

and the physical processes that may be responsive to suggestions. He believes that all symbolic images evoke some type of physiological response. He quotes Pavlov, who formulated the following principle.

As long as you think of a certain movement (i.e., you have a kinesthetic idea) you involuntarily perform it without noticing it. Thus, each time we think of a movement, we actually perform it abortively (p. 234).

It follows from the above principle that mental practice of a performance may smooth out the actual performance itself. There is some research evidence to suggest that such athletic performances as dart throwing and basketball shooting may be improved by daily mental practice (Suinn, 1976). One might facetiously speculate that Professor Harold Hill in the Broadway production *The Music Man* may not have been totally without justification when he frantically urged his Iowa school children to "think music."

In order to prepare oneself for the maximum benefits from autosuggestion, the body should be placed in a state of quiescence and passivity. Find a comfortable posture —usually a sitting or reclining position is best. Begin a set of relaxation exercises in which you alternately tense and relax each part of the body. A muscle relaxes more easily if it is first tensed. A suggested order for this is hands, arms, forehead, eyes, mouth, tongue, neck, shoulders, stomach, buttocks, thighs, calves, feet and toes. Tense the muscle, hold it for five to seven seconds, relax it, and then repeat the exercise. While the pattern may take twenty to thirty minutes at first, you will eventually be able to short-circuit it by combining muscle groups.

After the body feels relaxed, begin counting from ten to one, taking a deep breath for each number. When the count is completed, follow with a key word, such as "relax." If the relaxation exercises are followed enough times by the counting and the word "relax," you will soon be able to induce a similarly relaxed state merely by counting and repeating the word "relax."

Some people find it helpful to focus on an imaginary object, such as a spot in the middle of the eyebrows, to suppress other thoughts that might interfere with their concentration. Once the routine for relaxation has been mastered, the state may be achieved within a few minutes under most circumstances. The authors will have far more to say about such relaxation methods in chapter 8.

With the body and mind stilled, one can begin making self-suggestions. Sontged (1972) recommended four rules for enhancing the effects of self-suggestion:

1. *Make suggestions positive and permissive.* Most persons assume a resistive stance when pressed or coerced; therefore a permissive suggestion such as "I can . . ." is more likely to be carried out than a more domineering one such as "I will . . ."

2. *Repeat suggestions to increase their strength.* Suggestions should be repeated three or four times during a single session. This principle of repetition is well-respected in the advertising world. People tend to believe an idea if they hear it often enough.

3. *Phrase suggestions in the present perfect rather than in the present tense.* The Unconscious (Automatic Mechanism) needs time to act on suggestions. Rather than saying, "My headache is gone," it is more effective to say "My headache is beginning to clear up." Such a statement is more believable in this form, and it is only when one comes to believe a suggestion that it is acted upon by the unconscious.

4. *Employ visual images in suggestions whenever possible.* Imagine yourself subjectively experiencing the desired goal rather than objectively observing the activity.

These techniques are designed to influence a basic part of one's personality called the Unconscious, or the Automatic Mechanism. Most people are living out unconscious scripts that can lead either to success or failure.

People write their own scripts containing their own positive or negative goals and self-images. These techniques call for a frontal assault on inadequate and negative self-thoughts and feelings. If one persists at attending to specific, positive goals, rather than allowing one's mind to fret fearfully over the possibility of failure, if one constructs new, synthetic experiences to replace the old, hurtful ones by creatively imagining them vividly and in detail, if one properly prepares one's mind and body by relaxation for positive autosuggestions—if one does these things consistently and persistently over time—one may expect one's motivation for self-improvement to increase significantly.

# 4. Engineering Self-Change

*Give me the strength to accept with serenity*
*the things that cannot be changed.*
*Give me the courage to change the things*
*that can and should be changed.*
*And give me the wisdom to distinguish*
*one from the other.*

St. Francis of Assisi

Motivation to change dies a slow death without a map to guide one's efforts. Good intentions fade quickly when one blindly stumbles in attempts to bring about personal change. Quite often one builds up a head of steam for change only to watch it dissipate uselessly in self-recriminations and unenlightened false starts. One is able to harness constructively this energy only when one develops a careful plan for change—a plan that anticipates and successfully deals with blocks to be encountered within oneself and the environment. A convincing, detailed plan for personal change often awakens renewed hope, and hope unleashes enormous energy. In this chapter the authors will help the reader increase the motivation for personal change by anticipating blocks and by identifying key elements in any successful plan for change.

In preparing for self-engineered change, three questions require consideration: Can the situation be changed? What will it cost to change it? And how can it be changed if I decide to attempt to change it?

## Can the Situation Be Changed?

Some situations are extremely difficult to change. Persons sometimes find themselves caught up in human predicaments, common life straits imposed by human limitations. Moreover, cultural doublebinds—statements that prescribe mutually incompatible behavior—make paradoxical demands upon people; they are highly resistant to change and virtually impossible to escape. An example of a doublebind is the ancient theological riddle wherein an all-powerful God was to create a boulder so heavy that even He could not lift it. Watzlawick, Weakland, and Fisch (1974) refer to these predicaments and doublebinds as difficulties, to be distinguished from problems. According to them, a problem is solvable, whereas a difficulty eludes solution. One can only cope with it. After discussing the impasses created by human predicaments and cultural doublebinds, the authors will return to treat more fully the distinction between difficulties and problems.

### Human Predicaments

Erich Fromm (1959) suggested that many predicaments are occasioned by the unique position of the human being in the animal kingdom. People are the only animals capable of self-objectification. People alone are able to piece together a self-concept. Their ability to be aware of themselves is an endowment that follows from their position atop the phylogenetic scale. The new Brain, the cerebrum, contains an astounding associative network. The ten to twenty billion neurons housed in the new brain provide each person with the capability to make associations greater in number than the total combinations allowable by the celestial bodies in the known universe.

This amazing associational network would embarrass even the most complex of the computers developed to date. With this unique information storage and retrieval system, which Lilly (1972) calls the biocomputer, people are able to think in terms of past, present, and future; to engage in mental trial and error; to objectify themselves; and even to conceive of their own deaths. In addition to these remarkable mental gymnastics, the advanced brain makes it possible for people to experience anxiety, guilt, and loneliness.

As exhilarating as self-awareness may be, it nevertheless contributes to a sense of separateness and alienation. Lesser animals never experience this in the poignant manner in which humans feel it. Humans seem to know that they have cut the umbilical cord, their connection with unself-conscious nature, and are now on their own. One alternately whimpers dependently and then rails against the new-found freedom. One spends one's days seeking a substitute for the instantaneous and effortless gratification afforded by one's earlier intrauteral existence (Rank, 1936). An individual often appears willing to give up his birthright to freedom in exchange for a return to the painless paradise of the womb. Metaphorically speaking, when man ate of the Tree of Knowledge, and thus developed self-awareness, he was expelled from paradise. He had severed the umbilical cord that connected him to the rest of nature.

Self-awareness creates difficulties that cannot be solved. Separation resulting from the inability to be everywhere at once cannot be solved. Grief caused by the loss of a loved one cannot be solved. Concern for survival cannot be solved. Growing old cannot be solved. Having cancer or suffering an amputation cannot be solved. None of these conditions have solutions. They are inescapable, human predicaments with which one must learn to *cope*. Treating them as though they were problems that could be solved is a serious mistake.

According to Hans Selye, author of *Stress Without*.

*Distress* (1974), the human body recognizes the need merely to cope with certain stressors rather than to attack them. The body meets stressors with either syntoxic or catatoxic reactions. A syntoxic reaction triggers tissue tranquilizers, creating a state of passive tolerance or peaceful coexistence with the stressor. On the other hand, a catatoxic reaction triggers enzymes that attack the stressor. The same two reactions are appropriate at a psychological level. It is appropriate to attack some situations with a catatoxic-like reaction, but others must be coped with syntoxically. Catatoxic attacks upon stressors that can only be coped with will only further upset the psyche.

Other human predicaments are created by personal value systems. In order to change certain situations, it may be necessary to violate grossly these values, and in such cases, the situation may be impossible to change. Once a client who was a prisoner of her own value system complained to one of the authors that she was living with her husband in quiet desperation. She saw herself as vibrant, outgoing, and somewhat experimental, and she considered her husband as quite the opposite. He was a good, responsible man, but his needs for intimacy were minimal. She felt herself to be psychologically dying for lack of touch, warmth, and sharing. She had approached him many times about her incompleteness in this respect, but each time he had shown embarrassment and changed the subject.

Although divorce had crossed her mind many times, she did not feel free to do so. Her personal values effectively thwarted her in taking such action. She was a deeply committed Roman Catholic and respected the Church's proscription against divorce. Furthermore, it was important to her to think of herself as a kind, considerate person who could never hurt a husband who did not deserve such treatment. Moreover, she thought of herself as a loving, responsible mother who would not bring herself to cause suffering for her children in order

to meet her selfish needs. These values were as effective
as steel bands in restraining her from seeking a divorce,
and she was unwilling to give them up or even to modify
them. She was caught in a human predicament stemming
from her own value system. While she was trapped in a
relationship that offered little in the way of intimacy,
she was unwilling to terminate the relationship since she
had calculated the cost in terms of her personal values.
Ultimately we looked for ways in which she could achieve
closer ties with others without violating her values. This
predicament was not to be solved. The answer lay in coping as cleverly as possible.

## Cultural Doublebinds

Cultural prescriptions for behavior are not always
sane. The keen observer can usually spot within any
society certain cultural prescriptions that are paradoxical. One that is common to American culture is the command, "Be spontaneous!" The point is that one cannot
behave spontaneously while responding to a command.
American culture is replete with examples of doublebinds, many of which are thrust upon children by their
parents. Some parents are not content to force their
children to do what they require of them. They also demand evidence that the youngsters want to do it. At an
amusement park, a disconcerted mother was overheard
saying to her child, "I spent a lot of money getting you
in here, and you're going to enjoy it if I have to beat
you within an inch of your life!" Greenburg (1964:32)
offers the following example of another kind of parental
doublebind in his book, *How to Be a Jewish Mother*:
"Give your son, Marvin, two sport shirts as a present.
The first time he wears one of them, look at him sadly
and say in your Basic Tone of Voice: 'The other one you
didn't like?'"

American women are frequently caught in doublebind
demands. While they are exhorted to execute fully their
maternal duties by devoting themselves for years to the
rearing of their offspring, at the same time they are

scolded for clinging to the security of the home and urged to move out into the work world and assume their obligations. If the mother chooses to remain in the home with her children, she is likely to feel insipid, immature, and fearful. If she returns to the work world, she may see herself as a selfish, heartless, neglectful parent. In such doublebinds she is damned if she does and damned if she does not. She will find little salvation from her dilemma until she recognizes the insolvable nature of the doublebind.

## The Solution as the Problem

When one tries to treat difficulties arising out of inescapable human predicaments and cultural doublebinds as problems to be solved, the very steps taken to solve the problems are often problem-engendering. While thinking that the difficulty can be solved, one wastes enormous energy and creates endless unpleasantries for oneself and others by such ill-fated efforts. In such cases the solution is the problem (Watzlawick, Weakland, and Fisch, 1974).

The husband who fears being ignored more than death may demand attention from his wife to such an extent that she moves away from him. The more possessive he becomes of her time and attention, the more entrapped and consumed she feels. Consequently, she manufactures reasons for absenting herself from him. Thus, the very behaviors that he used to seek her attention cause her to ignore him in self-defense. His solution has become the problem.

A wife may be irritated by her husband's eternal pessimism and cynicism and may respond overly optimistically. He, in turn, may view her optimism as naive and attempt to moderate her views by repeatedly drawing her attention to the seamy, distressful side of life. The more they work on each other's problems, the greater the psychological distance between them becomes. As with so many marital and family problems, the solution has become the problem, and giving up on the problem sometimes makes things better. Sometimes couples rediscover and are reattracted to each other after they decide to get a divorce. At this point each gives up on the other, stops trying to make the other over, and the spontaneity and attractiveness sometimes returns.

There are, of course, many situations that can be changed. How does one distinguish the difficulties with which one must cope from the problems that can be solved? No simple rule works in every case, but there are a few aids one can employ in diagnosing the difference. One is usually dealing with a difficulty in the following instances:

If a trouble stems from biological limitations, such as shortness, unhandsome features, or congenital deformities.

If the only recognizable alternatives involve a clear violation of important values.

If the locus of responsibility for the troublesome behavior lies within others. If one is looking for other people to change to make one's life better, or if one is making unreasonable demands on others to meet one's needs, one is likely to be dealing with a difficulty. On the other hand, if one is looking to oneself to exercise all the options available to make one's life better, one is likely to be dealing with a problem that can be solved.

## What Will It Cost Me to Change?

Before embarking on an extensive program of self-change, ask yourself, "Do I really want to change?" Perhaps more appropriately, ask, "How *badly* do I want to change?" There is an old Spanish proverb that says, "Take what you will, but pay for it," and it is a wise person who realizes that everything has its price. One cannot take responsibility for a new course of action without first assessing the costs involved.

## Ambivalence about Change

Therapists quickly learn that the majority of clients are ambivalent about changing. They are miserable, confused by their symptoms, and therefore, driven to seek relief. They are even willing to expose their weaknesses to the therapist and to pay dearly for the privilege, but after all this, most clients are still ambivalent about changing. However self-defeating their symptoms may be in the long run, they tend to furnish some kind of immediate release from pent-up emotions. Consequently, clients sense that they must give up the familiar, immediate sources of nourishment in the hope that they will find more substantial sources within themselves and others. This is risky business. For this reason clients secretly embrace their symptoms as old friends and resist change in spite of their having come for therapy. The existential therapist, Kopp (1973:6), says the client often "prefers the security of known misery to the misery of unfamiliar insecurity." The therapist knows that no genuine progress will be experienced until the client is willing to loosen his grasp, to lift anchor, and to suffer through the change. We are all very much this way. We sense that growth does not come easily, that the old with its security must give way to allow for the new.

Seldom do significant personal changes occur without psychic pain of some sort. Perhaps the benchmark of a growing maturity is the willingness to suffer. To escape such anxiety, persons often deliver over their freedom to psychological authority figures—persons to whom they have imputed a control that is not inherently theirs. On the other hand, depression is the price of turning one's back on self-direction and self-creation. It seems healthier to suffer the pain that accompanies self-direction and self-creation than to suffer the pangs of self-recrimination that follow the decision to retreat from growth. Regarding this dilemma, Kopp (1973:144) wrote: "All his important decisions must be made on the basis of insufficient data. It is enough if a man accepts his freedom, takes his best shot, does what he can, faces the consequences of his acts, and makes no excuses."

Because being responsible for oneself is frightening, one often looks for parental substitutes to spare one the ordeal. One asks permission of others for actions that are clearly one's own options. One plaintively asks permission when it is clearly not the prerogative of the other person to grant it. One leans on the resources of others because one fears falling back on one's own. To do this, one elevates others—makes them authority figures. One makes parents out of them, gives them control over decisions, so that one is free to gripe and chafe, to attack them for not letting one do what one was afraid to do in the first place. Such authority figures can also be blamed for failures, and unfortunately, by the same token, they prevent one from honestly taking credit for successes.

Sometimes confession constitutes a request for permission. If one announces that one has a low boiling point, one may in reality be asking permission to explode when it suits one's purpose. This is a way of asking not to be held accountable for behavior.

A man who attempts to talk his wife into an open-marriage relationship so that he can have an affair with impunity is in effect seeking her permission. He wants to make her responsible for his behavior. He is capable of having an affair without her permission, but then he would have to be responsible for the consequences. Responsibility involves accepting the consequences before committing an act. And since responsibility is so frightening, one is often ambivalent about making even those changes that seem desirable.

## Destroying to Create

The Hindus perhaps originated the first systematic approach to personal change. They refer to God in three primary forms: *Brahma*, the creator; *Vishnu*, the preserver; and *Shiva*, the destroyer. It has always been a puzzle to the Western world that Shiva, who is a destroyer, should be deserving of worship. But with their total commitment to personal growth, the Hindus learned early that the old must be destroyed before the new can

**Figure 4–1.   The life cycle.**

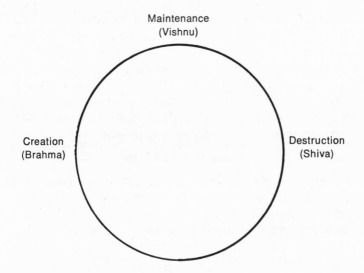

Maintenance
(Vishnu)

Creation
(Brahma)

Destruction
(Shiva)

be created. New life is always built upon the rubble of the old.

Similar processes operate within the human body, which replaces itself completely every seven years. The complementary processes of catabolism and anabolism are constantly at work. It is necessary to break down the old atomic patterns of the organic fuel through catabolism before the atoms can be reassembled through anabolism into life forms. Life-death, death-life—the cycle goes on endlessly. Each is necessary to the existence of the other. One must lift a foot off the secure rung below in order to climb a ladder. And one must give up some incomplete and self-defeating present comforts in order to gain the opportunity to try for more fulfilling life adjustments.

Growth or self-renewal sometimes requires the destruction of old relationships and old self-images. Some persons are locked into unsatisfying and unfulfilling marital relationships out of fear. Such persons may engage in obsequious behavior in order to maintain a relationship. They may suffer psychological and physical abuse rather than give up even the threadbare security of a demeaning relationship. Although divorce is often counterproductive, it can sometimes purchase the possibility of needed self-redefinition—a heavy price, but sometimes one that is better than the readjustment required to maintain an exploitative relationship.

## Playing Blind and Deaf

Unrealistic views of oneself and the world result in a blind-and-deaf approach to the world. Every thing, both animate and inanimate, is a kind of broadcasting station that is constantly sending signals—trying to tell us about our environment. The signals furnish vital information that can equip one to respect, enjoy, and use our world. Narrow, unrealistic views cause one to experience oneself and others in incomplete ways. One only picks up those aspects of the signal or message that are in accord with existing impressions.

The Hindus call this illusion *maya*. *Maya* furnishes a poor base from which to make life decisions; consequently, people often fail. Failure in turn causes one to become even more defensive in perceptual contacts with the world, and the resulting narrowness of perception leads to even more unrealistic views of self and the world. The antidote? *Shiva*. Destroy the old, unrealistic self-image in order to open up to more complete signals.

Swiss psychologist Jean Piaget suggests that there are two invariant functions by which one adjusts to the world: assimilation and accommodation. One assimilates a new experience when one forces its characteristics to fit within a category or concept that one has already hammered out. One accomodates when one forces changes in ready-made concepts to make them conform better to reality. An old concept may be enlarged or enriched, or a new one may be required. It is easier to assimilate than to accomodate. One is reluctant to change ready-made structure, and, consequently, one often ignores significant signals from experiences in order to assimilate these experiences within old concepts. The more one does this, the more one contributes to *maya,* that unrealistic and unworkable view of ourselves and the world.

The tendency to experience only enough of the signals to allow one to assimilate the experience within old concepts results in a general boredom. As a result, there are too many reruns in one's life. One just sits and stares. Similarly, when one forces new experiences into old frames, one is strangely detached from these experiences. People look for excitement in their lives because they fail to be receptive to their present perceptions. They tune out what does not fit their ready-made structure. William Blake said, "If the doors of perception were cleansed, everything would appear to man as it is, infinite. For man has closed himself up till he sees all through narrow chinks of his cavern." And Arthur Koestler in *The Sleepwalkers* states: "Every creative act involves ... a new innocence of perception, liberated from the cataract of accepted beliefs."

Sometimes one is forced by failure to change unrealistic views. An excellent example is the person who is fired from a job only to find that he moves into a much more rewarding position that he might not otherwise have sought. Failure, therefore, need not always be viewed as tragedy; failure can indeed contribute to the growth cycle if it prompts the destruction of inadequate frames of reference and stimulates the construction of more adequate ones.

An ancient Chinese saying warns that a crisis signals both danger and opportunity. Sometimes crises destroy old relationships that have been maintained at great expense to oneself. One may have held on to these relationships only out of fear that one would be unable to form more satisfying ones.

## How Does One Change?

Once one has resolved to change, one must settle on a strategy for bringing about the change. Very often one despairs of changing, since one believes that all available solutions have been tried. Unfortunately, this happens when one has locked oneself into a certain class of solutions, thereby failing to see other potential solutions.

### Changing a Mind-Set

Watzlawick, Weakland, and Fisch (1974) suggested that some problems are unresolvable as long as one limits oneself to first-order change. First-order change occurs when one vainly tries over and over again to use options only from within one class of solutions. One operates with a kind of tunnel vision and fails to see other possibilities. The situation can be changed only when one introduces second-order change, which occurs when one manages to break out of a mind-set, to go beyond the limited approaches to which one was unnecessarily chained.

Watzlawick, Weakland, and Fisch also demonstrated the need for second-order change with the use of the nine dot problem. The reader is asked to connect the nine dots shown in figure 4–2 using only four straight lines and without lifting the pencil from the paper or retracing any lines.

**Figure 4–2.   The nine dot problem.**

Most persons struggle at length with this problem because they operate within a mind-set. They assume that the dots define a square, and that one must not violate the sides of that square to find the solution. Once having made this assumption, one can repeatedly try differing combinations of four lines with the same inevitable result: one of the dots always remains unconnected.

Solution of the problem is possible only when the reader destroys his old mind-set. Then, and only then, is he free to try lines that extend beyond the square, which was, after all, only in his mind. The instructions for the problem certainly made no mention of a square. This problem parallels so many problems that persist only because of limiting, nonfunctional self-imposed assumptions. (The solution to the Nine Dot problem appears at the end of the chapter.)

Limiting oneself to an inadequate class of solutions is doubly hurtful, for it blinds one to potential solutions within other classes and sometimes results in maintaining a problem via the very solutions that are chosen.

Like millions of Americans, one of the authors has a problem with a lumbar vertebra. Approximately six years ago, the pain worsened as a result of prolonged physical labor that overly taxed his weak back muscles. He suffered severe, unmitigated pain for approximately three weeks. During this time, and for a few weeks thereafter, he received treatment from a well-known orthopedist. On the doctor's advice, he began an exercise regimen. As he slowly improved, he vowed that he would never again allow himself to become so out-of-shape. He extended the exercise regimen to several other routines, including jogging. He enjoyed the jogging and was psychologically rewarded for his self-discipline. He continued to build up mileage until he was running three to six miles a day. During this time he experienced only a residue of pain, which persisted and varied in its intensity. For six years he was required to make numerous life adjustments to cater to this condition. He asked himself whether the jogging and other physical routines could possibly be self-defeating, but had little evidence to conclude that it was. He even stopped for two or three days at a time to check out the results. The pain was unabated by these experiments, and so he concluded that he had been right in the design of physical fitness exercises —and that his back might be considerably worse off if he stopped the exercise.

One day, after jogging seven miles, his knees swelled painfully, forcing him to suspend the jogging for five months. Much to his surprise, the back condition improved considerably after the first few weeks. It gradually dawned on him that what he had intended as a solution, or at least as an aid, had greatly added to his pain. Unfortunately, it took another physical problem, inflamed knees, to bring about the second-order change.

In another example, one client, a middle-aged woman, complained that her husband was sabotaging her efforts to discipline their fifteen-year-old daughter. She had accumulated a great deal of resentment toward him and worried a great deal about the fate of her daughter. She asked for her husband's support, but he responded that she was too hard on the daughter. The wife concluded that it would be necessary for her to perform the disciplinary tasks of both father and mother if the daughter were to be salvaged. Assuming total responsibility, the mother became increasingly severe with the daughter. The more she disciplined her, however, the more the husband felt it necessary to erode her power base, and the more the husband and daughter aligned themselves against the mother.

A break in this disastrous cycle came when the mother realized that her behavior was actually contributing to the growing defection of both daughter and husband. She shared her insight with them and announced that she was delivering over to the husband the task of disciplining the daughter, since her efforts had clearly been self-defeating. She withdrew from potential conflicts, even when it pained her greatly. In the ensuing vacuum, the husband was forced to change his role with regard to his daughter, and, consequently, the previous alliance between husband and daughter loosened. The woman wisely refrained from "I told you so" scenes, and instead offered support to the husband when he shared his difficulty in properly managing the daughter. As a result of this second-order change technique, the relationship between wife and husband steadily improved. Previously, she had been locked into the common-sense notion that the way to control the daughter was to discipline her more.

Another common problem that is often solved by a change in thinking is the fear of public speaking. Many persons who must approach an audience to deliver a speech or confront an authority figure to make a request find themselves becoming increasingly nervous. Much energy is spent in trying to disguise the nervousness. People go to great lengths to prepare themselves for this ordeal. Such preparation is sometimes counterproductive. If one recognizes that trying to hide nervousness is, in a curious way, the problem itself, one may be en route to a creative solution for the problem. This writer has sometimes advised persons who are nervous in such situations to announce their nervousness. Once it is acknowledged, there is no further need to try to conceal it; one is freed to spend one's energy on the task at hand.

In summary, it is often helpful to change the mind-set with which a problem is approached. If one can recognize the limiting assumptions that have been made about classes of solutions, one can open oneself to more creative approaches.

Defining the Problem

From the discussion of second-order change, one can see clearly the importance of defining a problem properly. Quite often, one builds into a statement of a problem unnecessary parameters that severely limit the alternatives for action. The first and most important step in designing a strategy for self-change is to state the problem openly enough to prompt a consideration of competing classes of solutions.

The problem statement "How can I get into medical school with my C+ undergraduate grade point average?" may be unnecessarily restrictive. It is possible that the motivation behind this question is the search for an occupation that will offer many of the same financial and social rewards that are derived from the practice of medicine. In this eventuality, the problem statement might more appropriately become, "How can I identify and gain entrance into some occupation that will provide a high degree of financial success and social esteem?" Even in this form, the problem undoubtedly will be difficult to solve, but gaining entrance to medical school with a C+ average is all but impossible and, moreover, is unnecessary, if the second question is a more accurate statement of the problem.

Similarly, the problem statement "How can I get my spouse to become interested in tennis?" may be too restrictive. Perhaps a more apt statement of the problem would be: "How can I play tennis more often without feeling guilty about the time I am away from the family and without causing my spouse to become angry with me?" This broader statement allows for a larger number of potential solutions. One may never be able to interest one's spouse in the game, regardless of all the inducements one proposes. The spouse may be convinced that failure is inevitable, due to lack of coordination, and, consequently, the invitations are perceived as a form of badgering. Nevertheless, there are many classes of potential solutions to the second, more broadly worded, problem statement.

A problem statement must also be specific enough to be attackable. Do not settle for an ambiguous statement of the problem. Vague complaints must be translated into specific, attackable behaviors. The problem statement "I'm depressed and nothing seems to turn me on" is not attackable in its present form. Depression is often the result of perceived helplessness regarding the meeting of significant needs. For example, if a person feels the need for attention from members of the opposite sex, but believes that he is unlikely to get it, he is likely to become depressed. The nondirectional statement "I'm depressed and nothing seems to turn me on" must be made more specific. Upon further reflection, the statement may become: "I've tried and tried to screw up the courage to ask a classmate for a date, but I'm scared to death that she might turn me down, and, on the other hand, I'm scared to death that she might accept because I don't know how to talk to women alone." This statement is attackable on two fronts. One can attack the self-defeating talk, which says, "If she turned me down, that would be crushing—absolutely terrible. My ego couldn't cope with that!" And one can attack the problem of the lack of social skills.

Words are merely representatives of realities, and quite often, they are poor representatives at that. When persons fail to recognize this distinction, they treat words as though they were realities. While persons use words in trying to communicate what they want from others, it seldom occurs to them to check to see if a word or term means the same thing to the persons to whom they are speaking. One may say to a spouse, "You don't love me," but such allegations are seldom fruitful, since they do not tell the other person what he must do to please us. If, on the other hand, one says, "I am saddened because I have not been able to persuade you to go dancing more often," then the other person knows how to please if he cares to.

If one describes a problem as "laziness" or "incompetence," there is no clear direction for pursuing a solution. Once one uses such pejorative terms, one closes oneself off to other alternatives. It is easy, sloppy thinking to use such terms. It is better to define a problem in terms of "doings or happenings" rather than in abstract traits. Instead of concluding that one is lazy, if one says, "I have not yet located an approach to my work that seems likely to succeed," it is clear that one needs to seek consultation from others or to try other, new approaches.

A problem statement should also incorporate reasonable expectations for accomplishment. A natural tendency exists for persons who feel inadequate to overreact in goal setting—to make perfectionistic demands on themselves. When perfectionism is overcompensation for perceived weaknesses, it is merely a cop out, a mind trip one runs on oneself to delay starting the hard work required to change. If one assumes that the only goals worth pursuing are virtually impossible to achieve, then one can be excused for not trying at all. To dream the impossible dream may be noble and romantic, but it is hardly practical or likely to accomplish a desired change.

After several years of research regarding achievement motivation, David McClelland (1965) of Harvard concluded that successful persons tend to set moderate, rather than perfectionistic, goals. Since one borrows strength from past accomplishments for present endeavors, one is likely to bog down from insufficient motivation when one sets goals that require extremely difficult performances.

In summary, one is ready to plan a strategy for personal change only after one has stated the problem in a way that allows for as many solutions as possible, in a way that is specific enough to be attackable, and in a way that is modest enough to be achievable.

Focusing on Behavior

Attention is a powerful tool for personal change. Directing attention to a behavior quite often affects the frequency of the behavior. For this reason, automobile drivers are often told to direct their vision to the solid line along the right shoulder of the road when the lights of the approaching vehicle make it difficult to see. One is drawn toward the object of one's attention. If one were to look at the lights of the oncoming vehicle, one would be more likely to turn the nose of the car into its path. The act of directing attention is tantamount to directing the flow of energy.

The Soviet experimentation with Kirlian photography underscores this principle quite vividly. Kirlian photography, a lensless process of filming the electromagnetic field surrounding living bodies, has shown numerous flare points that correspond strikingly to the acupuncture points. Perhaps the most provocative outcome of Soviet research in this area is the ranking of stimuli according to their strength in influencing these flare points. In ascending order from least to most powerful these stimuli are: chemicals such as adrenaline, physical pressure, needles such as are used in acupuncture, electrical impulses, and laser beams. Moreover, more powerful than any of these is attention, or directed thought. If a person quietly directs attention to a part of the body, the radiation field shows a corresponding change.

Biofeedback experiments by scientists at Rockefeller University have demonstrated the ability of human subjects to cause specific cells of the body to fire at will. Some diabetics have been able to cause sluggish cells in the islet of Langerhans, a group of endocrine cells in the pancreas that contribute to secretion of insulin, to produce additional insulin.

Since cancerous cells have weaker electrical charges transversing their membranes than do normal cells, it is believed that these weaker charges are unable to inhibit DNA, the cells' programmer and production manager, from causing runaway growth. Some medical researchers speculate that, in the future, patients may be trained to increase the electrical charge by directing attention to such areas and, thus, arrest cancerous growths.

While these promising uses of therapeutic attention remain speculative at the moment, the uses of attention in personal change programs are well-documented (Mahoney and Thoresen, 1974). The frustration of past efforts to solve a problem has taught many persons to avoid thinking about a problem. People feel it is useless and self-punishing to think about problems, so they direct their attention to less disagreeable thoughts. Yet, attending to a problem in a constructive rather than in a morbid manner is helpful on two accounts: it helps one to understand the conditions that trigger and maintain the behavior, and it furnishes feedback on progress.

Behavior is always a response to a stimulus (a Latin word meaning "a goad" or "a prod"). The stimulus may come from the outside environment, or it may be self-initiated through thoughts and images. The influence of stimuli upon behavior can be most clearly seen in the one-celled life forms. Very little, if any, behavior in these organisms seems self-initiated. They move only as a reaction to outside stimuli, and their relationship to the environment is basically reactive.

A person's relationship to his environment, however, is much more complex and interactional. Behavior is quite often a response to internal stimulation, such as ideas, thoughts, beliefs, and images.

If one is to program one's own behavior, then one must influence the influencers, change the stimulus conditions that govern behavior.

There are two classes of stimuli: those that precede the behavior and are called cues and those that follow behavior and are called consequences. While both influence behavior, their functions are different. Cues are signals that prompt one either to avoid or to perform a given behavior, depending upon one's previous experience with the consequences of the behavior. If the consequences of the behavior are perceived as pleasant, then cues previously associated with the behavior flash a green light for the behavior; if the consequences are disagreeable, then a red light is signalled. Consequent stimuli are perceived as either rewarding or punishing. Behavior is largely governed by these consequences. Cues and consequences work together in controlling behavior.

## Changing the Cues

Cues are essential guides to behavior. Intelligent behavior requires a repertoire of skillful responses and a
sense of timing in the performance of these responses. It
is highly useful to be able to express affection, but it is not
always appropriate to do so. It is also useful to be able to
express irritation and anger, but the cost of doing so may
be dear if the situation is inappropriate. If one has been
fortunate, one's experiences have provided cues to assist
in recognizing the conditions in which such responses are
appropriate.

Unfortunately, not all experiences prepare one to perform appropriately. Some childhood training may have
taught inappropriate cues. For example, one may have
learned to cower, fawn, or otherwise appear helpless
when confronted by powerful people (parents or other
adults) who threaten. Some people learn to bellow and
intimidate when they are in a situation where others
control important resources.

The cues that trigger a child's responses may have
been quite functional for a child, but these same cues are
often inappropriate guides for adult behavior. A child
mistreated by a malevolent, uncaring father may learn
to respond cautiously and obsequiously in his presence.
His presence, then, becomes a cue to trigger fearful,
dependent behavior. One may find oneself still experiencing these same behaviors as an adult. Worse yet, the
tendency to defer may spread to other powerful figures
reminiscent, in some subconscious way, of one's father.
These cues have outlived their usefulness and now continue to cause discomfort in the presence of certain persons. Since such cues often function more or less sub-
consciously, one may not know why one freezes emotionally or responds with cowardice, or cannot think
straight and assert oneself on certain occasions.

One can discover the relationships between such cues
and behavior by attending to situations immediately pre-

ceding the disliked behavior. A cigarette machine, a coffee break, or being in the presence of someone smoking may constitute a strong cue to smoke. The sight of a refrigerator, a cookie jar or, in many cases, a TV set may serve as a cue for eating. If one can identify such cues, one can either avoid them or attempt to change their signal value.

Thoresen and Mahoney (1974) cite the efforts of Odysseus to avoid certain tempting cues for himself and his crewmen. It was the practice of the Sirens to lure passing seamen to their deaths with their enchanting calls. To avoid hearing the seductive Sirens, Odysseus commanded his men to fill their ears with beeswax and had himself tied to the mast. These precautions were maintained until the seamen were safely out of hearing range.

In a similar manner, one may choose to avoid certain cues that trigger undesirable behavior. Some time back one of the authors was interested in losing ten pounds. He analyzed his eating habits and concluded that during the daylight hours his intake of calories was actually less than the number required to maintain his weight. From 9:00 P.M. to 11:00 P.M., however, he ate continuously while watching television. He was often bored with the quality of the programming; consequently, he passed the hours pleasantly with the help of food. He decided to retire at 9:30 P.M. in order to avoid the nightly gorging. The plan worked splendidly, and he lost the ten pounds in fewer than six weeks. He successfully changed his behavior not by punishing the act of overeating, but by avoiding the stimuli that triggered it.

Behavior often occurs only in certain situations. If one can identify these situations and avoid them or remove them, one can effectively reduce the behavior in question.

Some time ago a youngster accused of being rebellious and disrespectful by a teacher was sent to one of the authors by his parents. The author was supposed to work on the boy to cause him to behave more appropriately in the classroom. After he had gained the child's confidence, he questioned him about his behavior in school. He found that he behaved acceptably in other classrooms, a fact later confirmed by the principal. Moreover, the author learned that the rebellious and disrespectful behavior always followed criticisms by the teacher of his personal grooming and sloppy handwriting. Upon learning this, the author decided that his real client was the teacher. He decided that the child's inappropriate behavior was, in fact, understandable in the light of the teacher's criticisms of his person and handwriting. The author tactfully shared this observation with the teacher, who made a concerted effort thereafter to avoid such adverse criticism. The happy result was that the child's rebelliousness predictably subsided. In this case the cue was removed, and the triggered behavior disappeared.

It is not always possible to avoid or remove a triggering cue. In such cases it is sometimes possible to change the signal value of such cues, that is, to destroy a cue's ability to trigger a behavior. It was noted earlier that the cue derives its ability to trigger avoidance or approach from its association with rewarding or punishing consequences following behavior. One of the authors has noted that his otherwise disgustingly independent cat rubs her fur across his legs and meows loudly when he approaches the refrigerator—provided she is hungry. She obviously has noticed that he goes to the refrigerator before placing food in her dish. His approach to the refrigerator, then, has become a signal that something very good is about to happen. This cue then triggers the cat to meow and rub against his legs, which, it must seem to the cat, encourages him to feed her. Indeed, the strategy often works. In this example, the approach to the refrigerator cues the cat's behavior, which, in turn, cues the author's obliging response. He supposes his reward is the sight of a satisfied cat—or could it be stopping her infernal racket?

If a cue derives its tendency to trigger behavior from the perceived consequences of the behavior, then one can extinguish a cue by changing the perceived consequences. The author suspects his cat would behave quite differently when he approached the refrigerator if it had been his habit to kick the cat each time he opened the refrigerator door. In this case, approaching the refrigerator would become a cue for the cat to scurry out of the room. Were he to institute this new behavior, he could change the signal value of the cue by changing the resulting consequences. This would be an example of aversion therapy.

Aversion therapy is a somewhat questionable technique in behavior therapy. It is sometimes used to treat alcoholism. Since the liquor bottle, liquor glass, and other paraphernalia associated with the habit are known to be cues for the act of drinking, the task of aversion therapy is to cause such paraphernalia to trigger a "stop drinking" response rather than a "drinking" one. Upon giving his consent, a client is wired so that a mildly disagreeable electrical current is directed to one of his fingers immediately following his movement toward such objects. The current stops when he moves away from the objects. Through this process these paraphernalia eventually come to trigger nondrinking rather than drinking behavior because their cue value has been changed.

## Changing the Consequences

It is also important to direct one's attention to the consequences of one's behavior. What happens after one gets angry, cries, apologizes or withdraws from an argument? One does what he gets paid for. If one continues a behavior, even one that grieves one sorely, it must be because it is in some sense rewarding. This concept is sometimes difficult to understand, for it seems that there are no rewards for some habits. How is one rewarded for the fit of anger that embarrasses, the flood of tears that makes one appear childish, or sickeningly compliant behavior in the face of demands by others? On cursory inspection such behaviors appear to hurt in every respect. Upon closer scrutiny, however, we may discover hidden rewards. The compliance that results in self-contempt may reduce the anxiety felt when one senses that confrontation is brewing. The tears that make one feel childish may bring the nurturing attention of persons important to us. And the anger that embarrasses may intimidate others and cause them to allow one to have one's way.

If one discovers the uses of one's behavior, one may decide that it is not really necessary to change it—at least not until some more acceptable way of accomplishing the same purpose is found. Both authors have foolishly spent considerable time attempting to help clients change behaviors that, in fact, they did not want to change. There were hidden purposes for the behavior, and the client was unconsciously resisting change since he was unaware of any good alternatives.

One is wise to attend to consequences, all consequences. When one discovers that undesirable habits are reinforced by hitherto unrecognized consequences, one is free to search for more acceptable ways of serving the same end. If one does not find more creative solutions, then one may choose to continue the habit.

Narciso and Burkett (1975) suggest that helplessness, suffering, and anger are learned techniques for getting one's way. When one claims helplessness, one is often avoiding self-responsibility. The built-in reward for helplessness is escape from personal accountability. When one demonstrates suffering, one is often instrumental in getting others either to pay attention, apologize, or feel guilty for having hurt one's feelings. And finally, when one demonstrates anger, one often frightens others into submission or, at least, one gets their attention. Each of these emotional behaviors is a self-serving technique calculated to get others to meet one's needs.

One finds that there is a small pay-off for some behavior that one wants to increase. If one examines the

consequences of such behaviors, it becomes obvious why
they have not been performed more often. It may be that
one no longer expresses irritation when others violate
one's rights because the consequences of earlier efforts
were perceived as being punishing. One may find it difficult to persist at homework assignments, because it may
appear that past study efforts did little to improve
grades. One may abandon efforts to get children to do
household chores because the resulting conflict is so
unpleasant. One may have difficulty motivating oneself
to apply for a better job if previous efforts were unsuccessful.

Whether one fails at assertion, improving study habits,
disciplining children, or seeking better employment, one
concludes that one is weak, lazy, or incompetent. Such
name-calling, in fact, does little to change behavior. It
is far better to question the particular behaviors used to
accomplish one's purposes. If one is unhappy with a
failure to stand up for personal rights, perhaps one
should attend a workshop on assertiveness training or
read books on the subject. If study habits need improving, perhaps one should compare one's habits with those
of students who earn better marks. Perhaps one would
be more successful in getting children to do chores by
examining the consequences when they do and do not
perform the chores. Children sometimes condition
a parent to give in by responding angrily and only half
completing a task. If this is the case and one concludes
that one still wants the children to do the chores, then
certain significant changes in the approach need to be
adopted. For example, one may wish to establish a rule
that the children cannot play until their work is done.
Obviously, any such move is attendant with hazards, but
the point is that one should question one's methods, *not
one's person*. One should understand that any person is
unlikely to perform any behavior consistently that does
not pay off. Either the behavior must change or an

attempt to change the consequences of the behavior must be made.

The reader will note that the authors have not recommended a pilgrimage into the distant past in order to understand individual behavior. In trying to eliminate self-defeating behaviors, it is seldom useful to search out their historical determinants. At best, the search concludes with a curious admixture of fact and fiction, since these determinants may not have been sufficiently logged in memory, and since time has a way of clouding the memory traces that are retained. Moreover, only that portion of the past that has resulted in reflexive habits or is retained in present memory currently influences behavior. If one somehow reifies the past as though it actually exists at present, as if it had been dragged along fully intact over the years, then one may convince oneself that behavior is beyond control. Alan Wheelis (1973) suggests that analytical therapy often overemphasizes the importance of the past. In writing of the analyst's efforts to make the client aware of the influences of the past, he concluded:

> ... whether this greater awareness will increase or diminish freedom will depend upon what it is we become aware of and how we use it. If the greater awareness is of unconscious forces which are postulated as determining causes and which remain outside our experience, and if we use that understanding of the past only to prove that we "had" to become what we are, then, since this view applies equally to the present, which is the unbroken extension of that determined past, therapy may become a way of establishing why we must continue to be what we have been, a way of disavowing choice with the apparent blessing of science, and the net effect will be a decrease in freedom (p. 117).

To some extent one is what one is because of what one

has been. People too frequently victimize themselves by recollections of personal histories. There are, of course, warm glowing parts of a past that can sustain and comfort, but for the person who feels the need for change, this is usually not the case.

Genetics supplies the most frequent and devastating argument for the past as prologue by demonstrating the relationship between physical characteristics and inheritance. Emotionally, the Freudian heritage has been a major factor in convincing people that their early childhood years bestow a great many conditions on them while they stand helplessly by. One is left with a pervasive belief that there is little or nothing that can be done to change short of psychoanalysis.

A simplistic but somewhat surprising truth about the past is that it no longer exists. Only the recollection and, more important, the perception, of the past exists. Under those conditions the past as a reality is academic and irrelevant, but perceptions of the past are extremely important. The eminent psychologist, Alfred Adler, deviated from Freud in his finding that individuals are held victim by the perceptions they have of their power, or lack thereof, as they grow up. His primary therapeutic striving was to help the individual come to grips with the fact that life does not have to be repeated according to one's recollections of the first act. Another of Adler's contributions was to use therapy to educate his clients, to teach them how they had learned to be powerless and to help them discover their own personal routes to responsible adult living.

Used in this way, knowledge of one's present perception of the past can provide insight regarding the ways one can best unlearn something or learn something new. It can tell one about one's learning style. The past never indicates an inability to learn.

In short, while the past-oriented "why" used in the question "Why have I become the way I am?" is of little help, there is a present-oriented "why" that is absolutely essential for designing any change strategy. It draws attention to present factors, to cues and consequences presently operating. The present-oriented "why" is much less likely to point to villains that one can blame for one's misery without having to take personal responsibility for a refusal to suffer through change.

The importance of focusing clearly on the present-oriented "why" can be seen in the following case. Ann sought therapy because of her inadequacy in dealing with her home situation. Her husband, Bob, had brought his mother to live with them following a long hospitalization for a broken hip. The mother-in-law always seemed to be in the way.

Ann and her mother-in-law clashed often over the manner in which the children were being reared. Ann thought her mother-in-law overindulged the children. She constantly gave them money, and while Ann did not confront her over this, she did make the children return the money.

Ann's mother-in-law also sided with the children in their rebellion at going to bed, but Ann ignored her and nagged the children until they finally went to bed. In many other situations, the mother-in-law greatly aggravated Ann's difficulties in handling the children. Whenever Ann complained of the situation, Bob became furious. Ann believed that it was bad for the children to see their father so angry with her; consequently, she would quickly apologize and avoid bringing up the issue again. Eventually, she could take it no longer. She would mention the problems again, and Bob would become angry again. She was intimidated, and the cycle began anew.

This situation could be approached without any investigation whatsoever of Ann's past. The problem could be viewed as her failure to assert herself effectively with her husband and mother-in-law. Even if she attempted to assert herself, she retreated under fire. One merely needed to identify the cues triggering her retreat and the consequences that followed. There were at least three cues that triggered her retreat: (1) her belief that the children should not see their father in a state of rage, (2) the angry retort of her husband, and (3) the fear that it aroused. The rewarding consequences of her retreat were a lessening of his anger and a subsequent reduction in her fear. The punishing consequences of her retreat were the continuing interference of the mother-in-law and the self-contempt that Ann experienced. By becoming aware of the nature of her behavior, Ann was able to deal more effectively with the situation.

Conditional Rewards

After one has properly defined a behavior and carefully attended to cues and consequences, one must plan to provide rewards for any intended change. One should do this on the same basis that it is done in business and industry. The rewards must be conditional, that is, they must be made contingent upon the desired performance.

The self-administration of rewards is a tricky matter. It is always possible to cheat, for who will know? One can partly take care of this problem by making public one's intentions. Most persons do better if they put pressure on themselves by informing others of their goals and progress. Nevertheless, under the most stringent precautions, there are still opportunities for cheating. And there is ultimately no foolproof antidote for this.

There are, however, some ways to inhibit cheating. Some rewards, for example, lose their meaning when self-administered. What real gain is there in taking money out of one pocket and placing it in another? Money is an ineffective reward under such circumstances. There is one way, however, in which money can be a meaningful reward. That is when one gives a significant sum to a trusted friend to be returned in agreed-upon amounts provided one meets one's goals. The money will be even more rewarding if the contract carries the proviso that it will be sent to a detested organization if one fails to meet the goals. This plan worked beautifully for a doctoral student who had difficulty finishing his dissertation.

There are four basic classes of rewards: (1) tangibles such as money, food, or other objects; (2) social attention such as compliments or expressions of affection; (3) enjoyable activities; and (4) feedback regarding progress. In the authors' experience, they have found the last two classes of rewards to be more useful than the first two in self-administered programs. Money and other tangibles are not usually rewarding when self-administered—for reasons already discussed. If compliments and expressions of affection are freely given by significant others, they are very motivating; indeed, they are among the most powerful of all rewards when given freely and spontaneously. Given at one's request, they appear contrived and forced and are less effective.

Favorite activities as rewards for behavior often work. A game of tennis, a few hours for loafing, an hour or two at the piano, going to the theater, and taking a trip are only a few of the possibilities. Such activities serve as rewards if one engages in them only after reaching a goal. First lose the excess weight, then take the trip. First do the required reading, then off to the tennis courts. First do the yoga exercises, then watch TV. Moreover, if such activities are to be rewarding, one must shut oneself off from them at all other times. If one is already watching TV extensively, further viewing is unrewarding. If one plays tennis several days a week, one more game is not likely to be sufficiently rewarding. In fact, it is wise to wean oneself off any activity for a reasonable period before attempting to use it as a reward.

The most natural of all self-administered rewards is feedback regarding one's progress. Very often persons who attempt self-change programs tire of other rewards, but continue to value feedback. Without feedback virtually no progress is made. While feedback sometimes comes from others in the form of praise or criticism, feedback can also take the form of records that reflect progress.

Finding the Starting Line

One needs to know where both the start and finish lines are before progress can be measured. If one has stated a problem specifically, the finish line, or goal, will be clearly in focus. It is also helpful in measuring progress to know where one started. One of the authors once had a client who refused to weigh herself before starting a diet. She said that she knew she was grossly overweight and did not want to punish herself by climbing on the scales. She managed to lose a modest amount of weight, but she was never quite certain how much. This kind of fuzziness about a starting line is usually discouraging, and it makes it difficult to know how well a plan is succeeding.

There are many ways of getting a reading on the frequency of a behavior. If one is trying to lose weight, then one can measure pounds, calories ingested, or snacks eaten. If one is trying to stop smoking, one can measure the number of cigarettes smoked in a twenty-four hour period, the number of hours in the day in which one did not smoke, or even the length of time spent smoking. If one is trying to become more outgoing, one can measure the number of times during the day that one initiates conversation with others or the amount of time spent in the company of others.

The Taste of Success

Few things are as rewarding as noting progress. The expression "Nothing succeeds like success" is particularly true in self-change programs. Feedback or knowledge of results, then, is crucial to personal change. It is for this reason that one is encouraged to keep continuous records of progress.

And one is unable to keep accurate records unless the behavior has been specifically defined. One must be able to identify instances and noninstances of behavior. Without such specificity efforts to chart progress or failure are likely to be grossly inexact.

The frequency and kind of records depend largely on the kind of behavior in question. As a rule, however, a full day is as long as one should go without some kind of evaluation or recording. When a behavior is very difficult to begin, more frequent recording may be necessary. The recording itself is often rewarding, as it provides immediate feedback. If one has to wait for long periods without feedback, there is a tendency for motivation to sag. Many educational psychologists think that the nine-week report card periods used by many schools have little to do with performance because this period is too long to motivate for most students. Daily grades are much more likely to influence behavior.

The recording of behavior is tedious, and there is a natural tendency for one to stop recording as soon as one has become thoroughly indoctrinated into a change program. But, as was pointed out in an earlier section, attention is a powerful reinforcer of behavior; remove the attention too early, and one may seriously reduce the frequency of the behavior.

This principle is frequently at work in public school classrooms. One author recalls advising a second-grade teacher to place five nonreading boys on a self-instructional program especially designed for nonreaders. The materials had a great deal of appeal to the boys, and they were soon making noticeable progress. When the teacher was convinced that the program was working, she decided to give her attention to other students. Approximately three days after she withdrew her attention, the boys complained of disinterest in the materials. The teacher took renewed interest in their performance and as a result, the boys resumed their progress at the task. The teacher had withdrawn her powerfully reinforcing attention too soon. Similarly, withdrawing attention from self-progress before the behavior becomes thoroughly habitual is often disastrous to the program. One must continue to monitor the behavior, to chart, to keep records, to endorse oneself, and to keep one's eye on the goal.

The human being is an information-processing animal. It depends upon feedback for the simplest performance. The body itself is a kind of self-correcting mechanism, which depends upon both exterior and interior feedback. Some of the feedback to guide behavior comes from the senses. One can see and/or hear the results of one's performances. Other feedback comes from interior nerve endings buried within muscles and organs. For example even with closed eyes, one is able to tell in what direction one has extended an arm. In such cases the feedback comes from the tiny interior nerve endings within the body.

One simply cannot hope to make serious progress toward a goal without feedback. If a program for change is working, then knowing about it increases one's resolve to continue. If it is not, then knowing about it allows one to make any necessary adjustments.

Plans for change often require adjustments when put into action. One may have anticipated a complete and perfect performance before it is likely, and one may need to accept instead some approximation to the full-blown performance. One may have planned for a desirable consequence that, in fact, one cannot provide, or that turns out to be less desirable in reality. One may find one has defined the problem behavior so abstractly that there is difficulty monitoring it.

Still, the need to structure a program remains. Structure is an effective antidote for the generalized anxiety that can result from the overwhelming ambiguity of some situations. One of the authors allows himself to become foolishly overcommitted. As a result, he becomes increasingly nervous over deadlines. Upon occasion the resulting anxiety is immobilizing. He sits staring aimlessly, looking for opportunities to be distracted, and generally accomplishing nothing of importance. It is only when introduced to some structure that his anxiety is assuaged. If he stops the cycle by carefully defining the full scope of the responsibilities assumed, if he establishes real time constraints under which he is working, and if he orders the enabling performances necessary for the accomplishment of the whole of them, then—and only then—does he feel any relief from the nagging uneasiness. It is only then that he can move his muscles in purposeful directions.

While it is true that a journey of a thousand miles starts from where one presently is, it is vital to know in which direction to drop the first foot. Establishing structure is tedious; it takes effort, and, for most persons, it is not fun. Nevertheless, seldom do persons carry through on important assignments without a reasonable degree of direction or structure. This is particularly important in the beginning. One may have failed several times at trying to change behavior, and unless one has a well-defined, reasonably convincing plan, one's present efforts are likely to suffer an early death for lack of sustaining motivation.

Beginning Efforts

When one begins a new behavior, two observations are quite likely. It may seem to take a lot of effort to get the new plan off the ground, and the new behavior quite likely will seem unnatural. There is a principle in mutual-fund investments called front-end loading. When first beginning an investment plan with many of these mutual funds, a disproportionate amount of the initial investment is taken for administrative fees. Later, the amount accruing to an account increases markedly. Self-change programs are similar. To get any behavior started to any noticeable degree may require a great deal of attention and effort. Later the behavior can be maintained with a fraction of the initial effort. Motorists recall the inital awkwardness of learning to drive an automobile. Each

maneuver, such as depressing the clutch and shifting
gears, at first completely absorbs one's full attention.
Later, however, a rhythm is established, and the most complex of tasks flows as a simple, effortless performance.

Persons often discourage themselves from change by
saying such things as, "This is ridiculous! It's just not
me. People tell me I'm acting." But in reality, who is the
real you or I? Behaviors that now seem natural were
themselves awkward initially. Behaviors, it is important
to remember, can be naturally good or naturally bad. One
often attempts change because one concludes that
a natural behavior is simply not functional. Swinging a
golf club as one swings a baseball bat may feel quite
natural to the beginner, but the trajectory of the ball hit
this way often indicates that the swing is nonfunctional.
The more one performs a new behavior, the more natural
it will become. One has only to decide who one wants to
be and to follow through with careful planning and consistent efforts.

Effects of Time and Practice

Considerable time and practice are necessary for
eliminating old responses and growing used to new ones.
Too often, a person develops an unrealistic time frame
within which to accomplish a change. While it is only
human nature to want to do something and get it over
with, most habits are highly resistant to change. They
even seem to return spontaneously after inadequate efforts to eliminate them. More often, persons fall prey to
fad diets, easy-to-swallow mood changers, and weekend,
personality-altering marathons.

On the other hand, the best, time-tested formula for
personal change looks something like this:

Motivation $(X)$ Program-For-Change $(X)$ Practice
$(X)$ Time $(=)$ Change

If any factor in the formula is inadequate, the resulting change will be meager. If any factor is nonexistent, everything to the right of the equal sign will be zero. Zero times anything is zero. Therefore the stronger the motivation, the more promising the program for change, the greater the practice, and the longer the program is maintained, the more significant the resulting change is likely to be.

## Rejecting Guilt

Once one is committed to a program of change, one should steadfastly resist the tendency to feel guilty over temporary backsliding. Guilt tends to be nonproductive. Furthermore, guilt is a depressor. It robs one of the motivation and energy necessary for change. Guilt often goes hand in hand with perfectionism. Both are usually counterproductive.

While it takes great courage to embark on the journey toward changing old habits, almost as much courage is needed to be imperfect along the way. This is not to be confused with planned imperfection, which is a world apart from the imperfection that is a natural by-product of any attempt at change. Without tolerance for such imperfection, one can never stand the journey, because of its unpredictability and the possibility of failure.

The usual path of self-change is like the flight of a bird. There is some wing flapping, some climbing, and then some coasting. Persons, too, work hard at change for a while, and then tend to coast for a while. If one requires perfectionism, one quits upon the first indication of backsliding or coasting. The Zen aphorism, "Gentle is the way," is good advice to counter these natural tendencies. One must be able to put backsliding into perspective. One must have a healthy respect for the difficulty involved in re-creation. The person who has the best chance for success is one who has come to accept oneself, whether climbing or coasting.

In summary, certain considerations are necessary to carry out well-designed plans for personal change. One

**Figure 4–3.    Solution to the nine dot problem.**

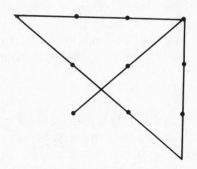

must define the problem openly enough to allow for competing classes of solutions and yet specifically enough to be attackable. One must discover the cues and consequences of behavior. One must attempt to remove or neutralize cues that trigger inappropriate behaviors and establish others that trigger appropriate ones. One must control, as much as possible, the consequences to insure that appropriate behavior is rewarded. These rewarding consequences must be made contingent upon performance of the desired behavior. And finally, we must continuously monitor progress for motivational purposes.

# 5. Choosing One's Company

*Bad company is loss, and good company is gain:*
*...In company with the wind the dust flies heaven-*
*ward; if it joins water, it becomes mud and sinks.*

Tulsi Das

*WARNING: If you don't have room in your living*
*room for an elephant—don't make friends with the*
*elephant trainer.*

Sufi mystic

Group pressure is a powerful influence on behavior. One is often dragged down from lofty resolutions by the company of persons disinclined to seek the same or similar goals. On the other hand, one is sometimes motivated to pursue nobler ends by the good examples of others. If one wishes to strengthen one's motivation to change, then one obviously should choose one's company wisely.

Associate with others seeking similar ends when you first attempt to break old habits and form new ones. Once you have firmly established the new behavior you may be able successfully to resist negative group influences, but it is foolhardy to subject oneself to unsympathetic audiences before the budding behavior has had a chance to become adequately rooted. The group's disinterest, or perhaps scorn, for a pursuit may strangle the early growth of improved habits.

Alvin Toffler, in his book *Future Shock* (1970), recognized the potential gain from group members sharing the same concern when he recommended "situational grouping" as a strategy for dealing with adjustment problems occasioned by the ever-increasing rate of change in modern society. He borrowed the idea from Gerjuoy who in an interview with him recommended that temporary groups be formed for "families caught in the upheaval of relocation, for men and women about to be divorced, for people about to lose a parent or a spouse, for those about to gain a child, for men preparing to switch to a new occupation, for families that have just moved into a community, for those about to marry off their last child, for those facing retirement—for anyone, in other words, who faces an important life change" (pp. 340–41)."

Social learning theorists (Bandura, 1969; Dollard, Doob, Miller and Sears, 1939) wrote extensively about the influence of groups on behavior. The behavioral pre- and proscriptions of groups important to an individual have a powerful impact on his behavior. The influence of street gangs upon the behavior of youth is all too well known to law enforcement personnel. These gangs often prescribe antisocial behaviors and proscribe snitching and other forms of cooperation with the authorities. Reference groups offer identification, support, and a feeling of importance to their members. Conversely, the desirable socializing influence of religious societies and civic groups upon members is widely believed to be uplifting and positive.

Persons are to a large extent social animals, and they depend heavily upon one another for support and guidance. There is a strong tendency to mimic the behavior of significant others. This imitative learning accounts for a significant amount of one's behavior, and, consequently, one is well advised to expose oneself to good behavioral models. A Sufi mystic aptly expressed the idea: "If you don't have room in your living room for an elephant, don't make friends with the elephant trainer."

Fortunately, there exist in many communities self-help groups formed to encourage members to change in desirable ways. They may be designed to help members lose weight, stop smoking, avoid alcohol or other drugs, stop gambling or child abuse, study more effectively, exercise, or gain political power. These nonprofessional self-help groups are open to the public. The costs are usually minimal or nonexistent, and members are often self-referred. Many of these groups are extremely helpful to persons wishing to make personal changes in their lives. There are a number of referral sources that can be consulted for assistance in locating an appropriate lay group.

## Choosing One's Company

Some states—Georgia, South Dakota, and North Carolina, for example—provide a state-wide referral service, which offers access to available services throughout the entire state. As an example of how these work, a caller in Georgia may dial the Tie-Line number, indicate the nature of his problem, and receive guidance as to the availability of assistance in his local community. Referral consultants who handle incoming calls are trained to cut through the usual red tape in an effort to provide an immediate link-up between the consumer and the service agency. A three-way conversation takes place between the consumer, the referral consultant, and a representative of the service agency.

Other agencies offer services similar to those provided by the statewide referral agencies, but referrals are limited to a geographical area. The number of a community referral agency can be obtained by telephoning the information number listed under city government or the local United Way.

One can often obtain expert referral assistance from a local branch of the National Association for Mental Health, which is a nationwide organization of citizens and consumers of mental health services; consequently,

it is likely to be less biased in its referrals than would be
the case if it were run by professionals. It is the business
of this organization to know what is available publicly
and privately. Some local branches also publish direc-
tories of community resources. One can usually locate the
branch number under the listing "Mental Health Association of . . ." in a telephone directory.

One of the more accessible referral sources is the Yellow Pages. Under the heading Social Service Organizations are listings of such services in most communities.

## Lay Self-Help Groups

A few of the more important national, self-help groups
are described below. The group's purpose, clientele, frequency of group contact, nature of the group's interaction, fees required, and suggested ways of contacting the
group are included.

### Weight-Regulation Groups

Losing weight is a difficult task for the more than
forty million overweight Americans. More difficult still
is keeping weight off once one has lost it. Roughly 80 percent of those who lose weight gain it back during the next
year. The need for social support in overcoming health
problems such as overweight is great. While some persons with iron wills appear to be able to accomplish the
task alone, many persons strongly need the support of
others. In addition, while most persons are bored with an
overeater's reports of indulgence or denial, fellow sufferers demonstrate a great interest, which may prove to
be the support necessary to persist in fighting this battle.
Two of the more successful self-help groups concerned
with weight reduction are Weight Watchers and Overeaters Anonymous. One or both are likely to be found in
any community.

### *Weight Watchers*

The best known of these groups is Weight Watchers.
This international organization that has helped millions

of persons was founded by Jean Nidetch (*The Story of Weight Watchers,* 1972) in her home when she sought the help of overweight friends in her efforts to diet. The purpose of the group is to offer support and encouragement for persons seeking to lose weight or to maintain previous weight losses. The organization distributes a monthly publication, *Weight Watchers Magazine,* and many supplementary dietary booklets.

Clientele include seriously overweight persons, mildly overweight persons having difficulty in further trimming, and persons wishing to maintain previous weight loss. Weekly meetings begin with a weigh-in. Members mix socially until all are weighed. Each member's weight is publicly announced, provided the weight represents a loss or a weight-loss maintenance. Each victory is applauded. The director leads a discussion of a weight-related topic, and low-calorie recipes are shared. New members are weighed, assigned a goal according to ideal weight tables, and oriented to a diet plan.

After one has lost the first ten pounds, he is rewarded with a pin and given an opportunity to testify before other members about the usefulness of the diet plan. Diet adjustments are made at each ten pound weight loss, and a member is shifted to a special leveling plan when within ten pounds of the ideal weight. Upon attaining the assigned goal, the member switches to the maintenance plan.

While the diet is useful, the magic of the program lies in the built-in social reinforcement. There is heavy group pressure for weight loss and weekly accountability. The weekly recognition of weight loss is a powerful aid to motivation. The membership fee is around $10, and a modest weekly fee is collected at each session. A reader may contact the local chapter by consulting the local telephone directory.

*Overeaters Anonymous*

Overeaters Anonymous is an international organization designed to help compulsive overeaters. It began in the 1960s and patterned itself after the successful Alcoholics Anonymous (A.A.) program. It has basically adapted the Twelve Step Program of Recovery of A.A. While the reader will have a much better idea of the Overeaters Anonymous program after reading the more detailed treatment given A.A. later in the chapter, a brief description here may be helpful.

The two-hour meeting is led by a volunteer leader, who may share a personal experience with the group. The format of the meeting usually calls for discussion, a panel of speakers, or group sharing of experiences. Unlike Weight Watchers, Overeaters Anonymous does not concern itself with food, menus, eating hints, or weighing-in. Like A.A., it rests largely on personal testimonies and social support and seeks to get at the basic causes for compulsive eating.

Members are urged to attend meetings several times a week, if possible, to be honest, open-minded, and willing to help others. There are no fees, but free-will offerings are taken. Consult a local telephone directory for a phone number.

Addiction-Control Groups

*Alcoholics Anonymous*

Certainly the best known of the self-help groups is Alcoholics Anonymous. The World Health Organization called it "the greatest therapeutic organization in the world" (St. Elizabeth's *Reporter,* 1972). This international organization, founded in the 1930s, has assisted thousands of persons to live sober, responsible lives. Alcoholics Anonymous often works where doctors, psychiatrists, psychologists, friends, and relatives fail. The most likely reason for its success is the generous social reinforcement afforded members by fellow sufferers. The purpose of the organization is aptly stated in its preamble:

Alcoholics Anonymous is a fellowship of men and women who share their experience, strength, and hope with each other that they may solve their common problem and help others to recover from alcoholism.

The only requirement for membership is a desire to stop drinking. There are no dues or fees for A.A. membership; we are self-supporting through our own contributions.

A.A. is not allied with any sect, denomination, political organization, or institution; does not wish to engage in any controversy; neither endorses nor opposes any causes. Our primary purpose is to stay sober and help other alcoholics to achieve sobriety. (Norris, 1970: 155)

The clientele of A.A. represents a cross-section of Americans. Alcoholism is a common problem, and for that reason, one finds in any local association a mixed group of persons, representing all professions and varying lifestyles. The organization has a definite religious flavor, although it is not affiliated with any particular religious faith. The religious emphasis is reflected in its Twelve Step Program of Recovery (Norris, 1970):

1. We admitted we were powerless over alcohol—that our lives had become unmanageable.
2. Came to believe that a Power greater than ourselves could restore us to sanity.
3. Made a decision to turn our will and our lives over to the care of God as we understood Him.
4. Made a searching and fearless moral inventory of ourselves.
5. Admitted to God, to ourselves and to another human being the exact nature of our wrongs.
6. Were entirely ready to have God remove all these defects of character.
7. Humbly asked Him to remove our shortcomings.
8. Made a list of all persons we had harmed, and became willing to make amends to them all.

9.  Made direct amends to such people wherever possible, except when to do so would injure them or others.
10. Continued to take personal inventory, and when we were wrong, promptly admitted it.
11. Sought through prayer and meditation to improve our conscious contact with God, as we understood Him, praying only for knowledge of His will for us and the power to carry that out.
12. Having had a spiritual awakening as the result of these steps, we tried to carry this message to alcoholics, and to practice these principles in all our affairs.

There are open and closed A.A. meetings. In a typical meeting, one is likely to hear the preamble read as well as some encouraging thoughts. The meeting usually includes several personal testimonials by members, which are generally nondefensive, poignant accounts of past bouts with drinking or present attempts to resist. The atmosphere is warm and supportive.

New members are urged to attend meetings every night for ninety days. Thereafter, it is customary to attend at least one meeting per week, but many members regularly attend two, three, or four meetings per week. Members are expected to help others seeking to break the habit at whatever the hour of the day or night. Members often testify during meetings of their trips across town to hold the hand of new members throughout the night as they try to kick the habit. Certainly this effort and the social reinforcement provided in the meetings contribute largely to the phenomenal success of A.A. Contact may be made with representatives through the local telephone directory. The national headquarters is at 468 Park Avenue South, New York, N.Y. 10022.

*Synanon*

Synanon is a self-help group for narcotics addicts. Although it began as an offshoot of Alcoholics Anonymous, its approach is radically different. It provides a form of community living for persons seeking a drug-free society. Its multimillion dollar operation includes live-in complexes, its own school system, interviewing centers, and a service station.

Group interaction seems harsh when compared with the nurturing provided by most other self-help groups. Group members are encouraged to relinquish excuse-making and blame-placing and to take responsibility for personal weaknesses. Members are confronted roughly if they try to escape personal responsibility for their habit.

The Synanon approach appears to be more successful in helping addicts than are other more conventional approaches (Davidson, 1970). It is clearly one of the best-known treatments for drug addiction. In cities where Synanon groups exist, representatives may be contacted under the regular listing in the telephone book or under "Narcotics" in the yellow pages. The national office is located at 2240 Twenty-Fourth Street, San Francisco, CA 94107.

## Gamblers Anonymous

Gamblers Anonymous is an international organization formed to help compulsive gamblers stop gambling. Gambling is as much an obsession for some persons as alcohol is for others. One member disclosed to the writers that he flew from Atlanta to Miami six times during one week to attend horse races. Many gamblers find that an association with others who share their problem is crucial to their recovery.

As the name would indicate, Gamblers Anonymous is patterned after Alcoholics Anonymous. The meetings follow the A.A. format—public confession and group support. The group practices 12 steps to recovery, which are similar to those of Alcoholics Anonymous. There appear to be three main ingredients of the program: (1) recognizing that one is powerless to break the habit, (2) dependence upon the mutual aid of the association, and

(3) missionary work to help other gamblers to break the habit. Again the interest and support of others are very important to this group, as they are to most other self-help groups.

New members are urged to attend meetings nightly, if possible. In some communities in New York, New Jersey, and California, this is possible due to the large number of local chapters. The organization is growing rapidly. There are no fees, but free-will offerings are taken. Representatives can be contacted through the local telephone directory in most large cities. National offices are located at P. O. Box 17173, Los Angeles, CA 90017, and P. O. Box 1404, New York, N. Y. 10001.

## Smokers' Groups

The authors were unable to locate any nationwide self-help groups for persons wishing to stop smoking. There are some public groups at the local level. Some chapters of the American Lung Association sponsor smoking-withdrawal workshops. One such group meets for five consecutive evenings. A leader recites the dangers involved in the habit and presents techniques for breaking the habit. A buddy system is used. The leader also makes telephone contact with members each day of the workshop. The fee, a modest $10, is charged to encourage attendance. Once again, social reinforcement seems to be the prime motivation. Contact the local chapter of the American Lung Association in any community for information regarding the existence of similar programs.

There is a growing number of commercial programs for smoking withdrawal. Since they are profit-making organizations, the expense involved is sometimes large. Smoke Enders has numerous offices in the United States and Canada. It charges $175 for a nine-week program. The weekly meetings last for two hours. This program is based upon many of the behavior principles covered in chapter 4. The address for the national office is Smoke Enders, Phillipsburg, N. J. 08865.

## Emotional Control Groups

Some self-help groups are concerned with helping members to better manage their emotions. Most of us have suffered the tyranny of runaway emotions at times, but some persons contend with more serious emotional disturbances. Recovery, Inc. and Neurotics Anonymous are well-known groups for persons with serious emotional problems.

### *Recovery, Inc.*

This is an international self-help group begun in Chicago in 1937 by Abraham A. Low, M.D. It has about ten thousand members in 1,025 chapters representing all fifty states as well as Canada and Puerto Rico (Park and Shapiro, 1976). It offers former mental patients a systematic method of self-help aftercare and assists other persons who consider themselves to be chronically nervous. Approximately half the members have never been hospitalized for mental illness, and 30 percent have never been treated for an emotional condition (Grosz, 1973). The range of members extends from those suffering from self-consciousness and tenseness to mental patients who at one time were hospitalized (Recovery, 1973). However, openly disturbed people are never invited to its meetings, which are held weekly. The Recovery method consists of: (1) independent study of his book, *Mental Health Through Will Training* (Low, 1950), and other publications by Dr. Low; (2) regular attendance at the weekly meetings; and (3) the practice of Recovery principles in daily life.

Meetings are open to the public and are led by a Recovery-trained volunteer. Mental health professionals cannot become leaders. Leaders are lay persons pursuing the Recovery method for their own emotional health. They have had training in the method at the Recovery training site and receive ongoing training throughout the year.

The meetings are quite structured. They begin with listening to one of Dr. Low's records or a reading from his book. Volunteers then offer recent examples of experiences that they have attempted to handle by the Recovery principles. These examples are presented in four structured steps described by Dr. Low. Each person is limited to five minutes and ten minutes are allotted to discussion of the example by remaining members. Each meeting lasts approximately one hour.

A brief social may follow the formal meeting. The conversation is expected to center on Recovery principles as they can be applied to daily living. Members may contact one another by telephone for aid at other times, but must limit the call to five minutes.

Recovery, Inc. is nonsectarian, is not intended to supplant the psychiatrist, doctor, or other mental health professional, and does not offer diagnosis or individual counseling. It merely attempts to apply the Recovery principles to those aspects of the person's life that allow for self-guidance. One member summed up his views of the organization in the following words:

> If you are not seeking some miraculous, easy way to good mental health and are ready to make a business of it, and if you think you could help yourself if you only knew how to go about it, then welcome to Recovery, Inc.—it offers a systematic way to help yourself. (Recovery, 1973)

There are no fees, although a free-will offering is taken at each meeting. One can make contact with a local chapter by consulting the telephone directory under Recovery, Inc. The national headquarters is located at 116 S. Michigan Avenue, Chicago, IL 60603.

*Neurotics Anonymous*

Neurotics Anonymous is an adaptation of Alcoholics Anonymous designed for mentally or emotionally disturbed persons. Anyone who is having or has had emotional problems is eligible to join. The basic ingredients for the weekly group meetings are the same as those used by Alcoholics Anonymous—public confession, and group support. Between meetings a member is expected to "affirm himself," to read assigned literature, and to call a group leader if he experiences difficulty applying the principles of Neurotics Anonymous. Some of the governing principles are as follows:

1. We, as members of Neurotics Anonymous, offer the program and our personal stories of recovery and insight gained. This is all we do in helping others.

2. We *never* attempt to psychoanalyze a person or diagnose him.

3. We *never* argue with anyone or any group over his or their beliefs. They are welcome to their beliefs as we are welcome to ours. If they wish to follow the Neurotics Anonymous program, that is their choice; they may still retain their other beliefs.

4. We *never* discuss religion, politics, national and international issues, or any other belief systems or policies. Neurotics Anonymous has no opinion on outside issues.

5. Neurotics Anonymous is a spiritual program but not a religious program. That is, it is not based on *any* formal system of religion. Anyone and everyone is welcome at Neurotics Anonymous. There is room in Neurotics for atheists, agnostics, and people of any faiths or of no faiths.

6. We only suggest a belief in a power greater than ourselves—*"God as we understand Him."* This understanding can be of a higher power, as human love, a force for good, evolution, the motions of atoms, gravity—anything at all.

7. We are friendly and warm to all people and make them welcome.

8. We never criticize anyone for anything. We do not judge. We look for the good and try to help bring it out.

9. We tell people how the program worked for us. We do not speak dogma and try to force our beliefs on other people.

10. The only purpose of Neurotics Anonymous is to help us stay well ourselves and to help others to get well and stay well. We lose ourselves in this endeavor. (Taken from *Some Principles of Neurotics Anonymous*, 1965.)

The group believes that a selfish life is not worth living, and that love as expressed through social interest is the key to mental and emotional health. There is a 24-hour telephone answering service for persons who need assistance. There are no dues or fees, but voluntary contributions are accepted. Contact may be made through the local telephone directory under Neurotics Anonymous. The address for the national headquarters is Room 426, Colorado Building, 1341 G Street NW, Washington, D.C. 20005.

Parent-Education Groups

Many persons experience difficulties in fulfilling the responsibilities associated with being a parent. Several groups offer assistance in parenting. Some of the more helpful are discussed below.

*Parent Effectiveness Training Groups (P.E.T.)*

This group is a profit-making program sponsored by Effectiveness Training Associates of Solana Beach, California. It is the brain-child of Thomas Gordon, Ph.D., and is based on humanistic psychology. Parent Effectiveness Training is the largest parenting group, having trained 8,000 instructors and 250,000 parents to date.

The program teaches parents to abandon power as a means of influencing the behavior of children. Children are to be treated with the respect normally accorded adults. Children do not misbehave; they merely behave in ways that are unacceptable to parents. Correct parenting is a matter of relating to children in such a way that the needs of both children and parents are respected. Three techniques are suggested for achieving this. When the child has a problem that does not conflict with the needs of the parent, active listening is recommended. Active listening is listening with deep understanding and responding in a way that lets the child know he is understood. No attempt is made to straighten him out or to solve his problem. If the child's behavior interferes with a parent's needs, then I-Messages are used. Sending an I-Message is a matter of letting the child know how his behavior inconveniences the parent—"I am unable to concentrate on my reading as long as you continue to bounce that ball in here." It is assumed that the child will care enough about the parent to make the necessary adjustments in his behavior. If the child persists after an I-Message, then a form of negotiation called the "no-lose method of problem-solving" becomes the appropriate technique. The program takes a respectful, optimistic view of human nature and the capacity to negotiate.

The course extends over eight to ten sessions; makes use of standard books, tapes, and charts; and costs between $50 and $90. You can make contact with group leaders through the local telephone directory under the listing Parent Effectiveness Training.

*Parent-Involvement Program*

Less well known is a program adapted from William Glasser's book, *Reality Therapy* (1967). The key to the approach is involvement, which means establishing and maintaining a warm, honest, and affectionate relationship with children. Irresponsible behavior results from lack of respect for oneself, from seeing oneself as a failure. The antidote is to convince the misbehaver that he is prized, that someone cares about him—but without engaging in indulgence.

The seven steps in this program may be briefly summarized as follows: (1) establish a warm, honest, affectionate relationship with the child largely through con-

versation on topics of mutual interest; (2) help the
child recognize what he is doing and accept responsibility
for it; (3) help the child judge the usefulness of his behavior in meeting his needs; (4) help him set moderate,
realistic goals for changing his behavior; (5) press him
gently for a commitment to his plans; (6) accept no excuses—but allow for revisions of the plan based upon a
reassessment of step 3; and (7) do not use the usual
types of punishment but rather, use reasonable consequences that are agreed to by the child.

Glasser's Parent Involvement Program is less widely
available to the public than is Gordon's Parent Effectiveness Training. Write William Glasser, M.D., at the Institute for Reality Therapy and Educator Training
Center, Los Angeles, California, or contact the depart-
ments of psychology or counseling at the nearest university for information about the program.

Adlerian parenting groups based upon Rudolph
Dreikurs' book, *Children: The Challenge* (1967), differ
from the two aforementioned groups in several respects.
It is assumed that misbehavior is really misguided behavior that represents a misguided attempt to find one's
place in the family, to gain a sense of belonging. The
misbehaving child has usually been discouraged in his
effort to find his place. All misbehavior is aimed at
realizing one of four goals: (1) attention, (2) power,
(3) revenge, or (4) overcoming inadequacy. The parent
is taught to identify which of these goals the child is pursuing by analyzing his own emotional reaction to the
child's misbehavior. Thereafter, the child is discouraged
from his dysfunctional behavior and encouraged to pursue a more enlightened approach. Emphasis is on cooperation and respect for the rights of others. There is
also a heavy emphasis on independence training for children. It is important that they develop confidence in
their own resources. The process of doing this is called
encouragement.

It may be difficult to make contact with these groups,

because they are not usually listed in the telephone directory. If you experience difficulty, write the Alfred Adler Institute, 333 Central Park West, New York, N.Y. 10025.

## Specialized Parent Groups

Two parenting groups with more specialized purposes are Parents Without Partners and Parents Anonymous. Parents Without Partners is a national self-help group for single parents. It holds semimonthly meetings and has a calendar of family events for each day of the month. It publishes *Single Parent Magazine*, which is included in the $16 annual membership fee. The group is listed in the local telephone directory.

Parents Anonymous is designed to assist child abusers. It is similar in many respects to Alcoholics Anonymous in that it provides education and support. Weekly meetings are held; there is 24-hour telephone support, and often free transportation and babysitting are provided. If a number is not listed in the local telephone directory, contact one of the national offices at 250 West Fifty-Seventh Street, New York, N.Y. 10019, or 2930 West Imperial Highway, Inglewood, CA 90303.

## The Genius of Self-Help Groups

Although self-help groups differ greatly in their approaches, most seem to work well for many kinds of persons. It is possible that the key to a group's success does not lie in the particular program offered, but rather, in the motivation of the person who seeks help. It seems likely that persons who will attend meetings, share testimonials of their successes and failures, and assist others to change will be highly motivated to bring about these same changes in themselves. If this is the case, then membership in these self-help groups is merely a sign of the will to change rather than its cause. The authors feel that this is not totally the case, that these groups do provide a powerful stimulant for personal change.

This powerful stimulant for personal change is the social reinforcement offered by membership in a group committed to the same behavioral goals. It is a great feeling to know that one is not alone with a problem. More helpful is to recognize that one is not unique in having a particular problem. To see others battling with scourges such as alcoholism, compulsive overeating, or the loneliness and sense of failure that accompany divorce somehow makes the trouble and pain feel less catastrophic. Moreover, the smiles, applause, and congratulations of friends who know what the problem is like can sustain motivation for personal change as little else can. People are social animals, and the warmth, interest, and approval of others are an organic fuel for our psyches. This social nourishment that typifies self-improvement groups is their genius.

### The Informal Alliance

While self-help groups are helpful for certain kinds of problems, they may not be appropriate for others. Moreover, a particular kind of self-help group may not exist in a community. In any event one may wish to strengthen one's resolve for personal change by deliberately choosing to spend time with specific persons whom one feels are influential in desirable ways. In this way one uses others' well-established habits to develop similar ones.

Parents show awareness of the influence of others when they encourage their children to associate with superior students. Likewise there is much folklore that tells of the woeful story of persons of good character turning bad out of attraction for persons of ill-fame. Translated into practical terms, this means that, if you are trying to stop the drinking habit, don't ride home with a friend who normally stops at the local bar on the way home; rather, seek out the company of persons unaddicted to drinking. If you are having trouble getting to work on time, drive with friends who arrive in plenty of time. If you are trying to lose weight, eat lunch with the gang that does the salad-and-yoghurt route. If you are trying to exercise more, join a neighbor who jogs each evening. If you trying to stop smoking, associate with others who have kicked the habit. Carefully selected company is a marvelous way of boosting the resolve to change.

Not only is company important when trying to make changes in behavior, but it is at least equally important as a source of nurturance and support for daily living. One needs the goodwill, warmth, and intimacy of others as much as one needs food and sleep. Lack of human support soon shows in one's energy level. Unfortunately, many persons have wired themselves into relationships that sap their energy rather than supplementing it. Negative persons are like bloodsuckers—they literally leave one tired and discouraged.

Most persons have some therapists among their primary relationships—spouses, parents, or friends. The amount of sustenance that one gains from a circle of friends and family members is truly incredible. Unfortunately, one seldom recognizes the importance of these relationships because they are so constant. Remove them, though, and one feels as though one's legs have been cut off. If these relationships are so vital to one's psychic well-being, then one should be prepared to invest richly in their maintenance and improvement.

There are some hazards, of course, in using friends and loved ones in this therapeutic mannner. If one admits them to the inner circle of one's psyches, one is somewhat vulnerable. Confidants may not carefully respect confidentiality, or they may use a disclosure to increase their own power base. These risks pall, however, when compared with the withering of the human spirit that results from lack of intimacy.

### Seeking Professional Assistance

In spite of efforts to lean on one's own resources or those of lay self-help groups, there may be occasions when one needs the assistance of a professional helper. Even in such cases, one is still exercising self-management, since it is up to each person to choose the form of professional therapy. Unfortunately, most people stumble into their contacts with therapists. They seldom inquire in depth about the training or kind of treatment used by the professional. Usually they depend on a recommendation from a friend or casually choose a name from the Yellow Pages. This is merely a form of Russian roulette. Even professionals now know that the effects of therapy can range from helpful to hurtful. Since choosing a therapist is a serious matter, there are a few considerations that may make one's selection a more profitable one.

## Become Acquainted with Available Resources

Be aware of the differences among mental health workers, which are likely to vary in occupational affiliation, work setting, degree of specialization, theoretical orientation, techniques, and personality. Psychiatrists differ from other mental health workers primarily in that they are licensed to practice medicine. This means that they can prescribe psychotropic medications such as tranquilizers, sedatives, and antidepressants. This can sometimes be an advantage, since this chemical assistance can prove valuable for some persons. Medication can impede therapy if used as a substitute for the more permanent effects of self-examination and the building of a repertoire of social skills. Skillful psychiatrists will use psychotropic medication as an adjunct to, rather than a substitute for, counseling. Other mental health workers include clinical psychologists, counseling psychologists, and psychiatric social workers. Clinical and counseling psychologists usually hold a doctorate. Psychiatric social workers usually have a masters degree in social work.

There are significant differences in the work settings of mental health practitioners. The basic breakdown is between public and private services. The one clear difference between them is the amount of money therapy will cost—seeking therapy at a clinic, for example, is significantly less expensive than is private counseling. Sources of low-cost aid are community mental health centers, college counseling centers, family and child service centers, schools, and state rehabilitation agencies.

Professionals also differ in regard to specialization. While the majority conduct general practice, some therapists specialize in family therapy, others, in sex therapy, and yet others, in group therapy. Group therapy, which costs about half that of individual therapy, is often a sound choice, since it offers the additional dimension of reality that is provided by other group members. Frequently, the most helpful insight will come from other group members. In our opinion the social nature of group treatment makes it less provincial and more representative of the real world. Group leaders vary widely in their approaches, and, as with other forms of therapy, the effect on a participant may be good, neutral, or bad.

Mental health practitioners also differ in regard to theoretical positions. These differences stem in part from variation in the types of clients seen by the various mental health workers, but they also indicate sharp differences in their views of the causes of human problems. Differences in theoretical orientations result in differences in technique. Although there is some reason to believe that the amount of experience of the therapist is a greater determinant of techniques used than theoretical background (Fiedler, 1950), it is, nevertheless, quite likely that theory also dictates practice. Consequently, it is important to ascertain a therapist's theoretical orientation before beginning therapy. While many theories are espoused by therapists, each is likely to fall into one of two broad categories: those seeking to alter personality and those seeking to alter behavior.

Most counseling theories are of the personality-altering varieties. These theories assume that basic, intangible internal causes of personality disturbance result in specific behavioral symptoms. The goal of therapy is to attack these basic causes in order to restructure the personality. The basic cause may be an imbalance between warring aspects of the personality, an inadequate self-concept, an overly oppressive conscience, lack of meaning, or an inferiority complex. Moreover, these theories assume that behavioral symptoms will disappear once the basic cause of a disease is removed. In this type of theory, the self-exploration stage of counseling is likely to be extensive, as it is necessary to establish and change the dynamics responsible for the personality disturbance. Symptoms are not usually dealt with directly; the therapist assumes they would merely be replaced by others if the basic disease is not cured.

Therapists who seek to alter behavior are generally more limited in their goals. Unlike the personality-altering types, the behavior-oriented therapist assumes no basic disease and, consequently, takes symptoms more seriously. He believes that symptoms are learned and that, therefore, they can be unlearned. He designs a direct frontal attack upon the symptoms.

The behavioral causes that interest these therapists are all in a person's present situation. They are uninterested in experiences out of the distant past that might be construed to be responsible for present behavior. They are interested in those present conditions in a person's life that trigger and maintain a behavior. These therapists engineer changes in a person's situation where possible. They may attempt to teach new social skills, rid the person of dysfunctional fears, reinforce more appropriate behavior or thoughts. In this type of therapy, one is likely to be far busier outside the counseling session than in personality-altering therapies. Since goals are more limited with this kind of therapy, fewer sessions are likely to be necessary.

The therapist's personality is likely to be a significant factor. In a well-controlled experiment with encounter groups, the ideal type of group leader was identified as being moderate in his stimulation of others to participate and in his need to control the group, high in caring and warmth, and accustomed to assisting clients in understanding what was happening to them. This ability to help clients understand the meaning of their own experiences was more closely associated with productive outcomes than was any other single trait (Lieberman, Yolom, and Miles, 1973).

The ability to understand the meaning of a client's experience is called accurate empathy. Most experts agree that accurate empathy, genuineness, and nonpossessive warmth form a trilogy of traits that characterize a good therapist (Truax and Carkhuff, 1967).

## Get the Specifics Before Beginning

One has a right to ask questions of a therapist before committing oneself to treatment. This reduces the likelihood of future disillusionment. There is a clear relationship between success in therapy and the degree to which counselor and client hold common expectations for the therapeutic process (Freed, Borus, Gonzales, Grant, Lightfoot, and Uribe, 1972). The Public Citizen's Health Research Group, one of Ralph Nader's groups, suggests 41 questions a potential client might put to a potential therapist (Adams and Orgel, 1975). While most of the questions are helpful in getting a good reading on the therapist, the total seems a bit too high. Persisting with such a lengthy questionnaire with most professionals is likely to trigger their ire, and, indeed, this is precisely what happened when the Health Research Group sent out 1,990 questionnaires to psychiatrists, psychologists, and psychiatric social workers in the Washington, D.C., area. Only 348 were returned. A few well-chosen questions, however, are likely to be answered courteously by most professionals, and the resulting information should prove helpful.

One might begin such an inquiry by stating: "If I commit myself to the process of therapy, I want to feel good about it, and it would help me to know a few things about you and the kind of experiences I am likely to be letting myself in for. Would you mind answering a few questions that are very important to me?" Such an approach is likely to receive a generous response from most professionals. Perhaps the most telling test would be for the professional to become defensive and to refuse to respond to the patient's questions. One may wish to raise questions about the following:

1. The therapist's credentials, training, and years of experience.
2. Theoretical orientation (be sure to ask what this means in terms of treatment).
3. The kinds of things that are likely to happen in therapy.
4. Financial arrangements, including (a) amount of time per session, (b) cost per session, (c) an estimate of the number of sessions that might be required, (d) when payment is due, and (e) penalties that might be assessed for a missed appointment.

Nader's group recommends drawing up a formal contract with all the above considerations and many more. Once again, this action may be more harmful than helpful to the therapeutic relationship, at least in the eyes of many professionals. Still, asking questions informally about the concerns mentioned is likely to put one's mind at rest and, therefore, to facilitate a higher degree of trust in the relationship.

## Summary

In this chapter, the importance of choosing one's company in order to strengthen one's resolve for personal change has been emphasized. Humans are social animals, and they are constantly faced with the values and behaviors of others. They should select friends carefully since they cannot fully escape the orbit of their influence. The social reinforcement of self-help groups can also be a powerful stimulant to attempts at personal change. Many of these groups have promising programs for recovery and growth. In spite of the potential of organized self-help groups and carefully selected friendships, some persons need professional assistance at times. A manner and method of choosing one has been outlined in this chapter.

# 6. Help from the Printed Page

*No man can be called friendless when he has God
and the companionship of books.*
                                    Elizabeth Barrett Browning

Bibliotherapy, also called bibliocounseling, refers to a type of therapy where the patient is assigned certain topics, books, or articles for the understanding or insight that they will bring to his therapy. While the use of books in counseling may be relatively new, persons have naturally used bibliotherapy probably as long as books have been available.

Reading has a tremendous influence on people. The results vary, however, from person to person. What may be inspiring and soothing to one individual may evoke anxiety and defensiveness in another. Sometimes the search for help from books backfires. Everyone has experienced the medical student syndrome, wherein one mysteriously develops the symptoms of a disease after having read about it.

While there are no ultimate guides to reading that can unerringly direct a reader to sources that are guaranteed to bring about intended effects, nevertheless, guidance in reading is offered in many instances. For example, one leading executive-development firm routinely assigns

*The Godfather* (Puzo, 1969) to clients whom they feel have difficulty facing the hard realities of the business world. They assign *Business as a Game* (Carr, 1969) to clients lacking an appreciation for the way in which one succeeds in the business world. Some therapists prescribe books by philosophers. The philotherapeutic approach is based on the assumption that most troubles encountered today have been addressed in the treatises of philosophers throughout the ages. Increasingly, therapists of all persuasions are supplementing the effects of their weekly sessions by homework assignments that quite often include prescribed reading.

The authors wish to share several sources that have proven helpful to their clients. While there are literally hundreds of appropriate volumes, the following ones have been chosen for their wide range of appeal. The reader can easily find many other useful books in each of the following categories. The books in this chapter have been selected for (1) their readability and general interest value, (2) their widespread use by therapists, (3) references to them in the professional literature, (4) their timeless quality, and (5) their availability.

This list is by no means exhaustive; it is just suggestive of some of the volumes that have proven helpful. The content of each of the works listed is well known to the authors and has been used on numerous occasions by psychologists and other helpers. The books are grouped by subject areas that are of great concern to a majority of persons. These concerns are not meant to comprise an exhaustive listing of human problems—they are merely representative of concerns commonly encountered in modern life.

## Negotiation in Marriage

Maladjustment in marriage often centers around patterns associated with the meeting of power and sexual needs. In every arena participants want to be involved in the decision-making process; marriages are no exception.

Narciso's and Burkett's volume, *Declare Yourself: Discovering the Me in Relationships* (1975), analyzes the basis for negotiation in interpersonal relationships. In many marriages one person plays the role of the Demander, while the other acts the part of the Deferrer. Even in marriages with an egalitarian base, one partner often makes more demands than the other. Most of the time the slight imbalance creates no discernable strain on the marriage; however, Deferrers in time begin to resent their position. If the resentment becomes severe enough, the Deferrer may defect, that is, begin to make extensive use of suffering, depression, and/or anger to strengthen his or her power base in the marriage.

Suffering, depression, and anger are selfish, attention-getting behaviors. The book suggests negotiation alternatives designed to lessen the Demander-Deferrer struggle in marital interaction.

Bach's and Wyden's *The Intimate Enemy: How to Fight Fair in Love and Marriage* (1968) views the universal traits of aggression and hostility between marital partners as healthy, growth-producing phenomena. Their premise is that all human beings have aggressive and hostile feelings and that to expect these to be shelved in marital interactions is not only unrealistic but damaging to understanding and growth in the relationship. Indeed, genuine intimacy can only be achieved through therapeutic aggression, and the authors present a set of guidelines for engaging in "constructive fighting."

Another book frequently assigned by marriage counselors is *The Mirages of Marriage* by Lederer and Jackson (1968). The authors take the position, based on experience and statistical evidence, that marriage is a severe disappointment to almost everyone within a few months of the wedding. They blame faulty assumptions for the ensuing unhappiness and, in a highly readable fashion, present an appealing and conclusive explanation of a systems approach to marriage. Marriage is seen as more than the sum of the personalities of the participants and, therefore, troubles that occur cannot be explained by examining each spouse. Rather, it is the system generated as the result of the interaction of these two personalities that needs to be understood and confronted.

The authors examine seven false assumptions that people consciously or unconsciously bring with them to the altar. For example, "Love is necessary for a satisfactory marriage," is an assumption challenged on the basis that spouses often confuse romance with love and are torn apart when the essentially selfish promises of romance are not fulfilled.

Most of the literature on marriage seems to imply that, once married, a couple must work it out, although statistics dramatically refute such a prescription. Simply put, many marriages are just not meant to be. Moreover, the legal and emotional commitment of marriage often leaves divorced persons exhausted, confused, and guilt-ridden at having failed in a major life endeavor. Krantzler's *Creative Divorce* (1973) turns such an attitude around and examines the positive and creative opportunities afforded by divorce. Everybody knows that there is a fine line in judging whether a marriage is "good" or "bad" or whether a couple should stay together or divorce. No simple formula is available to make that line vividly discernible, but Krantzler's book clearly helps those individuals who have resolved in their own minds that their marriage is no longer tenable. It also helps the reader to handle loneliness and the effects of divorce on children.

## Sexual Adjustment

Although the bumper sticker that proclaims "Give me the old days, when the air was clean and sex was dirty" describes some person's reactions to the current sexual revolution, few refute the notion that correct information regarding sexual functions is important. Belliveau's and Richter's *Understanding Human Sexual Inadequacy* (1970) outlines much of the voluminous research done by Masters and Johnson. The reader who is interested in an informative and fairly thorough summary of the causes of sexual failure will find much information in this volume. It is well written and tries to capture the psychological and social components of sexual functioning as they relate to the physical side.

*Our Bodies, Ourselves: A Book By and For Women* (1973) is an unusual and appealing grass roots version of women's liberation at its best. It began when a group of Boston women, frustrated by their experiences with physicians, talked and shared information with each other. The collective realization of how little they knew about their bodies led them to believe that such ignorance was probably widespread. The result was this book, with its comprehensive treatment of the physiological aspects of sexual and reproductive functions and also several sections on general health and nutrition.

The volume encourages openness and stresses the importance of getting and giving psychological support. In that spirit it necessarily includes a wide representation of value systems. Some readers may take exception to some parts, which seem to flaunt conventional mores; nonetheless, the volume is a storehouse of information not readily available elsewhere.

The sexual awakening of adolescents leaves many adults puzzled regarding their roles. Adults' recollections of adolescence are frequently meaningless, confusing, or painful, and the current trends in sexual values compete heavily for an adolescent's attention. Sol Gordon's *The Sexual Adolescent: Communicating with Teenagers about Sex* (1973) is expressly written to help parents and professionals become knowledgeable regarding current sexual issues and to be effective in discussing these with teenagers. Gordon squarely sides with the camp that believes teen-agers are going to make their own sexual decisions, and that the responsibility of adults is to be available, knowledgeable, and communicative. He pleads for parental openness and honesty regarding sexual matters, and he intensively strives to make the reader aware of the questions teen-agers have on their minds, whether or not they are asking them. The finer points of sexual morality are not avoided, but the emphasis is clearly on the more pragmatic issues of venereal disease, unwanted children, and exploitative sex. Included is a glossary of sexual slang and a bibliography.

Another excellent book, by the veteran psychologist-sex educator James McCary, is entitled *A Complete Sex Education for Parents, Teenagers, and Young Adults* (1973). All of McCary's writings on sex are dispassionate, scholarly, but extremely engaging and readable. This volume is outstanding in that it offers parents an accurate accounting of social and sexual issues with a minimum of moral judgment. As such it can be used as a catalyst for family discussion. The recounting of the mechanics of sex is complete and nontechnical. The varieties of sexual behaviors are examined, and common myths and fallacies are rebutted by facts. This book is also a fine resource for any young couple contemplating marriage.

## Parenting

Parents are frequently hounded and tormented by their own consciences for presumed faults regarding child-rearing. However hard they try, there always seems to be something else they could or should do, or should have done, in behalf of their offspring. Worse still, there never seem to be clear answers to the really critical issues: how much guidance to offer children, how much to require of them—and in what areas of their lives, how much to involve them in participatory management of family decisions, how open to be regarding sensitive topics, and the like.

Patterson and Gullion applied behavioral theory to child management in their programmed text, *Living with Children* (1968). It is based on the acknowledgement that people learn most of their behavior from other people. The book shows parents how to encourage desirable behavior and gradually eliminate undesirable behavior in their children. It offers step by step advice on handling such things as, "The Child Who Fights Too Often," "The 'I Don't Want To' Child," "The Overly Active, Noisy Child," "The Frightened Child," and "The Withdrawn Child." The principles are simple, easily understood, and likely to work *if they are used.* This handle on these child-management problems has given security and direction to many befuddled parents.

## Vocational Adjustment

One's life work is perhaps the most important issue to be resolved, with the possible exception of matters relating to marriage and family. How does one best integrate interests, abilities, and opportunities? How does one know what rewards to expect of a vocation before one commits oneself to long years of preparation? These and many other similar questions constitute legitimate concerns for both youth and adults.

Libraries are filled with books about working, yet the hapless reader searching the stacks for vocational insights will be disappointed more often than not. *What Color Is Your Parachute? A Practical Manual for Job-Hunters and Career Changers* by Richard Nelson Bolles (1975) delivers its readers from such anguish. Bolles has organized the methods and materials of vocational guidance into a highly readable and especially useful resource. He starts from the premise that getting a job can be a lot of work and then organizes the tasks and resources available to the career planner. How to find jobs, practical hints on getting a job, building a second career, a directory called "Help," which lists many free or inexpensive aids, and information on counseling agencies are just some of the topics included in the book. The bibliography is particularly helpful. Using it, a serious career planner can divide the task into subgoals and find books about interviewing, skill analysis, or even what to do when fired. Working and career planning are complex matters, and this volume successfully undercuts the part that chance plays and touts deliberate and intelligent job choices.

Another volume that can be helpful is John Holland's *Making Vocational Choices: A Theory of Careers* (1973). Holland posits the existence of six personality types—realistic, investigative, artistic, social, enterprising, and conventional—that provide the bases for determining which environments and types of people are most likely to be suited to each other. Holland believes that most persons can provide their own vocational guidance if they are exposed to the proper resources. Included in the book is the *Self-Directed Search,* a self-administering, self-scoring, and self-interpreting questionnaire. Upon completion of the questionnaire, one arrives at a three-letter code that represents a blend of the personality types. Using this code, an individual then turns to the Occupations Finder, a classification section that lists the occupational areas that are likely to be rewarding to the personality type. The reader is encouraged to begin his occupational investigation with the job areas that fit his personality.

## Handling Stress

Many persons are so exhausted by chronic anxiety and other forms of stress that they have little energy left to devote to the pleasurable pursuits of life. Consequently, they feel that life is passing them by, that they are so squeezed by the worries of the future and the regrets of the past that they do not have a present. It is difficult to concentrate, to attend, to be truly present with others. The ability to relax, as well as to cope effectively with mental feverishness, is a serious problem.

Hans Selye, perhaps the greatest living expert on stress, has written two volumes on the subject. His epic work, *The Stress of Life* (1956), greatly influenced the medical world's understanding of psychosomatic illnesses. Another volume, *Stress Without Distress* (1974), offers a prescription for minimizing psychic insults to the nervous system and suggests ways of using stress to achieve a rewarding lifestyle. In both volumes Selye convincingly demonstrates the physiological effects of coping with high stress. He explains these effects as stemming from the General Adaptation Syndrome. He suggests that a person has a limited amount of adaptive energy for coping, and when it is exhausted, death is a certainty. The rest of the volume is concerned with creative adjustments that conserve this precious energy. Reading these volumes is apt to cause the reader to recognize the futility and utter wastefulness of many habits.

Harvard professor Herbert Benson, M.D., has written a best-seller entitled *The Relaxation Response* (1975). Benson is one of the world's leading researchers on relaxation. Part of his research was conducted in his laboratory, and part was conducted in the library reading the vast amount of literature on meditation. He became convinced that meditative practices in Hinduism, Buddhism, Sufism, Taoism, Judaism, and Christianity all triggered identical physiological and psychological conditions. Each of these meditative practices activated the Relaxation Response, a protective mechanism that turns off harmful bodily effects created by overstress. It decreases heart rate, lowers metabolism, decreases rate of breathing, and restores a healthier balance to the body. The practice combines patterned breathing, muscle relaxation, and meditation in a simple, effortless exercise that requires 15 to 20 minutes, once or twice daily. Benson concludes that the physiologic changes elicited by this technique are similar to those induced by Transcendental Meditation, Zen, yoga, autogenic training, progressive relaxation, and hypnosis. Millions of persons have found that some form of these techniques significantly helps in reducing nervousness and stress.

### Asserting Oneself

Many people live with self-contempt because they feel unable to stand up for their rights. It seems that others make all their decisions. They feel overwhelmed by the forcefulness of others. Worse still, they feel frightened and even guilty when they try to assert themselves. They are unsure of their rights. They confuse self-respect with selfishness. Being unskillful and uncertain of their rights, they equivocate in expressing their preferences, and others find it quite easy to overrule them.

Alberti and Emmons have written a small and easily read book on assertiveness, entitled *Your Perfect Right* (1974). Early chapters assist the reader in overcoming guilt feelings about legitimate forms of self-assertion. Later chapters contain vignettes showing when assertive behavior is appropriate and offer examples of nonassertive, aggressive, and assertive responses to these situations. The book is useful in realigning thinking about the right to assert oneself and in providing illustrative examples of good taste in assertiveness.

More comprehensive than the Alberti and Emmons book, *I Am Worth It* (1979) by Kelley and Winship contains a three-part assertive response. It consists of empathy, conflict, and action. Very simply, it means that one should let others know that their views are understood and also share with them one's own thinking about a matter. Finally one should tell others what is going to happen (if it is one's choice) or what one would like to see happen (if it is another's choice). The use of this complete response pattern is respectful of the feelings of others and likely to make the assertive response effective and nonhurtful to the relationship.

Lazarus and Fay, in *I Can If I Want To* (1975), attack twenty nonfunctional beliefs common to American culture that effectively inhibit persons from asserting themselves. Beliefs such as "I am a victim of circumstances," "I must earn happiness," and "I must please other people to get along in this world" contribute to a feeling of powerlessness and worthlessness. These feelings, in turn, discourage one from sending clear signals to others about opinions, preferences, and values. Consequently, one is inadequate in negotiating with others for one's wants and needs since one fails to communicate directly to others what one really wants.

The authors identify basic erroneous themes that tend to ruin lives, reveal the faulty assumptions behind these themes, suggest a basis for more functional thinking about them, and prescribe corrective behavior. As an example, they suggest that one counter the belief that one is a helpless victim of circumstances by asking these questions: If I were offered $10,000 in cash to do the thing I say I can't do, would I do it? If a child of mine or the person closest to me were kidnaped and I knew that I would never see this person alive again if I didn't do the thing I say I can't do, would I do it? Answering such questions leads one to change "I can't" statements to "I choose to" statements and helps one to recognize that one can do what one wills, that one can do most things one wants to do if willing to pay the price.

This work is an ingenious and spirited book that has proved helpful to many of persons as they identified the common themes that have created tension and unhappiness in their lives.

In his book, *When I Say No, I Feel Guilty* (1975), Manuel J. Smith presents several techniques to enable persons to respond assertively to criticism and manipulative statements. One technique, Broken Record, involves repeating a request or wish for as long as necessary in a calm, relaxed voice while ignoring all side issues brought up by a critic. Fogging involves accepting manipulative criticism by calmly acknowledging the probability that there may be some truth in the criticism while clearly maintaining the right to do what one wants to about behavior. Negative Assertion is a matter of accepting responsibility for mistakes without apologizing for them. In Negative Inquiry, one invites further critical statements repeatedly until the other person is required to see the real basis for the criticism. And Self-Disclosure involves initiating and accepting discussion of both the positive and negative aspects of one's personality in order to encourage honest communication and to reduce manipulation and defensiveness. The brief descriptions of these techniques do not do them justice; Smith's forceful writing style and powerful illustrations make his techniques come alive on the printed page. The book is highly recommended for persons besieged with constant criticism from salespersons, casual acquaintances, business contacts, and others who are relatively unimportant to them.

Andrew Salter was one of the first to draw attention to the lack of assertiveness on the part of neurotics. In his book, *Conditioned Reflex Therapy* (1949), he faults conditioning by parents and society in general for nonassertive lifestyles. In the desire to be accepted and liked by everyone, persons become self-conscious, apologetic, and afraid of inconveniencing people. What appears to be courtesy becomes a fraud—one defers only because one is afraid of making others angry.

Salter suggests six ways to become a more assertive person: (1) become emotionally outspoken, expressing likes and dislikes, annoyance, regret, love, and other emotions; (2) show emotions by facial expressions; (3) contradict and attack when in disagreement rather than simulate agreeability; (4) use the word "I" as much as possible; (5) express agreement when praised; and (6) begin to act more spontaneously. While some of these suggestions may appear to be overcompensations in the opposite direction, Salter presumes that the reader's current tendency toward an inhibited lifestyle will result in a healthy compromise.

### Lack of Meaning

Many persons are plagued from time to time with a feeling that their lives lack meaning. While some persons appear to spend little time trying to resolve these questions, others are made restless by the need to relate themselves to their social and physical worlds. They tirelessly seek to construct a personal cosmology.

Frankl's book *Man's Search for Meaning* (1959) has been used by many therapists whose clients are unable to find personal meaning in life. Frankl, who suffered the travails of Auschwitz, impresses the reader in an unassuming way with his ideas regarding meaning and the suffering people endure in the pursuit of meaningful lives. Most persons are repelled by the thought or act of suicide, but Frankl asks, *"Why* don't you commit suicide?"* Each individual has his own unique answer to this question, and in this answer are found the beginnings of meaning and purpose in life.

The search for meaning in life leads people to create systems of belief. In *The Religions of Man* (1958) Huston Smith has written one of the clearer and fairer accounts of the world's great religions: Hinduism, Buddhism, Confucianism, Taoism, Islam, Judaism, and Christianity. Explained simply and sympathetically are the reasons that each of these religions has attracted millions of devout followers. While the authors are not interested in sponsoring any one religious position, they do realize that some readers may be in search of a more satisfying world view that can add meaning to their everyday lives, and a review of major religions may prove helpful.

## Depression

For many persons, depression is as uncontrollable as an eclipse of the sun. One's energy dips along with one's mood. Interest in appearance, sex, work, and community sags markedly. Feelings of guilt, worthlessness, and hopelessness mysteriously wash in like waves. Relations with others suffer enormously, and the joy of living evaporates. For some the greatest battle of their lives is with this dreaded ogre called depression.

*The New Guide to Rational Living* by Albert Ellis and R. Harper (1976) challenges habits of self-criticism. Most persons are their own worst enemies because they demand things of themselves and others that are unreasonable and often just plain stupid. The natural outcome of continual self-criticism is depression, and the cause of such a habit can be found in the faulty negative self-talk people engage in so frequently. Ellis attacks the assumptions upon which most depressing self-statements are based. He tries to convince readers that, for example, it is ridiculous indeed to believe that one must be loved by everyone. But, if so, why does one often act as if life is dreadful when someone expresses dislike? Such conclusions are reached by most people because of a faulty mechanism in their system of logical reasoning that betrays them time and again in their daily lives. Ellis helps the reader to redefine a system of logic so that helpful and satisfying conclusions about daily events and interpersonal relationships can lead to more functional and positive feelings.

### Self-Worth

Related to depression is concern about personal worth. Many persons run their lives as if they were on a neurotic treadmill, running like crazy to try to prove their self-worth. Inferiority feelings are extremely common. Although all persons experience the haunting pain of such feelings from time to time, some persons' lives are governed by an attempt to gain parity or superiority.

Thomas Harris, in *I'm OK—You're OK* (1967), applies the principles of transactional analysis to the development of self-worth. He analyzes four life positions underlying behavior: the immature person's anxious dependency, expressed as "I'm not OK—You're OK"; the despairing position, called "I'm not OK—You're not OK"; the criminal position, "I'm OK—You're not OK"; and the mature position, expressed as "I'm OK—You're OK."

He helps the reader examine the effect of his communication on others by drawing attention to three active facets in one's personality. The Parent personifies the "do's" and "don'ts" of one's life. The Child represents spontaneous emotion and behavior. Both Parent and Child must be governed by the Adult, the part of us that makes decisions based upon the objective facts. Coming at others from any one of these postures has predictable effects. One can often discover reasons for the disappointing responses one gets from others by analyzing the particular posture from which one is approaching them. Literally thousands of persons have found this book helpful in pursuing more positive feelings about themselves and relationships with others.

# Part III
# Sound Mind,
# Sound Body

After carefully researching the literature on placebos, Adam Smith, author of *Powers of Mind,* forwarded what he found to the National Institutes of Mental Health and asked them who was doing research on the subject. He received the surprising answer, "You are. Good luck. Please let us know what else you find."

The enigmatic relationship between mind and body has lured essayists, poets, philosophers, and scientists for thousands of years. In some ways it seems that people have not advanced greatly from the days of the early Greeks, who seemed to orchestrate the mind-soul-body trilogy so well.

Part 3 leads the reader through some of the current solutions to body and mind concerns. Chapter 7 tackles problems of physical functioning while chapter 8 deals with stress as a major body debilitator. In chapter 9, the authors show that the mind does indeed hold the key to many stress-reduction strategies.

# 7. The Functioning Body

*Every man is the builder of the temple called his body—we are all sculptors and painters, and our material is our own flesh and blood and bones. Any nobleness begins at once to refine a man's features.*
Henry David Thoreau

Millions punish their bodies through inactivity, overeating, overdrinking, smoking, or other habits of excess. They excuse themselves from personal responsibility with rationalizations such as, "It's all in the genes," "That's just the way I am," or "Each of us has been given just so many heartbeats in this life anyway." And such shibboleths are comforting cop-outs when one gives in to temptation.

The value one places on the welfare of one's body is a highly personal matter anyway. There are few laws regulating what one may or may not do to one's body. One cannot commit suicide legally, but one can do it slowly. Tobacco legislation, for example, seeks only to educate about the dangers of smoking, rather than to destroy the freedom to practice the habit. Similarly, while one cannot drink heavily and drive, one *is* free to drink heavily. Overall, one is free to destroy one's body or to protect and enhance its functioning. And Americans have abundant means of doing either.

In this chapter the authors present selected approaches designed to bring about changes in physical functioning. They have singled out weight control, physical conditioning, and alcohol and tobacco use for special attention, since these concerns are the most frequently cited problems. Moreover, they attempt to put the reader in contact with sources of medical information that should provide a better understanding of specific physical problems.

### Weight Control

For the vast majority of Americans, weight loss, rather than weight gain, is a primary concern. Entire industries play to the plight of the obese, and the array of diets is bewildering. The authors' approach is a nonpartisan one. They have found no approach that contains some simple mechanical technology that assures weight loss without concerted effort. Every diet has a particular appeal that may work for some but not for others. And since lifestyles can vary as much as handprints, the public is probably well served to have a variety of options.

If there is one crucial variable underlying the success of any diet, it is motivation. And the strength and endurance of motivation seem to be key aspects affecting the success of any diet. Fad diets, which allow a dieter to eat as much as desire dictates while restricting the kinds of food eaten, assume that a dieter may not be able to endure the moderation required by most long-term diets. Most diets have specific mechanical features designed to lessen the amount of willpower required of the dieter. The Stillman diet, for example, seeks to assuage the dieter's need for oral intake by substituting water. The Atkins diet discourages carbohydrate intake while ignoring calories and thus offers a no-hunger diet. The Weight Watchers approach supplements an individual's willpower with group approval and encouragement. The extent to which any diet works is directly related to the degree of motivation one brings to the diet.

Many persons seem to be perpetual dieters. A chart

showing weight loss would have a washboard look in that one loses a few pounds by dieting and then picks them up again. Yet, perfecting a set of reasonable eating habits that do not require conscious attention or adjustment is far healthier and less shocking to the system than depending on crash efforts that result in abrupt weight losses. For this reason the authors place far greater faith in any diet that is designed to accomplish weight loss over an extended period of time. A reasonable goal suggested by many sources is to lose one pound per week.

Another reasonable approach to weight control is the one-day-per-week fast that has been practiced by devotees of various religions for many centuries. One eats normally throughout the remainder of the week and marshalls one's total reserve of willpower exclusively for the waking hours of the one fast day. In this way one can dispense with calorie or carbohydrate counts, special food purchases, and other energy-consuming exercises. This practice is medically sound (Stillman and Baker, 1967). In practicing the one-day-per-week fast, one offers one's viscera its own sabbath and allows one's alimentary canal a chance to void more fully its contents.

Crash diets that require exceedingly low caloric intake (one thousand calories or less) appear merely to tease the system and comprise a very questionable motivational practice. Either a more moderate regimen designed to accomplish the same weight loss over a longer period of time or the one-day-per-week fast is likely to prove more tolerable for most persons.

## Setting Goals

Any serious attempt to control weight must have a definite end in mind. Out of desperation, many persons often set overly ambitious goals. They have been driven to such desperation out of self-contempt. They are appalled by the edemic image they see in the mirror. They feel stuffy and sluggish, and their clothes are too tight. They become angry with themselves for their indulgence

and vow to suffer bitterly to shed the excess weight. At
that moment they decide to lose a pound a day or some
other unreasonable amount. Yet, it is neither realistic nor
humane to expect to maintain for days and weeks the kind
of desperate motivation that would be required to lose
such an amount. Better by far to set a reasonable goal,
such as a pound a week, and thereby, to increase the
probability of success.

How does one know when one is really overweight?
Most persons have seen weight-height charts. Table 7-1,
the Metropolitan Life Insurance Company's chart, is one
such reference.

Another popular measure of overweight is the "pinch
an inch" test, whereby one calipers one's thumb and index finger against a fold in the stomach or ribcage. If the
pinch is an inch or more thick, some fat needs to come
off. Such measures are mimics of more precise calcula-
tions used in bariatric medicine or by conditioning specialists, a subject that will be discussed later.

Another way of measuring fatness for men is the waist
measurement. This test works only for men because they
tend to gather excess weight primarily around the waist,
whereas women deposit it more widely throughout the
body. Table 7-2 is a guide for judging overweight in
males.

Let us assume that in some way a discrepancy has been
noted between your ideal and actual weight and a weight-
loss goal has been set. It will be motivating to break down
the goal into weekly subgoals. A good way of doing this is
to plan to lose a pound a week or to lose an amount equal
to 1 percent of one's body weight per week.

As mentioned earlier, the number of popular diets
available is bewildering. The variety of approaches reflects the failure of the scientific and medical communities to agree on the finer points of weight control. The
techniques espoused here are based on the assumption
that one is in reasonably good health and has been encouraged to lose weight by a family physician.

## Table 7-1. Desirable Weights—Ages 25 and Over
Weight in pounds according to frame (in indoor clothing).

### Men

| Height (w/ shoes on) 1-inch heels Feet | Inches | Small Frame | Medium Frame | Large Frame |
|---|---|---|---|---|
| 5 | 2 | 112–120 | 118–129 | 126–141 |
| 5 | 3 | 115–123 | 121–133 | 129–144 |
| 5 | 4 | 118–126 | 124–136 | 132–148 |
| 5 | 5 | 121–129 | 127–139 | 135–152 |
| 5 | 6 | 124–133 | 130–143 | 138–156 |
| 5 | 7 | 128–137 | 134–147 | 142–161 |
| 5 | 8 | 132–141 | 138–152 | 147–166 |
| 5 | 9 | 136–145 | 142–156 | 151–170 |
| 5 | 10 | 140–150 | 146–160 | 155–174 |
| 5 | 11 | 144–154 | 150–165 | 159–179 |
| 6 | 0 | 148–158 | 154–170 | 164–184 |
| 6 | 1 | 152–162 | 158–175 | 168–189 |
| 6 | 2 | 156–167 | 162–180 | 173–194 |
| 6 | 3 | 160–171 | 167–185 | 178–199 |
| 6 | 4 | 164–175 | 172–190 | 182–204 |

### Women

| Height (w/ shoes on) 1-inch heels Feet | Inches | Small Frame | Medium Frame | Large Frame |
|---|---|---|---|---|
| 4 | 10 | 92– 98 | 96–107 | 104–119 |
| 4 | 11 | 94–101 | 98–110 | 106–122 |
| 5 | 0 | 96–104 | 101–113 | 109–125 |
| 5 | 1 | 99–107 | 104–116 | 112–128 |
| 5 | 2 | 102–110 | 107–119 | 115–131 |
| 5 | 3 | 105–113 | 110–122 | 118–134 |
| 5 | 4 | 108–116 | 113–126 | 121–138 |
| 5 | 5 | 111–119 | 116–130 | 125–142 |
| 5 | 6 | 114–123 | 120–135 | 129–146 |
| 5 | 7 | 118–127 | 124–139 | 133–150 |
| 5 | 8 | 122–131 | 128–143 | 137–154 |
| 5 | 9 | 126–135 | 132–147 | 141–158 |
| 5 | 10 | 130–140 | 136–151 | 145–163 |
| 5 | 11 | 134–144 | 140–155 | 149–168 |
| 6 | 0 | 138–148 | 144–159 | 153–173 |

For girls between 18 and 25, subtract 1 pound for each year under 25.

Courtesy of Metropolitan Life Insurance Company

### Table 7-2.  Fatness Guideline for Men

| If your nude weight is (pounds) | Your waistline girth should not exceed (inches) |
|---|---|
| 100 | 30 |
| 110 | 31 |
| 120 | 32 |
| 130 | 32 |
| 140 | 33 |
| 150 | 34 |
| 160 | 34 |
| 170 | 35 |
| 180 | 36 |
| 190 | 36 |
| 200 | 37 |
| 210 | 38 |
| 220 | 38 |
| 230 | 39 |
| 240 | 40 |
| 250 | 40 |

From *Total Fitness in 30 Minutes a Week* by Laurence E. Morehouse and Leonard Gross. Copyright © 1975 by Laurence E. Morehouse, Ph.D. Reprinted by permission of Simon & Schuster, a Division of Gulf and Western Corporation.

## Focusing on Behavior

A person does not *become* fat; one *makes* oneself fat. Weight is a natural and logical consequence of one's eating habits. It is the eater and not the food eaten that create fatness. Specifically, an average of one pound of fat is stored for every 3,500 calories consumed beyond what is needed for internal body processes and mobility. A person who gains weight is simply eating more than is required to maintain his or her current weight. That person must find our how much more he or she is eating in order to know where to start cutting back.

### Finding the Starting Line

Focusing on a daily routine that encompasses an over-eating pattern is the first step in interrupting this inappropriate behavior. A notebook is a good tool for recording eating habits. Select whatever size is convenient. One should make no attempt to alter eating behavior during the week in which one is establishing a baseline of normal eating. This is a time to find out how much one ordinarily eats. It may also be helpful to record activities in order to estimate energy expenditure. In this way a prospective dieter has a record of energy input and output. By carefully reviewing the record of weekly activities, one should be able to estimate an exertion level using the Table 7-3. Then use the correct exertion multiple to compute the number of daily calories needed to maintain body weight.

**Table 7-3. Calorie expenditure levels.**

| Level of Exertion | Exertion Multiple | Occupational Example |
|---|---|---|
| Extremely high | 17 | Construction Worker |
| Very high | 16 | Delivery Worker |
| Moderate | 15 | Occasional Jogger |
| Slight | 14 | Evening Walker |
| Sedentary | 13 | Office Worker |

To use the table, first decide on a level of exertion, then find the appropriate exertion multiple, and finally, multiply body weight by this number. This indicates the number of calories that must be consumed in order to maintain present weight. The table can be used to establish the number of calories needed daily in order to maintain an ideal weight. For example, one who wants to weigh 170 pounds and considers oneself to be slightly active would multiply 170 by 14 to get 2,380—the number of calories needed daily to maintain a weight of 170 pounds.

While carefully recording foods eaten during a baseline week, do not assign the number of calories to these foods until the end of the week. It is too easy to become impressed with the large number of calories one is consuming and to succumb to the temptation to change one's eating habits on the spot. This would destroy the purpose of the baseline period.

When assigning calories or carbohydrates to the foods eaten during the baseline week, do not guess—get the facts. The caloric and carbohydrate counts available on the labels of most packaged foods are helpful. For fresh foods, consult *The Dictionary of Calories and Carbohydrates* (Kraus, 1974), a frequently revised and fairly exhaustive reference that reports information by brand names and various weights and volumes. Armed with these references, plus a food scale, a serious dieter can accurately record a week's calorie intake. Table 7–4 shows one way of collecting the data. Notice that the log also includes a record of the time and occasion for each meal or snack, information that helps in uncovering patterns of overeating.

When the week's tally of caloric intake is completed, cut back in order to reach an ideal weight. Consult Table 7–3 in order to compute the number of calories that are needed to maintain an ideal weight. Subtract this number from the average number of calories eaten during the baseline week. The result is the number of calories overeaten.

One can arrive at the number of calories one wants to limit oneself to daily in one of two ways. Set the limit at the number necessary to maintain an ideal weight. Using this limit, compute the rate at which weight can be lost by the following steps. As mentioned earlier, compute the number of calories eaten beyond the daily number necessary to maintain an ideal weight. Divide this number into 3,500; the result is the number of days it will take to lose one pound. For example, if one is eating 1,750 calories a day more than is necessary to maintain an ideal weight, and one divides this number into 3,500, one finds that it will take two days to lose one pound. Actually, this means of calculating weight loss is slightly inaccurate, because every pound of fat burned results in a one-and-one-fourth to one-and-one-half pound loss in body weight since the

**Table 7-4. Sample daily log.**

|  |  | Calories | Carbo-hydrates |
|---|---|---|---|
| Breakfast | 4 oz. tomato juice | 22 | 4.9 |
| (at home) | ½ c. Raisin Bran | 104 | 22.7 |
| 7:30 | 1 egg | 81 | .4 |
|  | coffee |  |  |
|  | ½ c. 2 percent milk | 68 | 7.0 |
| Coffee break | coffee |  |  |
| (with boss) | 1 Hostess doughnut | 139 | 18.2 |
| 10:30 |  |  |  |
| Lunch | Big Mac | 600 | 35 |
| (with office crew | Choc. milk shake | 469 | 55 |
| at McDonalds) |  |  |  |
| 12:15 |  |  |  |
| Coffee break | coffee |  |  |
| (with Sam) | 4 oz. Spanish dry roasted | 700 | 13.6 |
| 2:30 | peanuts (Planters) |  |  |
| Dinner | 3 oz. Taylor Claret wine | 72 | 0 |
| (at home—alone) | 11½ oz. Swanson frozen | 371 | 30.3 |
| 6:00 | beef dinner |  |  |
|  | ½ c. canned green beans | 22 | 5.0 |
|  | coffee |  |  |
| Snack | 4 Betty Crocker macaroons | 232 | 35.2 |
| (at home with family | glass milk | 159 | 12 |
| watching TV) |  |  |  |
| 10:30 |  |  |  |
|  | Total | 3039 | 239.3 |

body also releases the water retained with the fat. Still, it seems best to ignore this technical adjustment and err conservatively when calculating desired caloric intake.

One can skip this whole procedure and decide to reduce caloric intake by a number equal to twice one's current body weight. Merely subtract this number from the average daily intake during the baseline week. To find the rate at which one will lose with this method, simply divide the number resulting from doubling current body weight into 3,500. This is the number of days it will take to lose one pound.

Ordinarily, no adult should eat fewer than 1,000 calories a day for an extended time, if destruction of muscles and organs is to be avoided. Moreover, the object is to make adjustments that are likely to lead to permanent changes in eating habits. The more drastic the change, the less likely it is to be permanent. Perfectionistic thinking, at this point, dooms one to failure.

Identify Triggering Situations

Once one has completed a tally of calories consumed and energy expended, one is ready to do some detective work. Begin to examine the conditions under which overeating occurs. A careful analysis of weekly eating habits should identify glaring patterns. In discovering such patterns, one can make changes that will assist in cutting down. One may find, for example, that one munches an astounding number of calories in the late evening while viewing television. Or one may be a social eater, only really eating on social occasions. If this is the case, willpower can be fortified by making changes in the way time is spent. Decide to retire earlier, take an evening walk with the family, or have fewer social engagements while dieting. In this way, some of the triggers for overeating are removed.

Moreover, by analyzing the foods one eats, one may discover that many of the offenders could be replaced with low-calorie foods of equal taste appeal. For instance, there are artificial substitutes for sugar, artificially sweetened soft drinks, and frozen yoghurts instead of ice cream.

Keeping Records

Keep careful daily records of caloric intake while dieting. Most persons do not want to believe that the body is the fierce accountant that it is, and taking the time to record calories draws attention to one's eating and serves as a reminder of one's game plan for losing weight. One also may do well during the week and forget the game plan on the weekend. When such caloric excesses are planned for, then such excursions will not affect the total weekly intake. Circumstances have much to do with eating behavior. For example, it may help to

—eat only in one room.

—use small plates.

—eat with a cocktail fork.

—chew food slower.

—always leave something on the plate.

—never eat while reading or watching television.

—take a drink of water when hungry.

One example is illustrated in the weight reduction program employed by the 12-year-old son of one of the authors. He decided to lose eight pounds over a one-month period. He calculated the daily reduction in calories necessary to accomplish the loss and charted both his actual weight and his desirable weight on a daily basis. Furthermore, he decided upon a series of activity rewards that would be contingent upon the accomplishment of weight loss. For example, he would not allow himself the scheduled reward unless his actual weight on that day was at or below the desirable weight. Table 7–5 shows his weight loss and reward system.

## Self-Rewards

While the knowledge that one is losing weight is likely to be highly rewarding, one may wish to plan for certain self-administered rewards. The most successful are preferred activities. If an activity is to be used as a reward, it cannot be engaged in except upon completion of a goal. If losing weight is really important, one might be willing to upset one's budget slightly to compensate oneself for the denial required.

## Establishing Contingencies

Once some rewards have been chosen, very carefully stipulate *when* the reward is due. Enjoying the rewards on a haphazard basis can destroy their usefulness as

**Table 7-5. Weight-loss chart.**

| | 1 | 2 | 3 | 4 | 5 | 6 | 7 | 8 | 9 | 10 | 11 | 12 | 13 | 14 | 15 | 16 | 17 | 18 | 19 | 20 | 21 | 22 | 23 | 24 | 25 | 26 | 27 | 28 |
|---|---|---|---|---|---|---|---|---|---|---|---|---|---|---|---|---|---|---|---|---|---|---|---|---|---|---|---|---|
| Actual Weight | 117 | 117 | 117 | 116 | 116 | 116 | 115 | 115 | 115 | 114 | 114 | 114 | 113 | 113 | 113 | 112 | 112 | 112 | 111 | 111 | 111 | 110 | 110 | 110 | 109 | 109 | 109 | 108 |
| Desirable Weight | 117 | 117 | 116 | 116 | 116 | 115 | 115 | 115 | 114 | 114 | 114 | 114 | 113 | 113 | 112 | 112 | 112 | 111 | 111 | 111 | 111 | 110 | 110 | 110 | 110 | 109 | 109 | 109 |
| Rewarding Event | | | | Movie | | | Ball Game (Atlanta Hawks) | | | | | | Ball Game (Atlanta Flames) | | | | | | Ice Skating | | | | Movie | | | Ball Game (Atlanta Hawks) | | |

motivators. Allow simple rewards for reaching short-range goals, such as three days of success in staying on the diet, and more exciting rewards for the accomplishment of long-range goals.

## Weight Gain

While obesity is a major problem in our culture, some persons actually need to gain weight. Only a generation ago, thinness was seen as a sign of malnutrition and poor health. Persons seeking to gain weight can use the same steps suggested for losing weight—the only difference, of course, is that they will eat more rather than less.

### Physical Conditioning

Although many Americans are out of shape, physical fitness for the kind of life that most people live can be gained without living a Spartan life. Unfortunately, most persons fall into one of two classes. Either they do nothing about their desire to get in shape, or they spasmodically adopt an excessive physical conditioning program that soon results in sore muscles and a lessening interest in the whole affair.

While physical conditioning is clearly related to good health, it is possible to have one without the other. One can be in excellent physical condition and yet have poor health. Now and then one reads of persons, sometimes even athletes, who appear to be in peak condition and yet succumb to disease. And some persons with terminal diseases manage, through discipline, to enjoy excellent control of their muscular and skeletal systems until shortly before death. It is also possible to enjoy relatively good health without good physical conditioning. Good conditioning, however, tends to contribute to good health. Moreover, physical conditioning contributes to a sense of self-control and positive body image. By keeping the machine in good running condition, one significantly decreases the likelihood of heart attack and stroke.

There are three major aspects of physical conditioning: muscle mass and strength, cardiovascular endurance, and skeletomuscular flexibility.

Muscle mass is a prerequisite to muscle strength. It is possible, however, to develop large muscle mass without a great deal of strength. Some hypertrophic, muscle-bound persons, despite their cosmetic appeal, actually have only modest strength. The process for building strength is different than that for building mass. One must first build mass, or "pack in the protein," as the athletes say, before beginning a program for building strength. Muscle mass is built through multiple repetitions—fifteen or twenty at a time—of an exercise that requires about 70 percent of maximum effort. On the other hand, muscle strength is built with fewer repetitions—four or five—that require maximum effort (Morehouse and Gross, 1975).

Cardiovascular endurance is perhaps even more important than muscle strength. It refers to the circulatory system, which consists of the heart and blood vessels. A strong cardiovascular system is good insurance against most forms of heart attack. One strengthens the heart by raising the heart rate for a few minutes at a time through exercise. The key to increasing heart strength is overload.

Overload involves increasing the amount of blood within the chambers of the heart so that the heart muscle must squeeze harder to pump it out. Increasing the heart rate through strong emotion *does not* strengthen the heart because this does not increase the amount of blood within the chambers. The rise in heart rate accompanying vigorous exercise, however, *does* increase the amount of blood in the chambers. Each muscle of the body is actually a kind of heart itself, since, when exercised, it squeezes the blood within it toward the heart. This constant squeezing by the body muscles lifts the blood from the lower limbs and torso and runs it back through the heart. The heart is thus gorged with blood and must squeeze extra hard to handle this overload. This extra effort strengthens the heart muscle considerably.

Skeletomuscular flexibility is important to graceful movement, to a feeling of well-being, and as a precaution against problems with strained muscles, tendons, and ligaments. Hatha yoga is an excellent method of flexing the spine as well as these muscles, tendons, and ligaments. The spine is the key to flexibility since it serves as a chassis upon which the other parts of the body are hung.

A perfectly acceptable level of physical conditioning with moderate effort can be achieved by following the basic steps listed here.

Setting Goals

First determine the degree of physical conditioning you are willing to maintain. It does little good to pursue a grueling exercise program to reach an advanced athletic build if the ten or more hours per week it takes to maintain the condition cannot be spared. Muscle mass and muscle strength disappear rapidly when one no longer puts the muscles under some strain. The only way to maintain a Tarzanlike appearance is to spend long periods weekly in weight lifting. Furthermore, you can lose up to 80 percent of this splendid conditioning within one month if an excessively sedentary lifestyle is adopted.

Before embarking on any program, answer these questions:

What do you want to be able to do in the way of physical activity?

How much endurance must you have in order to engage in the kinds of activities you wish to pursue?

Are you likely to become a tennis buff and play twelve to fifteen sets per week?

Are you planning on taking up mountain climbing as a sport?

Are you trying to prepare yourself for championship performance in a contact sport? *Or* are you merely concerned with attaining the kind of strength, endurance, and flexibility that will allow you to pursue a moderately active lifestyle with minimum exhaustion and suscepti- bility to heart attack?

How you answer these questions makes a significant difference in the design of a conditioning program.

Morehouse and Gross in their best-seller, *Total Fitness in 30 Minutes a Week* (1975), do a splendid job of advis- ing the reader to devise a fitness program that will meet his personal goals. Morehouse is a professor of exercise physiology and director of the Human Performance Laboratory at UCLA. His system for physical condition- ing is used by U.S. astronauts.

A couple of tests used by Morehouse to determine the current condition of subjects in the Human Performance Laboratory examine the amount of fat on the body frame and the rapidity of the pulse rate under standard condi- tions. The fatness tests for men and women were in- cluded under the section on weight control earlier in this chapter. In addition, the pulse rate correlates highly with heart rate. It is easily taken and is, according to More- house and Gross, "the body's most important single indi- cator of well-being, stress or illness" (p. 131). In order to evaluate one's present conditioning, one should check one's pulse rate under six conditions:

1. First get a resting pulse rate. The reading will be more accurate if one waits a few hours after eating, smoking, or drinking alcohol, coffee, or tea. The effect of coffee on the pulse rate is quite noticeable and may elevate it to ten beats per minute. Sit comfortably, at- tempt to relax the various muscle groups of the body, and breathe from your abdomen. Rest a few minutes in this condition and take the pulse.

There are several ways to find the pulse. It can be lo- cated in the wrist, in the temporal arteries next to the ear, in the carotid artery at the side of the neck or merely by placing a hand over the heart. A lower reading will be obtained in the morning than the evening since the beat rises from five to ten beats over the course of the day.

If the resting rate is 100 or more per minute, there is room for concern about one's condition. An average pulse rate for men ranges from 72–76, for women, 75–80, for boys, 80–84, and for girls, 82–89. If one finds a higher-than-normal rate, wait a few days and check again. If it remains high, consult a physician before attempting any physical conditioning program. If the count is below 100, go on to step 2.

2. Quietly stand in a resting position for one minute and take the pulse rate again. A standing count will likely increase over a sitting rate by as much as ten beats, but if the increase is twenty beats or more, discontinue the test and see a physician.

3. Now check the body's ability to recover from mild exercise. This check is called the Step Test, since the object is to step up and down rapidly to stimulate the system. The number of times one steps up and down is a function of the height of the step and one's body weight. It can be derived from the following table:

**Table 7–6.  Stepping rate (steps per minute).**

| | | Height of Step (inches) | | | | |
|---|---|---|---|---|---|---|
| | | 7 | 8 | 9 | 10 | 11 | 12 |
| | 100 | 30 | 30 | 30 | 30 | 30 | 30 |
| | 120 | 30 | 30 | 30 | 30 | 30 | 30 |
| Body Weight (pounds) | 140 | 30 | 30 | 30 | 30 | 20 | 20 |
| | 160 | 30 | 30 | 30 | 20 | 20 | 20 |
| | 180 | 30 | 30 | 20 | 20 | 20 | 20 |
| | 200 | 30 | 20 | 20 | 20 | 20 | 20 |
| | 220 | 20 | 20 | 20 | 20 | 20 | 20 |

From *Total Fitness in 30 Minutes a Week* by Laurence E. Morehouse and Leonard Gross. Copyright © 1975 by Laurence E. Morehouse, Ph. D. Reprinted by permission of Simon & Schuster, a Division of Gulf and Western Corporation.

Measure the height of the step and consult Table 7–6. If one weighs 180 pounds and the height of the step is ten inches, one should step 20 times in one minute. Step up with the left foot, then down with left, then repeat with right foot. Make certain that the cycle is completed the number of times per minute indicated in Table 7–6. Immediately sit down after completing the required number of steps and take the pulse. Since the pulse will generally drop slightly over a period of one minute, one needs to compute this pulse rate a bit differently. Count the beat for six seconds and add a zero. This prorates the figure over an entire minute and gives one a better indication of the rate immediately after the exercise. If the count is ten and one adds a zero, the pulse rate is 100. Discontinue the test if the rate is above 120 or if undue distress is experienced.

4. Repeat the one-minute exercise and again take the pulse immediately in a sitting position. Discontinue the test if the pulse exceeds 120 or if distress is experienced.

5. Once again, repeat the one-minute test and check the pulse rate while sitting. The count should be no higher than 120. Now wait one minute and take the pulse again. The count should decrease by ten or more beats. The second count should be no higher than 110 beats per minute. The greater the decrease, the better. This ability to recover from exertion in short order is an important indication of physical conditioning.

Morehouse and Gross conclude that one is in pretty good physical shape if one's pulse rate at no time exceeds 120 beats per minute and one recovers rapidly at the end of the test. If one flunks the test for either of these reasons, one would do well to consult a physician before beginning any conditioning program. Also, this test is not meant to replace a medical examination. It merely tells whether or not one is prepared for a moderate degree of physical exercise.

An immediate goal of physical conditioning should reflect one's response to the Step Test. If unable to complete the test, then one might accept as a goal a degree of physical conditioning that will allow one to pass the test.

One might express the goal in the following way: "To be able to pass the Step Test in three weeks time." Morehouse and Gross (pp. 155–156) suggest the following daily program for those unable to pass the Step Test:

1. Turn and twist the body joints to their near-maximum range of motion.

2. Stand for a total of two hours a day.

3. Lift something unusually heavy for five seconds.

4. Get the heart rate up to 120 beats a minute for at least three minutes.

5. Burn up 300 calories a day in physical activity.

In order to burn up 300 calories in physical activity each day, look for opportunities in ordinary routine that allow one to expend a little more energy. Walk up the stairs instead of riding the elevator. Get in the habit of standing more often than usual. When reading, rise and walk around the room every 15 or 20 minutes. Stand when answering the telephone. Many people find themselves performing a bit sharper mentally since they are getting more blood to their brains this way. A more concentrated form of exercise can be used by selecting one of the activities from Table 7–7.

Once one has met the minimum condition necessary to pass the Step Test, one might commit oneself to a more ambitious program that includes all three aspects of physical conditioning. In constructing a personal program, consult either Morehouse and Gross or *The Official YMCA Physical Fitness Handbook* (Myers, 1975).

Aids to developing flexibility can be found in *Be Young With Yoga* (Hittleman, 1962) or *Yoga for Physical Fitness* (Hittleman, 1964).

Once a decision is made on the degree of physical conditioning desired, one could express a goal either in terms of the goal sought or in terms of the means employed to reach the goal. If concentrating on a goal, it might be expressed as, "to be able to run a seven-minute mile," "to be able to swim (breaststroke) a mile in one

Table 7–7.    Calories expended in activity.

| Activity | Calories per minute |
|---|---|
| Walking, 2 mph | 2.8 |
| Walking, 3.5 mph | 4.8 |
| Bicycling, 5.5 mph | 3.2 |
| Bicycling rapidly | 6.9 |
| Running, 5.7 mph | 12.0 |
| Running, 7.0 mph | 14.5 |
| Running, 11.4 mph | 21.7 |
| Swimming (crawl), 2.2 mph | 26.7 |
| Swimming (breaststroke), 2.2 mph | 30.8 |
| Swimming (backstroke), 2.2 mph | 33.3 |
| Golf | 5.0 |
| Tennis | 7.1 |
| Table tennis | 5.8 |
| Dancing (fox trot) | 5.2 |

hour," or "to be able to play three sets of tennis without feeling unduly tired." Such goals are often too long-range to be sufficiently motivating. Consequently, goals are better expressed in terms of the means or process by which they will be obtained.

If stating a goal in terms of a process, it might include statements such as, "to jog twelve minutes every other day at a pace that will maintain pulse rate at 80 percent of my maximum heart rate." A good approximation of one's maximum heart rate can be obtained by subtracting one's age from 220. If one is thirty years old, the maximum heart rate is 190. The percentage depends on present conditioning. Providing one's conditioning is good enough to begin a program to improve cardiovascular endurance, begin with 60 percent for the first six to eight weeks, then 70 percent for the next six to eight weeks, and finally, at 80 percent for the duration of the program. For example, if you are thirty, your maximum heart rate is 190, and 60 percent of this figure is 114.

You can round off this figure upward to 120. Seventy percent is 133, and 80 percent, 152.

Using this process definition of a goal, one can compare one's progress against the norms described by Cooper (1970) in his book, *The New Aerobics*. Table 7–8 shows those figures. According to Table 7–8, if you are a thirty to thirty-nine year old female and you are able to run/jog 1.19 to 1.29 miles in twelve minutes, your condition would be rated "good." If your pulse rate is kept at the 60/70/80 percent figure for the length of the exercise, the heart and vascular system will be profiting maximally from the routine.

A program should include the three aspects of physical conditioning. A program for a forty-year-old person who easily passes the Step Test might include the following daily exercises:

### First Eight Weeks (daily exercises)

1. *Sit-ups*: Lie on back with knees up and feet flat on floor. Roll head, shoulders, and chest forward gently while allowing hands to gracefully glide up and over knees. Do ten during the first two weeks, and twenty during the third and fourth weeks.

During the fifth through eighth weeks, do ten of these sit-ups with hands cupped behind head.

2. *Push-ups*: Do ten push-ups daily on the following basis:

First week—Stand three feet from wall; lean with hands flat against wall and push away.

Second week—Stand four feet from wall; lean with hands flat against wall and push away.

Third week—Stand four feet from kitchen counter; lean with hands resting on counter and push away.

Fourth week—Stand four feet from 30-inch-high chair; lean with hands resting on chair and push away.

Fifth week—Stand four feet from footstool; lean with hands resting on stool and push away.

**Table 7–8. 12-Minute walking/running test.**
Distance (miles) covered in 12 minutes

*Fitness Category*

| | | Age (years) | | | | | |
|---|---|---|---|---|---|---|---|
| | | 13-19 | 20-29 | 30-39 | 40-49 | 50-59 | 60+ |
| I. Very poor | (men) | <1.30* | <1.22 | <1.18 | <1.14 | <1.03 | <.87 |
| | (women) | <1.0 | <.96 | <.94 | <.88 | <.84 | <.78 |
| II. Poor | (men) | 1.30-1.37 | 1.22-1.31 | 1.18-1.30 | 1.14-1.24 | 1.03-1.16 | .87-1.02 |
| | (women) | 1.00-1.18 | .96-1.11 | .95-1.05 | .88-.98 | .84-.93 | .78-.86 |
| III. Fair | (men) | 1.38-1.56 | 1.32-1.49 | 1.31-1.45 | 1.25-1.39 | 1.17-1.30 | 1.03-1.20 |
| | (women) | 1.19-1.29 | 1.12-1.22 | 1.06-1.18 | .99-1.11 | .94-1.05 | .87-.98 |
| IV. Good | (men) | 1.57-1.72 | 1.50-1.64 | 1.46-1.56 | 1.40-1.53 | 1.31-1.44 | 1.21-1.32 |
| | (women) | 1.30-1.43 | 1.23-1.34 | 1.19-1.29 | 1.12-1.24 | 1.06-1.18 | .99-1.09 |
| V. Excellent | (men) | 1.73-1.86 | 1.65-1.76 | 1.57-1.69 | 1.54-1.65 | 1.45-1.58 | 1.33-1.55 |
| | (women) | 1.44-1.51 | 1.35-1.45 | 1.30-1.39 | 1.25-1.34 | 1.19-1.30 | 1.10-1.18 |
| VI. Superior | (men) | >1.87 | >1.77 | >1.70 | >1.66 | >1.59 | >1.56 |
| | (women) | >1.52 | >1.46 | >1.40 | >1.35 | >1.31 | >1.19 |

* < Means "less than"; > means "more than."

From *The Aerobics Way* by Kenneth H. Cooper, M.D., M.P.H. Copyright © 1977 by
Kenneth H. Cooper, reprinted by permission of the publishers, M. Evans and Company,
Inc., New York, N.Y. 10017.

Sixth through eighth week—Stand five feet from a ten-inch-high step; lean with hands resting on step and push up.

3. *Ten minutes jogging* every other day at a rate that keeps the pulse rate at roughly 110 beats per minute.

4. *Fifteen minutes of yoga exercises* suggested in the graduated program by Hittleman (*Be Young With Yoga,* 1962).

### After Eight Weeks (daily exercises)

1. Twenty sit-ups with knees bent and hands cupped behind head.

2. Ten push-ups from the floor.

3. Ten minutes jogging every other day at a rate that keeps pulse rate at roughly 130 (eventually 150 as maximum).

4. Fifteen minutes of yoga exercises suggested in the graduated program by Hittleman (*Be Young With Yoga,* 1962).

### Focusing on Behavior

Drawing attention to a behavior tends to make it more likely to become habitual. Consequently, pay attention to any conditioning program. Imagine performing the habit, and imagine the payoff in terms of improved physical functioning. The more often one does this, the more likely one is to keep up one's routine. Furthermore, it is important to do some detective work to identify those conditions that encourage or discourage an exercise routine.

Finding the Starting Line

Motivation is helped if base rates of present conditioning are so established that one knows when one is making progress. One might ask how much work can be done while keeping a pulse rate of 60 percent of the maximum heart rate. This can be checked through any activity such as walking, running, cycling, or swimming. This is one way to find a starting line. Other indications of a starting line are performance on the Step Test, current weight, and the degree of flexibility as indicated by one's ability to perform basic yoga postures. Once the starting line is set, it is easy to measure progress—without it, one is likely to exaggerate or underrate early successes.

## Identifying Triggering Situations

When attempting to start a program, identify situations or conditions that affect performance: When are you least likely to exercise? When you are out of town? When you get home late from the office? When you are worried about some of the hassles experienced during the day? When it is cold outside? When you cannot get to the pool or gym? By anticipating any barriers, one may be able to do something about them. For instance, it helps to have an alternate plan in case a preferred form of exercise becomes difficult. One can skip rope inside a motel room or house if the weather is inclement. Persons who are too worried or tired to exercise in the evening can awake a half hour earlier and exercise in the morning.

Consider the circumstances that encourage consistency in pursuing an exercise program. A competitive person might challenge a friend who needs the exercises as much as he. Exercising together, however, can offer an excuse for not exercising. One might create social pressure on oneself by posting a "score" daily on the office door or on the refrigerator at home. Just remember that conditions that encourage one person may not encourage another.

The lunch hour is often the perfect time for a routine. One can lock the office door and shed outer garments. Many exercises can be used in an office. It is best to choose those routines that require few special trappings for their completion. On the other hand, one might like to get one's exercises in before beginning the work day. Carefully assess any habits and preferences, and select a time and conditions that will prove most conducive.

## Keeping Records

Keep some kind of daily record of progress. The exact nature of the record depends on the personal program. A record may prove more motivating if it requires a little time to complete (perhaps a minute or so), since this will rivet attention on the behavior being recorded. A basic rule is that anything that centers attention on a behavior will tend to encourage that behavior. After one has stuck with a program for awhile, the record-keeping will serve as a small daily reward.

### Choosing Self-Rewards

While a record of progress may be rewarding enough, one might also buttress this form of reward with others. Promises of special activities are generally more rewarding to adults than are tangible rewards such as money. The bad thing about using money as a reward is that it merely comes out of one pocket into another, if you are rewarding yourself. Draw up a list of favorite activities. It will probably include such things as tennis, golf, reading, partying, visiting friends, and going to the movies. Use these activities as rewards for faithful execution of the exercise program.

Establish some contingencies for administering self-rewards. As explained earlier, contingencies are the bases for rewarding conditions. If one is going to reward oneself by allowing oneself to read a novel or go to the movies, exactly when will the reward have been earned? A contingency might be, "If I stick with my exercise program from Monday through Friday, I will go to the movies on Friday evening." Take the contingencies seriously. The only way a reward is actually rewarding is if one enjoys it only after having met the conditions. If one goes to the movies Tuesday and Thursday irrespective of consistency in pursuing the program, then going to the movies on Friday is not likely to be motivating.

In summary, the first task in establishing a physical conditioning program is to set specific and moderate goals. These goals should take three aspects of physical conditioning into consideration: muscle mass and strength, cardiovascular endurance, and skeletal flexibility.

Next, it is important to get a reading on present conditioning so that progress can be measured against it. One needs to analyze conditions under which one is likely to be encouraged or discouraged and to attempt to keep the discouraging conditions at a minimum. Keeping daily records of progress helps. Select self-rewards with consistency and establish clear bases for allowing oneself to enjoy these rewards. If one follows these steps, one will be immensely pleased with oneself as rediscovered strength, endurance, and flexibility are experienced.

### Controlling Excessive Drinking

Millions of Americans have a drinking problem. Alcoholism is considered a problem that results in personal and social harm. The definition of "excessive drinking" is elusive, and even alcoholism has a variety of sometimes contradictory bases by which its presence is established. Even the theories regarding the origins of alcoholism and alcohol abuse in individuals are numerous enough to discourage the authors from offering any opinion. For those persons seeking some help in controlling their drinking, the following is an abbreviated adaptation of the foregoing plans for change.

Setting Goals

Alcohol abuse is the number one drug problem in the U.S. It is so prevalent that, as a subject, it has become firmly ensconced as a basic teaching unit in almost all of the health-education courses in schools. But like the lessons of drivers' training, the information is easily forgotten under peer pressure or some similar inducement. Alcohol has a familiar abuse pattern for most Americans.

Unless it has become a steady and frequent partner, its use is likely to become excessive during periods of stress and recreation. The cocktails after bowling, the martinis at the office party, a wedding, or a class reunion are all occasions of frequent alcohol overuse. Similarly, periods of stress beckon alcohol as a relief.

Assuming that complete abstinence is not a reasonable or necessary option for most individuals, the best major target seems to be to learn to drink safely and comfortably without incurring the long-range physical deterioration or the short-range conditions of drunkenness and hangovers. The amount of alcohol one can safely drink varies, depending on the following conditions:

1. *Rate of drinking.* Most adults can sip an alcoholic beverage containing the equivalent of one-half ounce of alcohol for one hour and the alcohol will be burned up at the same rate that the bloodstream is absorbing it. If the drink is gulped, the drinker will quickly feel it, and the effects will last an hour or so.

2. *Food eaten.* Food in the stomach slows down the rate at which alcohol is absorbed into the bloodstream, thus affecting the rate at which the alcohol reaches the brain.

3. *Type of beverage.* Beer and wine contain nutrients and other substances that make the absorption rate somewhat slower than for liquor.

4. *Body weight.* The more a drinker weighs, the greater the amount of blood and other fluids that are present to dilute the alcohol, thus affecting the speed and extent of the effect on the drinker.

5. *Body chemistry.* Individual body differences can affect any of the four conditions just described.

In addition to these physical factors, psychological factors also influence the effect of alcohol on a person. Some of the factors most clearly influencing the resulting effects are:

1. *Mood.* Tension or anger may pressure a drinker to

overdrink as an escape mechanism. Furthermore, one's mood can either exaggerate or lessen the effect of alcohol on behavior.

2. *Attitudes.* Very strict familial or religious proscriptions against drinking sometimes have a boomerang effect. When persons who have been subjected to such teaching early in their lives take up the use of alcohol, they sometimes drink to excess. Perhaps this early training induces guilt, and the drinker decides to drink even more to drown out the internal harping. Training that leads to too frequent or too casual use may lead to alcoholism.

3. *Situation.* Depending on where one is and with whom, one may regulate one's drinking behavior.

4. *Drinking experience.* A person who is used to alcohol can recognize when judgment and coordination are being impaired and act accordingly to avoid intoxication or abuse.

The above factors suggest reasons for the wide variety of alcohol consumption patterns that exist among drinkers. They also explain some of the confusion regarding the definition of alcoholism. Such confusion often causes the media to portray an alcoholic as a stumbling victim of all of these factors when any one of them, if overlooked or mishandled, may spell trouble.

Considering one's own personality and drinking habits allows a person to decide whether it is time to cut down or cut off drinking altogether. One must be very specific about change. Vague goals about consumption habits related to eating and drinking are generally worthless. While cutting out drinking altogether is a specific goal, cutting down is not. One must specify the exact amount that one will allow oneself, or one is most likely to find oneself overdoing it. One method is to set a limit on daily intake. The actual amount of alcohol varies depending upon whether beer, wine, or hard liquors is being consumed.

## Focusing on Behavior

Begin to pay attention to drinking habits. Drawing attention to drinking patterns will likely increase the motivation to either quit or drink in moderation. To know how much to cut down, one should first accurately discover one's current base rate of drinking.

### Finding the Starting Line

For one week record every drink taken. Indicate the circumstances under which it is taken, as well as one's companions, the activity, what was drunk, and where it was drunk. At the end of one week the record should show how much one normally drinks. A person is ready to determine exactly how much cutting down is needed.

### Identifying Triggering Situations

The records of normal drinking behavior collected during a baseline week also tell a lot about the conditions under which one is led to drink. When attempting to cut down, change in routine sometimes boosts willpower. Someone who tends to overdrink in the company of certain persons may decide to see less of them. Someone who overdrinks on the way home may decide to forgo the stopover. A person who takes in more alcohol when drinking hard liquor may decide to limit himself to beer and wine. One who tends to overdrink when worried or tired may seek another way of handling the tension. A careful analysis of the conditions under which one overdrinks will put one in a position to make certain changes in routine that may result in greater moderation. Getting the facts helps considerably.

### Keeping Records

It is important to continue to keep a record of alcohol use for a fairly long time. This method of personal accountability makes it more difficult to slip back into old drinking habits. It also serves as a constant reminder of progress in handling this problem.

## Self-Rewards

While one may wish to compensate oneself for denial with certain activities that are very much enjoyed, it is a mistake to make alcohol the reward. This practice militates against the overall goal, and it further establishes a rewarding nature of drinking.

As mentioned earlier, it is important to allow rewards only if one meets certain specific requirements of self-denial set beforehand. The rewards are contingent upon adherence to self-imposed limits on drinking.

## Controlling of Smoking

Reasons for controlling or eliminating smoking are so legion and hackneyed that there is no need for another statistic indicting the lowly weed. In spite of all the reasons for quitting, however, more cigarettes are being smoked each year. Likewise, pipe and cigar smoking are here to stay, frequently serving as substitutes for cigarettes.

For a commodity that has attained the vilified status that it so recently has, tobacco has a fairly long and venerable history. Columbus found tobacco when he arrived in America. The Indians cultivated, smoked, chewed, and snuffed it. Its spread throughout the world was phenomenal. It became the most important product of the colonies and even served as a means of monetary exchange. The introduction of cigarettes in the seventeenth century was little noticed, and their use did not become widespread until World War I, when women also began smoking.

Given its history of economic profit, it is easy to understand why cigarettes were not seriously indicted earlier. Their relatively mild flavor encouraged the smoker to inhale deep into the lungs. The small size, light weight and quick-burning qualities encouraged users to light cigarette after cigarette, and the factory production of the twentieth century put them within reach of the masses.

Pipes and cigars are also not blameless. Their involvement in mouth and lip cancers is considerable, and if one inhales, the other dangers attributed to cigarettes apply equally, given the same rate of use. Tobacco contains three poisonous elements: nicotine, tar, and carbon monoxide. Nicotine and carbon monoxide contribute to heart and artery disease, while tar contributes to emphysema and cancer. In addition, nicotine acts first as a stimulant and then as a depressant. A single cigarette increases cardiovascular indices for approximately one half hour, and then a letdown occurs, which serves to trigger further smoking. The carbon monoxide in tobacco is the same ingredient that is lethal in concentrated amounts in auto exhaust. The combined effects of these poisons can reduce the life expectancy of a fifty-year-old who has smoked a pack of cigarettes a day for thirty years by eight-and-a-half years (Myers, 1975).

Setting Goals

One must first decide whether one's goal is to reduce the number of cigarettes or to eliminate them altogether. Many persons find that there is no in-between for them. They cannot smoke one or two cigarettes per day year in and year out. The amount always seems to increase gradually until they are smoking a pack or more a day. For them, smoking in moderation is like being pregnant in moderation—impossible.

If the decision is to quit entirely, one must decide whether to eliminate the habit step by step or to go "cold turkey." While it is possible gradually to wean oneself from the habit, many people consider this method little more than a constant tease. For many persons, the pain of cold turkey is no greater than the torturous nature of the gradual process. Cutting off the habit quickly frees a person to concentrate on the substitute activities and satisfaction that one has arranged as disassociative mechanisms and rewards.

Whatever the choice—to smoke moderately or not at all—be absolutely clear about the matter. If the choice is to cut down, specify exactly how many cigarettes are allowed. In deciding to give it up altogether, there is obviously no ambiguity involved.

Focusing on Behavior

As mentioned earlier, it is extremely important to direct attention to the behavior. Attention is a powerful form of energy that can be harnessed to resist inner urges.

*Finding the Starting Line*

While most smokers pretty well know what they are facing, they should not omit the task of establishing a baseline. It will prove helpful to know exactly how many cigarettes are smoked before beginning efforts to stop. Keeping records is the way to be sure. Note when and under what circumstances each cigarette is puffed for a whole week before mounting an offensive. Some research shows that the simple process of monitoring has a retarding effect on smoking, but for this first week, make absolutely no effort to reduce smoking. This baseline measure will become the basis for calculating the degree of progress made at various times during the effort to stop.

*Identifying Triggering Stimuli*

It is important to identify those conditions under which one is most encouraged to smoke. One may associate smoking with drinking coffee, after-dinner behavior, reading, working, conversing, playing cards, and other activities. Smoking may follow such activities so often that they now trigger the smoking. One may not even be aware of the triggering effect of these activities.

One may rather automatically reach for a cigarette at their prompting.

There are many such triggers for this unconscious behavior. The National Institute of Health has a cigarette habit-breaking program that attempts to limit these triggers to a single trigger over which a smoker has control. The program requires the purchase of a cigarette case with a built-in alarm. The smoker discovers from baseline data how frequently he smokes. He then sets the alarm so that it automatically goes off slightly more frequently than he normally smokes. For instance, if he normally smokes every half hour, he is to set the alarm for every 20 minutes. When the alarm goes off, he is to smoke regardless of the inconvenience and regardless of his desire to do so. Moreover, he is not to smoke at any other time. Since the smoking intervals are at first set so frequently, it requires no act of will to limit the smoking to these times. Slowly the smoker lengthens the smoking intervals, continuing to limit the smoking to these triggers. In the process the association between smoking and all its associated activities (coffee, dinner, reading, and the like) is broken, and the sole remaining trigger is one that is under the control of the smoker. This program is packaged by and inexpensively available from the National Institute of Health, Washington, D.C.

Whether or not one chooses to use the program, it is important to identify any triggers and attempt to remove as many of them as possible. Control will be somewhat limited, however, without the program from the National Institute of Health.

Choosing Self-Rewards

Quite likely the greatest reward for one's efforts to stop smoking will be the data that reflects progress. One experiences a sense of self-endorsement when recording the lower number of cigarettes one is smoking. One may, however, wish to add other forms of encouragement. As mentioned earlier, one may wish to select certain interesting activities as rewards, or one may wish to allow oneself to purchase some item that one has wanted for quite some time.

## Establishing Contingencies

It is important to reserve the chosen self-rewards. One should not allow oneself to enjoy them unless the requirements have been met. These rewards should be spaced in such a way as to provide significant encouragement early in the program. Since data will probably be collected on a daily basis, it may provide some form of reward for the earlier successes. Both the recording and the self-rewards will tend to focus attention on nonsmoking behavior, and such attention tends to further reinforce one's efforts.

## A Final Word

While the authors realize that the most accepted professional advice regarding medical care is to work through a family physician, they are also aware that many persons feel hopelessly ignorant about their medical problems. Some persons have attempted to obtain a fuller base of information about a condition from a physician only to feel that such inquiries are viewed as being inappropriate. Perhaps the physician has answered the question to his satisfaction, but the patient is left with the most fragmentary understanding of a condition. He would like to be more fully informed. He would like to be in possession of information that would allow him to assess his problem.

In the spirit of this self-help volume, the authors would like to make the reader aware of a few reference volumes that might be reviewed in order to obtain some guidance through the maze of medical information and treatments available. In no way will this information allow one to flout the advice of a physician, but these books may furnish one with a fuller understanding of any health problems that one is likely to get from a hurried interview with a physician.

One of the most popular guides for the layman is *Black's Medical Dictionary* (1974). First published in 1906, this work has been revised thirty times and is therefore reliably up-to-date. One of its premises is that patients consult their family doctor about many minor ailments that they could well cope with on their own. It thoroughly describes the way the body functions in health and disease and what one should do about a specific condition.

Better Homes and Gardens' *Family Medical Guide* (1973) is another good reference. Compiled through the efforts of many respected medical specialists, it is intended to serve as a supplement to family medical counsel. It is written in readable language and style. Although it does not avoid technical terms, it does provide a dictionary and encyclopedia of medical terms for easy reference. It is richly and attractively illustrated and family members of almost any age are likely to enjoy scanning and selectively reading its contents.

The *Child Health Encyclopedia* (1975) recognizes that the parent is on the front line in providing health care to children. This volume, or a facsimile, is a must for every parent. Even though a parent may be well educated, the medical aspects of child rearing are often not within the scope of a general education. The coverage of this volume is thorough and wide-ranging.

# 8. Physical Approaches to Stress Reduction

*Nothing can so pierce the soul as the uttermost sigh of the body.*

George Santayana

*He will be the slave of many masters who is his body's slave.*

Seneca

Stress exacts a frightful price. The World Health Organization reports that yearly fifteen million people threaten suicide, three million attempt it, three hundred sixty five thousand succeed, and of this number five hundred are children. One of every ten Americans suffers serious mental or emotional problems, and one of every ten American families has an alcoholic. Billions of dollars are spent annually on tranquilizers, and drug abuse is a leading cause of death. Moreover, stress is a prime factor in such psychosomatic illnesses as migraine headaches, tachycardia, colitis, asthma, and ulcerated conditions.

Hans Selye, the author of *The Stress of Life* (1956) and *Stress Without Distress* (1974), defines stress as the nonspecific response of the body to any demand made on it. It makes no difference whether the demands are imposed by infection, hemorrhage, heat or freezing temperatures, trauma, nervous irritation, frustration, or anxiety; all are forms of stress. Two psychiatrists, Holmes and Rahe (1967), attempted to list in order the relative stress occasioned by certain life changes. While the list (see Table 8–1) undoubtedly suffers from the usual imprecision resulting from sampling research, it is nevertheless suggestive of the kinds of stressors to which persons are commonly subjected.

The mean value for each life event listed in the table represents the amount, duration, and severity of the change that is believed to be necessary to cope with the event. These figures represent responses from hundreds of people interviewed by Holmes and Rahe. Marriage was arbitrarily assigned a rating of 50 points, and persons interviewed were asked to rate all other events in comparison with marriage. For example, the death of a spouse was believed to be twice as stressful as marriage, and so it was given a mean rating of 100; a change in living conditions, on the other hand, was viewed as half as stressful, and so it was given a rating of 25.

Holmes and Rahe suggest that one can add up the scores for all the events on the list that happened to him or her during the past year in order to estimate the risk of psychological disturbance or psychosomatic illness. Their simple guide suggests that a rating of less than 150 points results in about a one in three chance of a serious health problem in the next two years; a total between 150 and 300 points raises the chances to about one out of two, and a total above 300 points raises the chances to almost nine out of ten.

There is no doubt that many of these stressors tax coping resources severely. It is known, for example, that in the first year after the death of a spouse, the death rate of the remaining spouse is ten times higher than for other persons of the same age, and in the first year following divorce, divorced persons have an illness rate twelve times greater than that of married persons (Benson, 1975).

While the specific effects of these stressors differ significantly, their nonspecific effects are the same. The organism's predictable, nonspecific reaction to stress is what Selye (1974) called the General Adaptation Syndrome. This syndrome is the organism's typical manner of dealing with demands made upon it. It includes three stages: alarm, resistance, and exhaustion.

**Table 8-1.   Social readjustment rating scale.***

| Life Event | Mean Value |
|---|---|
| 1.  Death of spouse | 100 |
| 2.  Divorce | 73 |
| 3.  Marital separation | 65 |
| 4.  Jail term | 63 |
| 5.  Death of close family member | 63 |
| 6.  Personal injury or illness | 53 |
| 7.  Marriage | 50 |
| 8.  Fired at work | 47 |
| 9.  Marital reconciliation | 45 |
| 10.  Retirement | 45 |
| 11.  Change in health of family member | 44 |
| 12.  Pregnancy | 40 |
| 13.  Sex difficulties | 39 |
| 14.  Gain of new family member | 39 |
| 15.  Business readjustment | 39 |
| 16.  Change in financial state | 38 |
| 17.  Death of close friend | 37 |
| 18.  Change to different line of work | 36 |
| 19.  Change in number of arguments with spouse | 36 |
| 20.  Mortgage over $10,000 | 31 |
| 21.  Foreclosure of mortgage or loan | 30 |
| 22.  Change in responsibilities at work | 29 |
| 23.  Son or daughter leaving home | 29 |
| 24.  Trouble with in-laws | 29 |
| 25.  Outstanding personal achievement | 28 |
| 26.  Wife begins or stops work | 26 |
| 27.  Begin or end school | 26 |
| 28.  Change in living conditions | 25 |
| 29.  Revision of personal habits | 24 |
| 30.  Trouble with boss | 23 |
| 31.  Change in work hours or conditions | 20 |
| 32.  Change in residence | 20 |
| 33.  Change in schools | 20 |
| 34.  Change in recreation | 19 |

| | | |
|---|---|---|
| 35. | Change in church activities | 19 |
| 36. | Change in social activities | 18 |
| 37. | Mortgage or loan less than $10,000 | 17 |
| 38. | Change in sleeping habits | 16 |
| 39. | Change in number of family get-togethers | 15 |
| 40. | Change in eating habits | 15 |
| 41. | Vacation | 13 |
| 42. | Christmas | 12 |
| 43. | Minor violations of the law | 11 |

*See T. H. Holmes and R. H. Rahe , The Social Adjustment Rating Scale, *Journal of Psychosomatic Research,* 11:213-18, 1967, for complete wording of the items. Reproduced by permission of the exclusive licensee for Pergamon back volumes Microforms International Marketing Corporation.

When a stressor attacks, the nervous system signals a general alarm. While the process is not understood fully, it is clear that the hypothalamus (a part of the limbic system located at the base of the skull), the pituitary gland (located in the brain directly behind the forehead), and the adrenal glands (located on the tips of the kidneys) are vitally involved. The sensory input indicating danger is translated into an electrochemical signal that is carried along the afferent nervous system to the cerebral cortex, a kind of executive in charge of the organism's response. The signal is then compared with internally generated signals (memories) and interpreted in the light of these memories.

This worked-over signal is transmitted to the hypothalamus, which mobilizes emotions and muscles for appropriate action. The hypothalamus performs this vital function with the aid of the pituitary and adrenal glands. The hypothalamus stimulates the pituitary to produce ACTH (adrenocorticotrophic hormone), which, in turn, stimulates the adrenal glands to produce epinephrine, norepinephrine, and the corticoids. These hormones create a general preparedness on the part of the body for handling stressors. The resulting internal reaction to these hormones is swift and predictable. The pupils dilate, salivation decreases, heart rate elevates, blood supply to voluntary muscles increases, the trachea and bronchi dilate to increase air flow, glycogen is converted into glucose (a more usable form of energy), and blood supply to stomach and intestines decreases.

The stage of alarm is followed by the stage of resistance. The mobilized state of the organism triggered in the alarm stage is maintained during the resistance stage. This resistance to the stressor is expensive in terms of the limited adaptive energy that heredity has provided. If the stressor persists until the adaptive energy is depleted, the resulting stage, exhaustion, leads to death.

Although it seems that persons bounce back after a bout with illness, excessive worry, depression, or some other form of stress, they are never quite the same again, since some small amount of this intangible energy has forever escaped. It is as though they have both a temporary storage tank and a reserve tank. They may *seem* as well as ever, since the temporary storage tank has replenished itself from the dwindling supply in the reserve tank. They may feel full of energy again, but the limited supply in the reserve tank now holds less than it did. In a very graphic way, aging can be seen as a fuel gauge with a limited reserve supply.

According to Selye, stress leaves a residue of metabolic debris that clogs up the machinery of the body and interferes with its functioning. Aging is related to this clogging—the greater the clogging, the faster the aging process. This metabolic debris takes three major forms. There are the insoluble pigments that accumulate in certain cells, such as those in the liver and the heart. There are the calcium deposits in the joints and arteries, and there is the rigidification of elastic connective tissue as a probable result of the accumulation of stable waste products that form cross-linkages between these tissues. This clogging and binding places increasing strain upon normal functioning. With enough of this metabolic debris, death becomes a certainty.

The excessive hormonal activity accompanying stress

tends to create various physical problems. Fatty acids (cholesterol) are released into the blood system and, through a gradual build-up, eventually line the vessels. Resulting circulatory difficulties lead to migraine headaches, tachycardia, and heart attacks. The elevated hydrochloric acid level in the gastrointestinal tract increases the chances of peptic ulcers and colitis. The body's natural immune response is inhibited, and the result is increased susceptibility to disease. Moreover, urinary difficulties and sexual dysfunctions are often observed. These physical reactions are often accompanied by certain psychological symptoms such as irritability, restlessness, anxiety, and insomnia.

A certain amount of stress is unavoidable, and some stress is even healthy. In the same way that an automobile engine wears more while idling than while in gear and running at moderate speed, a body lasts longer if subjected to modest demands than if subjected to enforced inactivity. On the other hand, most persons live with far more stress than is healthy. Mishandling stress only adds to the problem. Stress is mishandled when one allows demands made to exact a greater price in adaptive energy than is necessary. Consequently, it is important that one learn to cope successfully with stress.

One cannot monitor one's hormonal activity, but, fortunately, there are other signs of the body's reaction to stress. There is the rapid heart rate, the flushed skin, and the taut muscles. The feeling of taut muscles results from tension and, quite often, from anxiety. Muscle tone, so necessary for well-being, is not considered tension; neither are muscles appropriately poised for necessary action. Tension occurs when muscles and neurons are poised at a level higher than normal to accomplish a task (Gutwirth, 1975).

Tensed, overworked muscles are accompanied by the build-up of lactic acid (lactate), a residue of neuron firing in muscle tissue. While normal functioning increases the amount of lactate in the system, rest will decrease it.

A neuron synapse, or firing, is analogous to the firing of compressed gases in the compression chamber of an automobile cylinder. Both create usable energy, and both require the proper admixture of fuels. The combustible engine requires the proper admixture of gasoline vapor and air. If the automatic choke malfunctions (the "butterfly" remains closed), the air supply is cut off, and the automobile runs on pure gasoline vapor. The resulting carbon deposits in the chamber and on the valves increase markedly over the amount that accumulates as a result of normal firing. Similarly, for efficient neuronal firing in the human body, the proper amount of oxygen must be present, along with the organic fuel. If the ratio of oxygen to organic fuel is disturbed, there is abnormal build-up of lactate—the body's equivalent to carbon deposits. When one is operating under physical or mental forms of stress, this ratio is disturbed, and lactate builds up at a faster-than-normal rate.

If the build-up of lactate is too great, it can kill the surrounding muscle tissue. The body has a remarkable fail-safe system that protects it from such damage. When a certain level of lactate accumulates, the muscle is said to fatigue; that is, the embedded neurons are inhibited from further firing until the blood removes the lactate. There is evidence that the accumulation of lactate is accompanied by the feeling of anxiety. The greater the amount of lactate, the more intense is the experience of anxiety. Indeed, calm persons can be made to feel anxious with an injection of lactate (Smith, 1975).

If one can learn to monitor the early build-up of neuromuscular hypertension, one can take steps to combat successfully the punishing effects. The key is early detection, and the prime focus is on the muscles. Once the tension has built to disastrous levels, it is exceedingly difficult to lower. Caught early in the cycle, building tension can be successfully countered by the skillful use of certain relaxation methods.

## Deep-Muscle Relaxation

Dr. Edmund Jacobson researched the physiological effects of tension in his Harvard laboratory early in the twentieth century. His investigation led to a practical approach to tension reduction, which he called progressive relaxation and described in his 1938 volume by the same title. Very simply, the technique calls for learning to recognize the feeling of tension and the feeling of relaxation. One first tenses a muscle in order to study the resulting tension; then one releases the muscle and studies the growing relaxation. The following adaptation of his technique is self-administered, absolutely harmless, and has proven of great value to thousands of persons.

A nervous or anxious person will often say, "I'm all tied up in knots." This offhand expression is fairly accurate. Muscles have become all bunched up. The sharply contracted condition of these tense muscles pinches nerves, which send pain signals. Contracted muscles lead to the sensation of tension, and lengthened muscles lead to the sensation of relaxation. Contracted and lengthened muscles are not figures of speech; muscles actually contract and lengthen depending upon the amount of stress experienced. Figure 8–1 depicts these conditions of the muscle fibers.

There are 16 major muscle groups that can be systematically tensed and relaxed. While there are many variants of the practice, the following adaptation has proven helpful to many clients who have serious trouble with nervousness. Indeed, one client has recently found these deep-muscle relaxation exercises, together with prescribed breathing (to be discussed later), to be an effective preventive measure against chronic migraine headaches. As a vice-president of a well-known corporation, he occupies a sensitive position. He had suffered from one to three migraine attacks each week for the thirteen years prior to his treatment. Since beginning his

**Figure 8–1.  Tensed, normal and relaxed conditions of muscle fibers.**

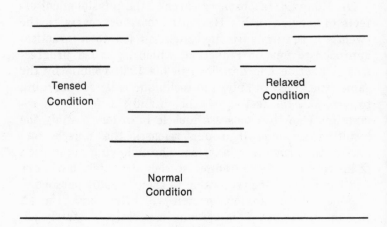

Tensed
Condition

Relaxed
Condition

Normal
Condition

relaxation regimen several months ago, he has not suffered a single attack, a feat beyond his wildest hopes.
Yet, his case is not unusual. If consistently practiced,
these simple exercises can provide effective relief from
tension and its debilitating effects. The sixteen muscle
groups are listed in Table 8–3.

The steps involved in deep-muscle relaxation are
simple. Move systematically through the sixteen muscle
groups, first tensing a muscle, then releasing it. It may
seem strange to be asked to tense a muscle in order to
relax it, but there are two reasons for this practice. First,
it is important to learn the feeling of a tense muscle in
order to be able to detect tension early in the cycle. Tensing a muscle for a few seconds and studying the specific
sites of the resulting tension is excellent practice for developing a heightened sensitivity to incipient tension. In
this way, one is able to begin self-treatment before the
tension builds to excessive levels. Second, the muscle will
automatically lengthen more easily if it has first been
contracted. The effect is roughly analogous to lifting the
pendulum of a clock to its maximum height on one side,

**Table 8–3.** **Major muscle groups.**

| Muscle Group | Exercise |
|---|---|
| Dominant fist and lower arm | Clinch the fist. |
| Dominant biceps | Touch shoulder with fingers. |
| Non-dominant fist and lower arm | Clinch the fist. |
| Non-dominant biceps | Touch shoulder with fingers. |
| Forehead | Lift eyebrows high. |
| Mouth, tongue and jaws | Pull corners of mouth back toward ears. Press tongue into palate. Clinch molar teeth. |
| Neck | Pull chin to within one inch of chest; then push down and pull back at same time. |
| Shoulders | Hunch shoulders toward ears. |
| Chest and upper back | Pull shoulder blades together in back. |
| Abdomen | Attempt to touch spinal column with stomach. |
| Dominant thigh | Lift heel of out-streched leg six inches off floor. |
| Dominant calf | Pull toes toward knee. |
| Dominant foot | Curl toes downward toward heel. |
| Non-dominant thigh | Lift heel of out-stretched leg six inches off floor. |
| Non-dominant calf | Pull toes toward knee. |
| Non-dominant foot | Curl toes downward toward heel. |

thereby causing it to swing completely to the opposite side upon its release. A contracted muscle automatically lengthens when it is released.

Hold the tensed muscle for five to seven seconds while studying the sources of tension. Then release the muscle. Do not release the muscle gradually; release it all at once. It is sometimes helpful to hold one's breath while tensing the muscle and then to release the air and muscle together. There will be a sudden surge of relaxation, lasting approximately one to two seconds. Study this sense of relaxation. Notice the difference between the feelings of a tensed and a relaxed muscle. There may be an accompanying feeling of warmth in the relaxed muscle. Now imagine these relaxed muscles getting longer and looser, more and more deeply relaxed. The desired effect is not to be limited to the immediate surge of relaxation following the release of the tensed muscle, but rather, to a sensation of deeper relaxation that follows several minutes of sustained inactivity subsequent to the release of the muscle. Go on to exercise another muscle. As each muscle is finished, imagine that it is being put away on a shelf for a while.

These exercises will be more valuable if one is properly prepared. Use a comfortable, padded chair. Sit upright, but not rigidly. Let the weight of the body rest solidly upon the spine. Do not cross arms or legs. Remove such constraining items as watches, rings, eyeglasses, contact lenses, and shoes. Loosen ties and unbutton collars. Seek a quiet, dimly lit place.

The routine requires 20 to 30 minutes. The pace calls for tensing a muscle 5 to 7 seconds and releasing it for 20 to 30 seconds before going on to the next muscle. Certain favorable outcomes are predictable. In general, the body will feel heavier. Persons who have been quite nervous before beginning the exercises will note that their foreheads will become somewhat cooler and their palms somewhat warmer. Heartbeat and breathing rate will slow. Facial muscles may feel as though they are sagging. One will be reluctant to stir once again since the sensation of relaxation will be so pleasant. Moreover, one will develop greater sensitivity to muscle condition, and will even be able to point out the condition of a given muscle with relative accuracy.

Practicing these exercises on a daily basis will result in a significant decrease in the amount of energy that need be expended throughout a day. The extent of the help to be gained is directly related to the consistency with which one practices the exercises.

### Prescribed Breathing

Perhaps the quickest way of reducing heightened physiological arousal is through proper breathing. The effect is more immediate than that derived from deep-muscle relaxation, but the effect is not as profound, nor does it last as long. Its cost in units of time is considerably less, but so are its benefits. Often a person gets into tense situations that cause immobilizing anxiety. One may go into a supervisor's office to share a new idea, for example, and upon gaining his undivided attention, freeze. Or one may sense that a discussion is approaching a serious confrontation and feel obliged to choose between acquiescing or being overwhelmed. In such situations, it is important to remain calm, to use one's faculties without suffering the inhibiting effects of anxiety.

If one can remain calm for the first few minutes while getting into a subject, one can often create a reaction in others that puts one at ease. If feedback in these first few critical moments suggests that the performance is appropriate and well-received, it is easier to maintain composure. Very often, then, what is needed is merely a temporary kind of control over anxiety. For this purpose, the prescribed breathing technique seems ideal.

Persons generally breathe properly when sleeping, but frequently breathe improperly when under stress. The lungs are pear-shaped organs with the enlarged portion resting on the diaphragm at about the lateral midpoint of the abdomen. During proper breathing, the diaphragm, which rests in a concave position during exhalation, contracts downward, pulling the partially collapsed lungs down-and-outward, thus forming a vacuum. This vacuum causes inhalation. When one employs the diaphragm properly in breathing, the stomach protrudes, the rib cage expands, and the shoulders lift slightly at the end of the cycle.

When under stress, this natural rhythm is disturbed. One may breathe rapidly and shallowly, setting up a condition called hyperventilation, or one may breathe too slowly or inefficiently, setting up a condition known as hypoxia. In both cases the natural pH (hydrogen-ion concentration) condition of the blood is disturbed.

Hyperventilation causes neurons to fire wildly and the

muscles to become tight and rigid (tetany). The accompanying emotional state is anxiety. One can help to restore the natural pH condition and thereby relieve the anxiety by prescribed breathing exercises. While breathing in a paper sack (a time-honored cure) will increase the amount of carbon dioxide in the blood, and thus lower anxiety, this temporary cure does little to teach one the process of balanced breathing. Pranayama, on the other hand, a type of breathing prescribed by Hindu gurus, reduces anxiety through a perfectly balanced breathing ratio, expressed as 1–4–2. One also learns the feeling of proper breathing.

The 1–4–2 ratio involves holding one's breath for a period four times as long as it takes to inhale and then taking twice as long to exhale as to inhale. Since three seconds are usually required to inhale sufficiently, one can hold one's breath for twelve seconds and take six seconds to exhale it. Holding one's breath allows the alveoli of the bronchial tree to adequately absorb the oxygen. With proper breathing, the inhaled air, normally containing 21 percent oxygen, contains only 12 percent upon exhalation.

One should prepare for these breathing exercises in much the same way as for Deep-Muscle Relaxation. Sit comfortably with feet firmly planted on the floor, body weight evenly distributed along the spine, eyes closed, and tight garments appropriately loosened.

Before beginning, a pulse count should be taken in the following way: turn the palm of one hand upward and reach around the wrist with the other hand. Locate the pulse beat approximately an inch in from the top side of the wrist. Count the beats for thirty seconds; then double the number in order to get the pulse rate per minute.

Run through six cycles of the 3–12–6 breathing. On the seventh cycle, hold the breath for a count of twenty; then exhale explosively. Sit quietly for one minute while the breathing returns to its normal level. Before opening the eyes and moving around, once again take the pulse.

Ordinarily the pulse rate will drop three or more beats, but the count may drop ten or more beats per minute in an extremely nervous person. This drop in heart rate will help to convince one of the quietening effects of this kind of breathing.

Practicing this exercise daily should increase one's confidence in it as an effective antidote for anxiety. Persons who are aware of their nervousness at an early stage will most likely find noticeable relief after a few minutes of such breathing. Since the difference between fear and panic is the feeling of helplessness, just having a technique for coping may tend to lower physiological arousal and increase feelings of control.

## Meditation

The West is currently rediscovering the religiotherapeutic practices of the East. While certain trailblazers such as William James, Ralph Waldo Emerson, Henry David Thoreau, and Carl Jung attempted to translate these practices into Western mind-sets, the richness of Eastern myth and methods has remained relatively obscure to Westerners. Until recently there was little receptivity to the Eastern way of viewing human experience. American psychology, the science that might have been expected to translate Eastern practices into Western forms, ruled out introspection as a tool for studying private thoughts for most of this century. Out of its insecurity as a science, American psychology identified with the experimental methods of the physical sciences. It was instead committed to logical positivism, a philosophy of science that asserted that no subject was worthy of investigation that could not be studied via one of the five senses. If one could not see it, hear it, feel it, smell it, or taste it, it did not for scientific purposes exist. With the growth of the Human Potential Movement, however, this situation is changing, and once again, private experience has become a legitimate subject for investigation.

Americans have been far too busy impressing their

wills upon the external environment to share Easterners' concern for the delicate nature of internal experience. While the West was busy mastering the external world, the East was at work mastering the internal world. While the West pursued dichotomies—light and darkness, male and female, good and bad, life and death, the East pursued oneness. Westerners sought God largely outside themselves; Easterners turned inward in an attempt to transcend the struggle to change the external world via the realization that they and the world were one. This gave them quite a head start at the new spiritual frontier, the conquest of the inner world. Recently, many wise men from the East, gurus, have come to teach us to pursue centeredness, serenity, and integration.

The part of this Eastern practice that is of interest in this chapter is meditation. Meditation is practiced in Hinduism, Buddhism, Taoism, Sufism, and some sects of Christianity and Judaism. Naranjo and Ornstein (1971) point out that there are many variations in the practice of meditation:

> Thus, while certain techniques (like those in the Tibetan Tantra) emphasize mental images, others discourage paying attention to any imagery; some involve sense organs and use visual forms (Mandalas) or music, others emphasize a complete withdrawal from the senses; some call for complete inaction, and others involve action (mantra), gestures (mudra), walking or other activities. Again, some forms of meditation require the summoning up of specific feeling states, while others encourage an indifference beyond the identification with any particular illusion (p. 7).

While meditation takes many forms, the concentrative types always involve dwelling upon something. It is not the *object* of meditation that is important, but, rather, the *process*. The trick is to be aware of the object without consciously thinking about it. Consciously thinking about the object is counterproductive. The idea is to let go, to develop a detached awareness of one's internal experiencing. One accomplishes this state by directing one's attention to something with such regularity that it loses its capacity to stimulate. The less meaningful and stimulating an object is, the more useful it is as an object of meditation.

If one accepts a psychological rather than a religious interpretation of meditation, two chief benefits can be derived from the practice. Researchers now know that meditation leads to a recuperative and pleasant state of relaxation *and* to an altered state of consciousness. Both outcomes appear to be useful in reducing stress.

## The Relaxation Response

Nobel Prize-winning physiologist Walter Hess discovered two centers within the brain that are associated with mutually incompatible emotional reactions. If the ergotropic center is triggered, an organism is prepared for fight or flight; if the trophotropic center is triggered, an organism experiences a high degree of relaxation. Herbert Benson, associate professor of medicine at Harvard Medical School, concluded that the practice of meditation triggers the trophotropic center and results in a sense of relaxation and well-being. It would seem that self-administered, meditative treatment is able to activate, without unfortunate side effects, a degree of muscular relaxation similar to that provided by psychoactive medication. Benson calls this trophotropic reaction the relaxation response and he has written about it in a book by the same title (1975).

Benson's technique is similar to Transcendental Meditation (TM). After some early research on the physiological effects of the practice of TM with Keith Wallace (1972), who later became the president of Maharishi International University, Benson studied similar practices found within the literature of psychology and religion. He concluded that the effects of Transcendental Meditation, Zen and Yoga, autogenic training, progressive relaxation, hypnosis, and sentic cycles were quite similar.

The relaxation response is a natural and innate protective mechanism that allows one to turn off harmful bodily effects due to excessive stress and to bring on bodily changes that decrease heart rate, lower metabolism, decrease rate of breathing, and bring the body back into a healthier balance. Consequently it is an effective antidote for the pervasive anxiety that is so much a part of modern living. Benson pieced together the technique mainly from the yogic forms of meditation. The resulting practice is likely to appeal to Westerners more than the yogic forms themselves, because it is shorn of mystical elements and expressed in familiar terms. Moreover, the practice is supported by a great deal of physiological research about oxygen consumption, respiratory rate, heartbeat, alpha waves, blood pressure, and muscle tension. The net outcome of this line of research is to suggest that certain psychosomatic problems, such as hypertension and migraine headaches, and certain addictive problems, such as alcoholism and drug abuse, are likely to be lessened by the regular use of the relaxation response.

Four Basic Elements

Benson points out that there are four basic elements necessary to evoke the relaxation response: a quiet environment, an object to dwell upon, a passive attitude, and a comfortable position. To get into the experience fully, it is necessary to screen out external sources of stimulation and to center one's attention on internal experiencing. Consequently, a quiet place is best for the practice of meditation. It is quite possible to meditate in a noisy place, but it is easier with quiet. One of the authors has often induced the relaxation response while riding to and from the university on the rapid transit express by merely assuming a comfortable position, shutting the eyes (hidden behind sunglasses), and beginning his mantram (a word repeated inaudibly). By the time he reaches his stop, he is well rested. It is easier and more agreeable, however, to meditate in the quiet of a bedroom or study.

To meditate is to dwell upon something. The something is usually a sound (mantram) or a visual figure (mandala). Most persons will find it easier to focus upon a sound than on a visual figure. We tend to be visually oriented and, therefore, find it difficult to screen out visual activity. Transcendental meditation followers suggest that it is important to choose the right sound. For this purpose they go back to the Hindu Vedic literature. The words selected tend to be those that set up a vibration that can be felt in the cheek bones, words with the consonants "m," "n," "h," or "ng." The mantra (plural for mantram) tend to be euphonious and rhythmical— sharp sounds such as "k" or "ch" are avoided. Examples of common mantra are "om," "aum," "shiam," and "aing." It should not require much effort to make the sound. Benson suggests that practically any word will do. The word he has chosen for the relaxation response is "one."

In pursuing the relaxation response, one meditates on a mantram to drown out distracting thoughts. In repeating the mantram, one soon enough becomes habituated to it, but one may still be paying enough attention to it to let it tie up the mind. Every thought is accompanied by weak muscle activity, that is, the thought causes limited firing of neurons terminating in muscle tissue. The firing may not be enough to cause movement, but it does use energy, and it does involve muscle contraction. If one can preempt tension-arousing thoughts by tying up the mind with low intensity, habituated repetition, muscle tension is reduced.

The muscle contraction following the increased firing of embedded neurons often pinches blood vessels, making it more difficult for the circulatory system to carry off harmful lactate. The relaxation response appears to activate the parasympathetic system, which, in turn, dilates the blood vessels. The increased blood flow cleans out the lactate sludge, and the result is the feeling of relaxation.

Moreover, activating the trophotropic center by the relaxation response has an effect upon the body similar to that of a neural inhibitor. In order for a neuron to fire, to send its electrical charge across the gap between itself and the muscle tissue, it must have the services of a neural transmitter—a chemical that bridges the gap. The hormonal changes accompanying anxiety appear to increase the supply of neural transmitters such as norepinephrine, serotonin, and copamine. The result is a wild twitching of the neurons. A neural inhibitor neutralizes the effects of transmitters and terminates the wild firing. Sedatives and tranquilizers are used extensively to slow down the firing, but some are addictive and many have possible side effects. Meditation, however, appears to slow down the wild firing in a very healthy way. It involves no outside chemicals, no possible trauma to the system, no negative side effects, and a resulting healthy addiction (if one is lucky).

Perhaps the most important ingredient in the formula for inducing the relaxation response is a passive attitude. We are to "let go," to "go negative," to "not try." The Zen roshis advise, "Gentle is the way." We are not to fight extraneous thoughts. If one's mind wanders, one merely returns to the silent repetition of the mantram. Very often, beginners at meditating worry that they are unable to stop thinking. One is urged to stop worrying, to assume an attitude of detached awareness. Merely observe the flight of ideas and gently bring your attention back to the mantram.

It is important to keep disturbing thoughts out of mind long enough for the body to become deeply relaxed. Afterward, the association of troublesome thoughts with this state of deep relaxation actually may defuse them. The Harvard psychologist, Goleman (1971), refers to meditation as a "natural, global self-desensitization." It seems that one becomes aware that the mind has wandered when the thoughts and images threaten the state of relaxation. It may be that there is a kind of built-in wisdom, or thermostat, that makes one aware of such thoughts when they threaten to disturb a state of relaxation. If this is the case, then the mind wandering may actually desensitize one to anxious thoughts by associating them with the feeling of deep relaxation and thereby lead to a less stressful life.

The last of Benson's four basic elements necessary to evoke the relaxation response is a comfortable position. Easterners prefer to sit in the cross-legged lotus position. But this posture is quite painful for anyone with tight muscles. Sitting in an erect posture with the weight of the body resting on the spine and the arms lying loosely on one's lap appears to be a very good posture for most Westerners. While lying down would seem to have built-in advantages for relaxing, one risks falling asleep. And in the terms of the degree of recuperation derived, meditation appears to be better than a comparable amount of time spent in sleeping. Wallace and Benson (1972) referred to the meditative state as a "wakeful hypometabolic physiologic state." While the state is wakeful, it also appears to be more hypometabolic than is sleep; that is, the system appears to be resting more deeply than during sleep, at which time one has no control over thoughts. Oxygen consumption drops almost immediately with meditation, whereas it takes a couple of hours during sleep to drop. Skin resistance to outside stimulation is greater during meditation than it is during sleep (Brown, 1975).

The technique for inducing the relaxation response is disarmingly simple. Indeed, there are some who might take meditation more seriously if it appeared to be more difficult. Such persons confuse complexity with value. Zen teaches that what is truly valuable is the ordinary, the simple, the uncomplicated. One of the more valuable of all human experiences, according to Zen practitioners, is the act of sitting. In all fairness, however, it should be pointed out that just sitting is not as simple and easy as it seems. Similarly, Benson's method is not quite as simple as it seems. It does require some persistence, but soon it will become second nature to the practitioner.

The Sequence of Steps

Benson (1975:114–15) incorporates the four basic elements of the method in his steps for triggering the relaxation response. He suggests that one should:

1. Sit quietly in a comfortable position with the eyes closed.
2. Relax deeply by imagining the muscles relaxed, beginning with the feet and working up to the face.
3. Breathe easily and naturally through one's nose. Each time one exhales one is to silently repeat the word *one*.
4. Continue the practice for ten to twenty minutes, and when finished, sit quietly for several minutes.
5. Maintain a passive attitude throughout. Do not try too hard. Ignore distracting thoughts and merely return to the rhythmic breathing and the repetition of the word *one* after each exhalation. Allow the relaxation to occur at its own pace.
6. Repeat this practice once or twice a day. Since the digestive processes appear to interfere with the relaxation response, allow two hours after any meal before beginning the practice.

Benson stresses the physiologic effects of the practice of meditation. However, the originators of the practice, the Yogin, would have been disappointed with this emphasis. The practice also induces significant perceptual and sensory effects that the Yogin felt were preludes to rising consciousness and spiritual integration. If one analyzes these perceptual and sensory effects in psychological terms, one discovers that the practice indeed leads to an altered state of consciousness.

## An Altered State of Consciousness

Humans are always searching for something more. They are dissatisfied with their conditioned way of viewing things and with their habitual emotional responses. They intuit that there is something else to be experienced, but they feel cut off from this something else. It is as though one knows it is there, one is looking at it, yet one cannot bring it into focus—one cannot see it.

Religions everywhere have been concerned with assisting persons to reconnect with what is significant to them. Indeed, the word *religion* etymologically means "to connect again or to bind back." The word *god* is used for the something that is significant to humans. Religion, then, is concerned with the human being's relationship to this something that is significant. Most of religious ritual is an attempt to help one to experience this union and, thereby, to rid oneself of estrangement, isolation, and loneliness.

While rituals have taken many forms, chief among them are such practices as chanting, dancing, praying, and meditating. All of these practices seem designed to bring about a certain state of mind, an altered state of consciousness; to help one to change one's view of nature and one's place in it. Psychoactive drugs such as peyote have often been used in religious ritual to assist in raising the devotee's consciousness. Modern users of these drugs report that the prime benefit gained from their use is a change in consciousness. They report that things look different, that the boundary between the observer and the object appears to blur, and that they feel a sense of oneness with the objects they are experiencing.

The brain performs two main functions: awareness and thinking. The thinking function was developed rather recently on the evolutionary scale, and it comes late in individual human development. Early mental operations were largely matters of sensing, or of becoming aware. Swiss developmental psychologist Jean Piaget has spent a lifetime studying the cognitive development of humans. He concludes that development moves from early sensory impressions to concrete and then to abstract categories of thinking (1961). It seems that he has rediscovered what the mental astronauts of the Eastern religions had earlier discovered: that awareness and thinking are two different mental functions.

Developmentally, awareness is primary, while thinking is secondary. In thinking one uses categories. Categories are abstracted commonalities that one has discovered among one's observations. For example, one notes that tomatoes, oranges, cereals, breads, fish, and beef can all be eaten, and that in terms of the function called "eating," they are all the same; therefore, they are all categorized as *foods*.

The use of categories becomes a mental shorthand allowing one to process large quantities of observations economically. This shorthand is efficient. It allows one to communicate quickly with oneself and with others about a wide range of topics. But one engages in gross "rounding off" of errors when one forces objects and events into ready-made categories for our use.

As we grow older, more and more is demanded of us, and the use of mental abstractions becomes more and more important. Consequently, the original order of awareness and thinking becomes reversed: thinking now becomes primary, and awareness is reduced to a secondary function. One is aware of an object only long enough to see it as an instance of some category that has already developed. All the uniqueness of the object is lost in the rush to categorize it. Only its criterial attributes are noticed. In a sense one becomes a prisoner of one's own mental conditioning, one's own categorization process. One is no longer open to experiences. One is in touch with one's environment only through preconceived, and sometimes erroneous, impressions of it. Experiences become so routine, so automatic, so much the same that one no longer feels vibrantly alive.

If one can stop thinking for awhile, one may be able to expand one's awareness. Perhaps then we can have a new, more direct experience of reality. The goal of meditation is to stop thinking and to expand awareness, to receive the *other* signals from experience that are arbitrarily tuned out when one prematurely assigns one's experiences to categories. The Hindu swami, Patanjali, around 150 B.C., wrote: "Yoga is the stopping of the spontaneous activities of the mind." Fritz Perls, the founder of gestalt therapy, said that the goal of therapy is to "lose your mind to gain your senses" (1970). All forms of meditation lead to a detached awareness—an awareness of oneself and of the objects of one's experiencing.

Meditation is a vehicle for consciousness-raising. It is called this because the resulting alteration in consciousness allows a practitioner to transcend everyday, partial experiencing. Past conditioning results in standard ways of viewing experience. As one grows older, conditioning becomes so complete that one is no longer open to new experiences. The assignment of potentially new experiences to ready-made categories shuts one off to these new experiences. As a result, there is a predictable sameness to experiencing. More and more experiences take on the quality of playbacks or reruns. The novelty and freshness of experience disappears, and one is consigned to live in gray-land.

The important thing about meditation is that the thinking part of the mind focuses on the smallest possible target so that awareness can expand. During meditation, awareness precludes thinking. The goal is single-minded attention, a sense of being in touch moment after moment, a sustained openness to the present. The tumultuous waves stirred up by the thinking processes must be calmed, and the mind must become a stilled lake so it can faithfully mirror its surroundings.

The normal churning condition of the mind militates against such serenity. There are too many waves; there is too much short-circuiting, too much twitching. In this condition the mind is not a friend. Eastern mystics compared it to a drunken monkey, doing all sorts of crazy, useless things. One discovers this all too well when one attempts to meditate. One is likely to find it extremely difficult to focus one's mind upon any target for long. Once the mantram is started, attention flits back and forth over an endless array of nonsense.

Meditation is a way of life for many Eastern practitioners. It is designed to bring about a fresh contact with the now and the ordinary. The good life is to be found in the here and now, not in the there and then. The there and then constitute the Great Illusion—fantasized, romantic notions about how life *should* be. Gestalt therapy, a Western adaptation of Zen Buddhism, maintains that attention should be directed to the obvious. Awareness of the obvious requires suppression of fantasized future scenarios, reminiscences of the past, and feverish conceptual activity. Many poets and writers of sacred literature were also impressed with the importance of living in the present. Longfellow wrote:

> Trust no future, howe'er pleasant,
> Let the dead Past bury its dead!
> Act, act in the living Present!
> Heart within and God o'erhead.

The *Pali Canon* attributes Buddha with the saying, "Do not hark back to things that passed, and for the future cherish no fond hopes."

The New Testament quotes Jesus as saying, "Take, therefore, no thought of the morrow, for the morrow shall take thoughts for the things of itself."

And Emerson said:

> These roses under my window make no reference to former roses or to better ones; they are for what they are; they exist with God today. There is not time to them. There is simply the rose; it is perfect in every moment of its existence . . . but man postpones and

remembers. He cannot be happy and strong until he, too, lives with nature in the present, above time.

Present-centeredness implies a high degree of involvement in what one is doing at the moment. Pirsig in *Zen and the Art of Motorcycle Maintenance* (1974) was to equate this involvement with quality, a characteristic grossly missing in much of what is produced today. The early Greek Sophists referred to involvement when they spoke of *arete*. The Shakers believed in the religious value of "concentrated labor," of focusing their attention on their work. The Buddhist tradition calls for everyday activities to be pursued with "bare attention," attention uncluttered by regrets from the past or worries from the future.

Present-centeredness, detached awareness, involvement in one's present actions—these are the altered forms of consciousness pursued by the meditative arts. This unhurried, serene, celebrative attitude toward the present would serve as a splendid antidote for the stressful kind of existence so typical of modern living.

While meditation as a vehicle for arriving at an altered state is being discovered by large number of Americans these days, it has a more Americanized version in alpha training, which uses brain-wave feedback and offers yet another way of reducing the stress of daily living.

### Alpha Training

The brain continuously emits electrical microwaves. Hans Berger, a German psychiatrist and researcher, discovered two distinct patterns in these waves. The slower pattern, which consisted of roughly 10 cycles per second, he called alpha; the faster pattern, 12 or more cycles per second, he called beta. With equipment sensitive to these tiny waves, researchers have since identified two additional patterns: the theta pattern emits 4 to 7 cycles, and the delta pattern, from 1 to 3 cycles. Figure 8–7 shows these waves visually.

Sound Mind, Sound Body

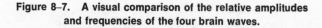

**Figure 8–7.  A visual comparison of the relative amplitudes
and frequencies of the four brain waves.**

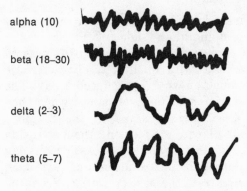

alpha (10)

beta (18–30)

delta (2–3)

theta (5–7)

1 second
wave amplitude

A great deal about the relationship of these patterns
to mental activities is now known. Researchers know that
beta is associated with worry and active problem-solving,
alpha is associated with relaxation (and some say with
the synthesis of previously acquired bits of information),
and theta and delta are associated with conditions of
sleep. The sleep cycle involves roughly ninety minutes in
a theta and delta cycle before bouncing back up to an
alpha-beta cycle for 20 minutes or so. We know that these
twenty minute periods are accompanied by rapid eye
movements (REM) and that REM is associated with
dreaming.

Contrary to common belief, it appears that the dreaming phases of sleep are possibly the most recuperative
periods. Because there are more eye and wave movements
during these dreaming periods, the assumption was made
that these periods were less restful than the periods of
deeper sleep. It is now known that the body is more
hypometabolic during dreaming periods than when the
brain is giving off theta and delta waves. It seems that
the body is deriving its greatest rest when the brain is
giving off waves that more nearly approximate alpha.

Smith (1975) has shown that when an accomplished meditator is hooked up to biofeedback equipment used to measure brain waves, he or she gives off a great deal more alpha both before and while meditating than do persons who have not meditated. It appears that meditation helps one to move into the nonstressful alpha state. There is a clear connection between the states of consciousness associated with Eastern meditation and Western alpha. An early alpha experimenter, Kamiya (1973), recognized this connection when he said, "We seem to have backed into something that the East has known for centuries."

A great deal of research is currently being done to speed up the process of producing an alpha state with the use of biofeedback equipment. The simpler forms of this equipment record the brain waves with the help of electrodes attached to the back of the head and to the ear lobes. Results are reported to the person visually and audibly. Visual signals generally take the form of lights. A red light is used in beta; yellow when moving toward alpha; and green when in alpha. A beeping sound is registered in the earphone when alpha bursts are given off. One tries to get the green light to come on and stay on or to increase the frequency of beeps.

Experiments have demonstrated the ability of the human subject to exercise control over a single group of cells in the viscera. Diabetics were taught to produce insulin by directing their attention to this activity. They were given feedback regarding the firing of the neurons in the islet of Langerhans and were able to increase the firing so as to produce more insulin (Miller, 1969). Kamiya (1969), Brown (1974), and others have demonstrated repeatedly the ability of the human subject to increase the production of alpha waves. While the particular technique used by a person to create alpha waves is quite difficult to communicate, it seems that the same passive attitude pursued in meditation is important to alpha production. Subjects sometimes report that they "let go," "go negative," or "merely stare at the light." Moreover, relaxing seems to be a significant aid as well. This almost seems self-evident since the state of alpha is one of deep relaxation. The subject is asked to relax as much as he can. Very often, the subject is asked to undergo a shortened version of the deep-muscle relaxation exercises discussed earlier in this chapter.

It now appears that some persons are able to move into alpha more readily with the aid of biofeedback. When the green light appears or the beeping sound begins, one can monitor what one is aware of at that time.

Many unsubstantiated claims have been made for the alpha state. Some declare that it is a state of creativity, that it allows the unconscious, artistic elements of the right brain to emerge into consciousness. Regardless of the truth of these claims, it is clear that the alpha state is one of deep relaxation. It is impossible to be in alpha and worry at the same time. Consequently, persons would be helped by being able to move into alpha as an antidote for excessive anxiety and other wasteful energy states.

It is possible to purchase an alpha training machine for self-treatment. Simple models sell for roughly $100 and come with relatively simple instructions. Generally, instructions involve the following steps:

1. Training relaxation.
2. Establishing a training level by identifying the machine setting at which the subject is emitting low levels of alpha.
3. Monitoring alpha in the normal waking brain patterns of the individual. Each individual has a unique alpha pattern, with which he can become familiar. The subject is to become familiar with the pattern as a base line for recognizing progress toward greater amounts of alpha.
4. Training in suggestive methods for inducing greater amounts of alpha. This training may include concentrating on one's breathing, imagining oneself falling back into the water, listening to soft

music, concentrating on a relaxing scene, or concentrating on a drop of water placed on the forehead.

Alpha training usually begins with the eyes closed
since alpha is more easily induced in this way. Next the
eyes are opened while the room is darkened. Then one sits
under dimly lighted conditions while staring at a blank
wall. Then one sits in bright light while staring at a
blank wall. Next one sits in a bright light with stationary
objects. Finally, in bright light with moving objects. The
ultimate goal is to be able to maintain higher-than-
average amounts of alpha while pursuing activities. The
relaxed state accompanying alpha renders persons less
defensive and more open to experiences.

## Summary

Mishandled stress is expensive because each person has
only a limited amount of adaptive energy. Deep-muscle
relaxation, prescribed breathing, meditation, and alpha
training are promising ways of reducing stress and returning the body to a more relaxed condition. One of
these techniques may have more appeal than the others.
Each individual must follow his instincts in this matter.
All are worthwhile skills for coping. One would do well
to experiment with each before settling upon a favorite.
Although this will require a fair amount of time, by doing this the authors found that their current favorite is
not the one they would have chosen originally. All the
methods will result in increased relaxation; all will lead
to a less feverish approach to daily activities; all are
likely to prove rewarding if they are given a fair trial.

# 9. Mental Approaches to Stress Reduction

*The mind is its own place, and one can make a heaven of hell, a hell of heaven.*

John Milton
*Paradise Lost*

An early Roman philosopher, Epictetus (60 A.D.), once said, "Men are disturbed not by things, but by the view which they take of them. When we meet with troubles, become anxious or depressed, let us never blame anyone but ... our opinions about things." Much stress is self-generated. It results from views of what is happening to one. It appears that one is constantly carrying on a one-way conversation with oneself about the meaning of experience. This self-talk is strongly influenced by our beliefs about ourselves, the world, and ourselves in relation to the world. One chooses self-talk based on these beliefs, and the self-talk appears to determine one's emotional response to the experience. In one of the passages from Castaneda's *A Separate Reality* (1972), Don Juan says:

> The world is such-and-such or so-and-so only because we tell ourselves that that is the way it is. ... You talk to yourself. You're not unique at that. Every one of us does that. We carry on internal talk. ... In fact we maintain our world with our internal talk.

Farber (1963) made the same point when he said, "The one thing psychologists can count on is that their subjects or clients will talk, if only to themselves; and not infrequently, whether relevant or irrelevant, the things people say to themselves determine the rest of the things they do."

Many current therapies emphasize the importance of beliefs in determining stress levels. The Individual Psychology of Alfred Adler, the Rational Emotive Therapy of Albert Ellis, the Transactional Analysis of Berne, and the cognitive restructuring of modern behaviorists all stress the crucial role played by beliefs in creating stressful emotions.

The idea that behavior can be changed by thought control is hardly new. It has been stated time and again in the world's great literature. In Shakespeare's play, Hamlet says: "There is nothing either good or bad but thinking makes it so." In the Old Testament one reads, "As a man thinketh in his heart, so is he," and in the New Testament "Finally, brethren, whatsoever things are true ... honest, ... just, ... pure, ... lovely, ... of good report; if there be any virtue, and if there be any praise, think on these things." Right thinking is one of the chief practices recommended by Buddhists for a good life. Faith in the importance of thinking as a guide to behavior underlies the practice of advertising, political brainwashing, and more legitimate forms of education.

Behavior is largely a function of expectations of future events. If one wants to write poetry, try out for the varsity football team, or begin a business, and one believes one has no talent for such things, one probably will not try. Talent is, of course, important, but expectations frequently make the difference. Very often believing is seeing. Rosenthal (1966) called this phenomenon the self-fulfilling prophesy. If one tells oneself convincingly enough that one is going to fail, this expectation is likely to become reality. A promising way of reducing the amount of stress with which one must cope is to replace nonfunctional self-talk, which stems from irrational beliefs, with more functional self-talk.

Two Russians, Vygotsky (1962) and Luria (1965), have had a great deal to say about the governance of behavior by self-talk. Luria investigated the manner in which language instigates and inhibits behavior. Luria noted that the effects of language on behavior begin with meaningful commands on the part of parents and eventually become internalized. The developmental process is something like this:

1. Parents issue commands audibly, and the child responds.
2. The child issues simple commands aloud to himself and responds appropriately.
3. The commands become inaudible, but the child continues to respond.

Commands are not learned at random. They express the training of parents and other significant persons. Unfortunately, not all talk learned from parents is functional. Some of it leads to emotional disturbance. The effects of self-talk are truly great. Ellis (1962:68) says, "For all practical purposes the phrases and sentences that we keep telling ourselves frequently *are* or *become* our thoughts and emotions."

Some recent research supports the assumption that beliefs, and their resulting self-talk responses, influence emotions. Typical of many research studies investigating the effects of manipulative beliefs upon emotions are the studies by Schachter and Singer (1962) and Nisbett and Schachter (1966). Schachter and Singer injected their subjects with epinephrine, a hormone that heightens physiological arousal. Some of their subjects were informed about the physiological effects resulting from the hormone while the remaining subjects were either misinformed or not informed at all. All subjects were then exposed to situations that were contrived to induce alternately anger, euphoria, and amusement. The research was to determine if the effects of these contrived situations would depend upon the explanations (beliefs) available to subjects. In each situation the group informed of the effects of epinephrine appeared to be less influenced than were other groups. While the informed group believed that their arousal was a direct result of the epinephrine, the other groups attributed their arousal to cues furnished by the situations. These latter groups reported greater anger, greater euphoria, and greater amusement.

Nisbett and Schachter gave their subjects a placebo and then subjected them to mild electrical shock. Half of these subjects were told that their emotional arousal following the shock was largely a result of the properties of the pill. Subsequently, these subjects tolerated four times more shock than remaining subjects. Expectations arising from beliefs appear to influence strongly the amount of emotional stress.

These studies suggest that beliefs influence the labels that are used for reactions to stressors. This labeling appears to affect the level of physiological arousal. Velton (1968) asked his subjects to read statements selected for their presumed ability to elicit certain emotional responses. One group read "elated" statements, another "depressed," and yet another "neutral" statements. He presumed that the emotional effects of reading these statements would be reflected in their subsequent performances on several behavioral measures. On the majority of these tasks, the "elated" group out-performed the other two.

In a similar study Rimm and Litvak (1969) found that subjects reading emotionally loaded statements registered greater arousal on standard physiological measures than did subjects reading emotionally neutral statements. Words are powerful stimulants to emotionality. The choice of words used to label experiences is important. If one explains one's reactions with labels such as "hopping mad" or "scared to death," one is more likely to increase one's physiological arousal than if one uses labels

such as "irritated" or "excited." The important thing is
that one must believe the explanation. One cannot change
self-talk without changing the beliefs underlying the self-
talk and thereby bring about a hoped-for emotional result.

## Checking Logic

Persons assume quite naturally that emotional reactions are a direct response to some unpleasant situation.
One is angry *because* the mechanic failed to properly repair one's automobile, or one is afraid *because* one must
speak before a class. A person may talk as though the
mechanic and the class have the power to cause one to be
angry or fearful. In reality, however, such things do not
cause anger or fear; rather, persons cause themselves to
become angry or fearful by what they say to themselves
about these events. In the case of the mechanic, one might
say, "Darn him, I doubt that he even touched those
brakes. Probably just left the car in the stall for a couple
of hours and then turned the ticket in to the cashier as
though the repair had been made." This anger, then, is
a function of believing that the mechanic's intentions
were malevolent, and that one was purposefully
exploited. Similarly, the fear of addressing a class is a
function of what one is saying to oneself about their response. When one probably says something like this: "I'm
going to make a fool out of myself. I'm not going to be able
to remember a thing, and they are going to make fun of
me," it is not the group, but one's thoughts that make one
fearful.

Alternative explanations of these events that would
lead to different emotional responses are available. Of
the mechanic's failure we could have said, "It's an honest
mistake. He was probably pushed and, without knowing
it, failed to complete the repair." And of the class we
could have said, "They know how it is; their turn is coming. They are pulling for me. They must want me to give
them an excuse for applauding me." This form of self-
talk undoubtedly leads to less stressful reactions. Figure

9–1 summarizes the relationship between events, self-talk, and emotional response.

**Figure 9–1.  Relationship among various factors leading to emotional response.**

It is clear from Figure 9–1 that the labelling of emotional responses does not follow directly from an actual event. The key to the situation appears to be the self-talk, the explanation that one gives oneself of the event. This explanation is followed by an appropriate degree of physiological arousal, which in turn is followed by some emotional label. Figures 9–2 and 9–3 show the emotional responses in the case of the mechanic and the class speech.

The revelation that one can punish oneself with self-talk opens up the possibility of far greater emotional control than might have been thought possible otherwise. It places a person at the center of the universe with almost full responsibility for his fate. It is one's choice to become seriously disturbed over the events in one's life. In a very real sense, the words and most actions of others can hurt only if one lets them. Verbal abuse can have its intended result only if it is taken seriously. Although one might say of someone who stares in a puzzling manner, "He makes me so angry when he looks at me with that silly smirk on his face," this angry response is not actually a reaction to the facial expression, but rather, it is an explanation of the expression. A person can upset

Figure 9–2.  Relationship among factors in mechanic's case.

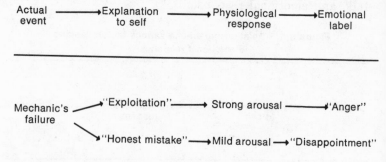

Figure 9–3.  Relationship among factors in class speech case.

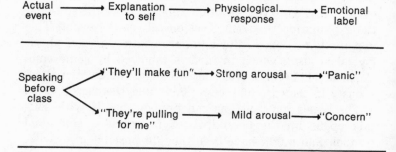

himself in this way, or he can realize that control over emotional reactions resides in one's head rather than in one's actions. One is free to change an emotional reaction by changing one's perception of an event. For example, an emotional response would be quite different if one adopted the following explanation, "He reacts with a silly, self-complacent smile because he's stumped and embarrassed by his inability to think of an appropriate comeback, and his smile is his only defense."

Ellis (1962:61) suggests that persons choose hurtful explanations because of basic, nonfunctional beliefs that they have adopted from society. Such nonfunctional beliefs, several of which are said to be universally inculcated in Western society, can lead to widespread neurosis. Ellis describes 11 such statement-myths commonly held by Westerners:

1. It is essential that one be loved or approved by virtually everyone in his community.
2. One must be perfectly competent, adequate, and achieving to consider oneself worthwhile.
3. Some people are bad, wicked, or villainous and therefore should be blamed and punished.
4. It is a terrible catastrophe when things are not as one wants them to be.
5. Unhappiness is caused by outside circumstances, and the individual has no control over it.
6. Dangerous or fearsome persons or events are causes for great concern, and the possibility of their existence must be continually dwelt upon.
7. It is easier to avoid certain difficulties and self-responsibilities than to face them.
8. One should be dependent on others, and one must have someone stronger on whom to rely.
9. Past experiences and events are the determiners of present behavior; the influence of the past cannot be eradicated.
10. One should be quite upset over other people's problems and disturbances.
11. There is always a right or perfect solution to every problem, and it must be found or the results will be catastrophic.

The perfectionism and excessiveness of these statements are easily recognized. In a recent publication Ellis (1973) suggests that these eleven nonfunctional statements can be reduced to three:

1. One should be perfectly competent and masterful, and one is a worthless individual if one is not.
2. One should be approved and loved by everybody, and one is a rotten person if one is not.
3. Life should be made up of pleasure without pain, and pain is intolerable when it comes.

Ellis (1962) maintains that these irrational ideas, when accepted and reinforced by continuous self-indoctrination, lead to emotional disturbance because they cannot be lived up to successfully. He wrote:

> Once a human being believes the kind of nonsense included in these notions, he will inevitably tend to become inhibited, hostile, defensive, guilty, ineffective, inert, uncontrolled, unhappy. If, on the other hand, he could become thoroughly released from all these fundamental kinds of illogical thinking, it would be exceptionally difficult for him to become intensely emotionally upset, or at least to sustain his disturbance for any extended period (p. 63).

Since the explanations for things that happen are often determined by such nonfunctional beliefs, one often takes normally occurring experiences and turns them into significant stressors. These faulty editorials about the news in one's life triggers strong emotions. If one can ferret out these culprits—these faulty editorials, and exchange them for more reasonable ones, one can greatly reduce the stress and misery in one's life. With a little detective work, anyone can begin to spot the irrationality in self-talk, which may take one or more of the following common forms.

1. *Blow up.* Many persons have a tendency to exaggerate or magnify the meaning of an event all out of proportion to the actual situation. Such a tendency can lead one to make statements such as, "Uncle Cecil hasn't answered my letter. I just know he hates me" or "Jack's a big snob. He didn't come over to speak with me after the meeting." In such cases one takes small bits of in-

formation and assigns enormous importance to them. In so doing one often makes unjustifiable jumps in logic and draws conclusions from evidence that is either lacking or actually contrary to the conclusion reached. Persons tend to create general rules from single incidents.

2. *All-or-nothing thinking.* Persons often think in extremes. In these cases only two possibilities are allowed: right or wrong, good or bad, always or never. One says things such as, "I *always* mess up on exams" or "People *never* have a good time with me." Such dichotomous thinking obscures the many alternatives of opinion made possible by more discriminating thinking. If one says, "People *sometimes* seem to be bored with my company," then one can begin to seek additional facts that may make it possible to experience more rewarding relationships with others. If one discovers when others are bored with one and when they are interested, then one may choose whether or not one wishes to engage in the kinds of behaviors that interest others. This kind of discriminating thinking often leads to more functional outcomes than does all-or-nothing thinking.

3. *Projective thinking.* Persons sometimes project the responsibility for their emotional states and personal worth onto others. They say, "He makes me so angry I could belt him one" or "I would be a stable person today if my father hadn't been such a drunkard." Wanting to escape responsibility for their own behavior, they project the responsibility onto others. In the first example it is easier to blame the other person for one's anger than it is to recognize that one is making oneself angry. In the second example one makes use of a favorite villain—in this case, one's father. One attributes a lack of dependability to poor parenting.

4. *Perfectionist thinking.* Persons sometimes demonstrate a brittle kind of perfectionism in their thinking. Nothing short of a perfect performance is worthwhile. Such an attitude is exemplified by comments such as, "So what if I got an A. It was barely over the line" or "Being

second may be good enough for Avis, but let me tell you, nobody worth their salt will settle for coming in second."

5. *Self-punishing thinking.* Sometimes one becomes so disappointed with oneself that one loses sight of the task. One mopes while opportunities for improvement pass by. This self-punishment results in a poor self-image, and the acceptance of defeat is inevitable. Statements such as, "I usually don't remember names, so there is really no use in trying now" or "I'm so dumb; that's the third straight shot I've missed" are clues to this attitude. Anything that diverts attention from the task is likely to be self-defeating, and self-punishing thoughts are no exceptions. Persons with this attitude would be much better off if they spent their time trying to correct an error rather than in lowering their confidence by punishing self-talk.

### Correcting Self-Talk

All this is not to suggest that one is likely to turn disaster into triumph or depression into euphoria by changing one's self-talk. Nevertheless, the degree of stress suffered does depend in part upon one's explanation of what is going on. More discriminating editorials about the facts may make the difference between depression and disappointment, rage and irritation, or fear and concern. One can often learn about one's own self-talk problems by attempting to identify traces of dysfunctionality in the self-talk of others. Study the examples below. First decide whether or not the statement seems to be dysfunctional, then decide whether it is an example of blow-up, all-or-nothing thinking, projective thinking, perfectionist thinking, or self-punishing thinking. The answers are listed at the end of the chapter.

Obviously the important thing is to be able to discriminate between nonfunctional self-sentences and functional self-sentences. Consequently one's score in the no/yes column is considerably more important than one's

# Self-Sentences

TYPE

—  —  1. OK, so I don't always get A's. That doesn't ____
mean I'm a bad student.

—  —  2. I'm so damn stupid. No wonder people hate ____
me.

—  —  3. Mrs. Smith doesn't like me because she lets ____
John tell his answer and won't let me tell
mine.

—  —  4. Darn it, the cake fell. Guess I'd better read ____
the instructions next time.

—  —  5. I'm doing it again! I always talk too much ____
every single time I meet somebody.

—  —  6. So June turned me down. That's disap- ____
pointing, but there are other girls I can ask.

—  —  7. John hasn't called me from the convention ____
yet. I can image how pressured he is by
that committee assignment.

—  —  8. The reason I'm reluctant to express my ____
opinion is because I know how people like to
put others down.

—  —  9. If I can't clear up every single blemish, then ____
I simply won't go to the wedding.

—  —  10. That proves it! I won't be able to pass any ____
of those tests no matter how long I study.

—  —  11. Until I can memorize every line without any ____
errors, I refuse to try to give a speech to
that class again.

—  —  12. I never make a good first impression. So I ____
might as well brace myself for their reaction.

—  —  13. He's made me so damn upset there's no way ____
I'm going to be able to play decent tennis.

—  —  14. So what if I can play basketball pretty ____
good. I'm no athlete cause I can't play hand-
ball or tennis worth beans.

—  —  15. Whoops! Missed that move, but, then, I've ____
'pulled off' some good ones earlier in this
game.

score in the type column. (In fact, the types may even have two or more suitable answers.) After scoring the answers with the help of the scoring key at the end of the chapter, consult the interpretive key below.

Interpretive Key

CORRECT
    15      Brilliant! A modern Socrates.
  12–14     Outstanding perspicacity.
   9–11     Good work (entitled to one free massage from whomever you can con into doing it).
   7–8      Brush up on your detective work.
6 or less   Let's get with it!

When one understands that one strongly influences one's emotional states by covert explanations, then one can realize the importance of correcting self-talk so that it will accord more closely with reality. The following steps for dealing with self-talk may prove useful.
1. When experiencing stress, listen to the internal monologue. You may not actually hear yourself saying the words, but you can ask, "What could I be saying to myself that would account for my emotional response."
2. Decide whether or not a self-talk explanation is nonfunctional in one or more of the above-mentioned ways; that is, does the explanation make use of Blow-Up, All-Or-Nothing Thinking, Projective Thinking, Perfectionist Thinking or Self-Punishing Thinking?
3. Take a second look at the actual situation—just the specifics, never mind the interpretation or explanation.
4. Generate alternative explanations for the actual situation.
5. Choose a more functional explanation from among these alternatives and begin to operate on the basis of it. Often the evidence is not overwhelming, and you are left with a number of equally plausible

explanations. Choose any one that will lead to more satisfying results—one that is less self-punishing and that leads to more promising action.

6. Attempt to convince others of the relationship between their faulty explanations (editorials) and their own emotional grief. One of the best ways of learning is to teach others. Self-help groups such as Alcoholics Anonymous fully appreciate this principle and strongly urge their members to share their testimonials with others who are attempting to break the drinking habit.

Now apply these steps to a common experience. Jones has just received a test score from an instructor, and his reaction is highly self-punishing: "I flunked the damned exam! How stupid! No one as dumb as I am ought to be going to college anyway. Maybe I had better hang it up." This is step 1. This kind of talk is extremely nonfunctional. It does not suggest constructive action, and it is disheartening. This is clearly an example of Blow-Up. The results of this one examination led Jones to conclude that he was stupid, dumb, and unable to measure up in college. Moreover, Jones also engaged in Self-Punishing Thinking. All this talk about being stupid and dumb misdirects his attention from the task to his presumed worthlessness. It is unlikely to lead to constructive action, and it is likely to injure further his self image, as described in step 2.

Taking a second look at the actual situation may suggest that Jones did not flunk the examination at all. Sometimes a grade such as 75 or 80 is taken as failure, provided one's self-expectations are high. Perhaps Jones would conclude, on second look, that, in reality, he had made a C or B rather than a failing grade, which is indicative of step 3.

Alternative explanations for a performance also may be as reasonable as the one Jones has given himself. Perhaps Jones is not so dumb as he thought. Perhaps the exam was really poorly written, perhaps the instructor allowed the date of the examination to slip up on him, and he used an old and somewhat inappropriate examination. Or perhaps Jones did not study enough or did not study the right things. If Jones chooses to believe that the exam was a bad one, at least he can turn self-deprecation into irritation toward the instructor for his slipshod work. If Jones chooses to believe that he has studied too little or inappropriately, then he can talk with other students or the instructor to see what he might have studied or how long he should have devoted to preparation. This latter alternative is likely to prove more helpful in coping with similar situations in the future than either of the other two (step 4). At this point all that remains to be done is to select the more promising of these alternative explanations and to begin to take the appropriate action that would follow for this explanation (step 5).

In summary, irrational ideas result in a kind of self-talk that influences one's emotional responses to stress. People need to monitor this self-talk and change it when it is nonfunctional. It can be changed by taking a more realistic look at the actual specifics of a troublesome situation, by generating alternative explanations for the event, and by behaving on the basis of the most likely alternative explanation.

## Stress Inoculation

Meichenbaum and Cameron (1974) devised a psychological approach to anxiety control, which they call stress inoculation. Their hope is that clients can learn a set of coping instructions that will immunize them against the more serious effects of anxiety. The assumption underlying the technique is that people frequently give themselves covert instructions on how to behave and that, quite frequently, these instructions militate against one's best adjustment. Persons find themselves in a stressful situation and automatically start the mental audiotape that has inappropriately instructed them in similar situations on other occasions. The instructions have become so routine that they are mostly unaware that they are reciting them. Since the instructions are habitual, and since resulting behavior has been self-defeating for so long, they experience a general sense of helplessness everytime they encounter the stressor. Stress inoculation is designed to move people from a sense of learned helplessness to a sense of learned resourcefulness.

Everytime a person experiences something novel, he gives himself instructions on coping with it. Sometimes, in the early stages, one actually repeats the self-instructions aloud. One of the authors recently noticed his son instructing himself aloud in driving a car. The son half-whispered the following directions: "Let's see, I put the key in the ignition. Now I put my foot on the clutch. Make certain the gear is in neutral. Turn the key. Give it a little gas." He was consciously instructing himself in this new performance. One can only assume that these audible instructions soon become inaudible and finally so routine as to be virtually embedded in his muscles. People can and do program themselves for social occasions as well as for such motor performances. And some of the time the programming is nonfunctional.

Stress inoculation is designed to teach a process that can be used in stressful situations. While the content of the self-instructions must be changed from situation to situation, the basic steps remain the same.

When one becomes anxious, one's attention wanders from the topic at hand to physiological symptoms. One becomes aware of one's increasing tension and begins to say things to oneself that tend to heighten anxiety. A self-defeating cycle develops in which the more anxious one becomes, the more anxiety-engendering and nonfunctional are the self-instructions one gives oneself, and the more nonfunctional the self-instructions, the greater the failure and resulting anxiety. We must intervene in this cycle.

The   physiological   arousal   (increased   heart   rate,

flushed face, etc.) must become a cue to begin the intervention. One must learn to see this arousal as facilitative rather than debilitative, as a friendly early-warning network designed to detect future painful consequences. Intervention in the disastrous anxiety cycle begins by using the arousal as a cue to recite functional self-instructions that take the place of self-defeating ones. New self-instructions move the focus away from the arousal and toward response alternatives. Essentially one says, "I feel myself getting anxious. Good, I'm glad I discovered it early because now I can begin to cope." Obviously, however, such self-talk offers little assurance unless the person has a well-developed coping strategy in mind.

The strategy involves neutralizing the negative self-instructions one has used repeatedly in such situations in the past with more functional self-instructions. When a person ties up his mind with functional self-instructions, he effectively inhibits anxiety-engendering ones. The functional self-instructions accomplish three purposes: (1) they provide a means of directly lowering the physiological arousal; (2) they direct attention to the relevant dimensions of the task; and (3) they provide a form of self-endorsement for having used these improved self-instructions.

Anxiety is often related to ambiguity. The authors noticed that anxiety regarding the writing of a chapter in this book lowered considerably once they had a clear outline of what they wanted to cover. Getting a handle on a problem greatly lessens ambiguity and anxiety.

Self-Instruction 1. *Relax.* The physiological arousal is to become a cue for relaxing. Since one ordinarily does not spend a great deal of time in stressful situations, the prescribed breathing technique dealt with in the preceding chapter is the preferred method of relaxing for most persons. Fall back on the patterned breathing using a 1–4–2 ratio. Hold the breath four times longer than it took to inhale it. As indicated in the previous chapter, most persons will find it comfortable to inhale for 3 seconds, hold for 12 seconds and exhale for 6 seconds. This patterned breathing is helpful in lowering physiological arousal. At this point the self-instruction may go like this: "OK, I see I'm getting anxious, so it's time for my controlled breathing."

Self-Instruction 2. *Remain task-relevant.* Now one turns one's attention away from the arousal to the specifics of the task. Under stress the mind tends to wander away from the task and onto one's symptoms. One can reverse this by directing one's attention to the actual performance required. If one is taking an examination, the self-instruction may look something like this: "The breathing is helping a bit, so now I'm ready to look at the task. What is this question asking? What are the options? Which seem most likely?" In constructing instructions at this point, one may attempt to anticipate trouble spots and be prepared for them. One may notice others working their way through an exam more quickly, and one may begin to get increasingly nervous as a result. In this event one may instruct oneself to remain calm. One might say, "It's not important how quickly others finish. If I continue to use my coping process, I'll have plenty of time."

One may have other instructions ready for the resurgence of anxiety during a performance. One might say, "I have to remember to pause when I'm getting anxious like this and focus my attention on the present task—I won't focus on the anxious symptoms. Now what is it I have to do?"

Self-instructions at this point may take widely varying forms, depending on the task at hand and on the person's preferences. The important thing is to have some meaningful structure with which to combat ambiguity and anxiety. Perhaps the most important point is task relevancy. One must be able to get back to a task, to be discriminating in one's perception of what has to be done.

Self-Instruction 3. *Endorse yourself.* What one says to

oneself about newly acquired behaviors largely deter-
mines whether or not the behavioral change is maintained. As one changes in such situations, one elicits
different reactions from others. What one says to oneself
and what one imagines about these reactions influences
the permanence of the change. It is important to engage
in self-endorsement after one has made use of one's new
self-instructions. One might say something like "OK, I
did it! I managed to go through the scene with my full
attention on the task. I consciously directed my response
rather than remaining helplessly adrift in all that anxiety. From here on out things should get better."

These instructions may seem mundane to some readers.
Indeed, they almost seem too simple to work. Still, many
persons in therapy have found such self-instructions to
be enormously helpful in countering the self-defeating
scripts they have been reciting. At least, a new script will
divert one's attention from old anxiety-engendering instructions. As one practices these three forms of self-
instruction in stress-inducing situations, one gains confidence. A person who becomes good enough at using positive self-instructions will be relatively immune to many
stressful situations.

## Symptom Prescription

Sometimes therapy consists of prescribing the very
symptom or behavior that causes one stress. Dunlap
(1932) first did this with stutterers in order to help
them overcome their nervous response. Even today this
technique remains one of the primary ways speech therapists work with stutterers. The use of this technique assumes that fear of committing the behavior is the chief
cause of the behavior itself. Hence, if a person can bring
a behavior under conscious control, the automatic nature
of the behavior is destroyed. Stutterers carrying out the
prescription purposefully stutter while purchasing items
in a department store, while talking on the telephone, or
while speaking in class. If one can will oneself to stutter,

so the argument goes, one can will oneself to stop stuttering.

Symptom prescription has been used with persons suffering other involuntary nervous symptoms. The authors once used the technique with an impotent husband. He was so fearful that he would be unable to have an erection that he could not even attempt intercourse. In the presence of his wife, we instructed him to refrain from having intercourse during the coming week. We also instructed the two of them during the week to shower together, massage each other, and to engage in other kinds of activities that had been sexually arousing earlier in their marriage. But even if they had the urge to do so, they were not under any circumstances to engage in intercourse. The couple smiled and good-naturedly agreed to the prescription. The couple returned the following week and sheepishly told us that they had been unable to respect the contract. Asking them not to have intercourse had lowered the husband's anxiety, and the prescribed playful activities had aroused him sufficiently to perform. Earlier, feeling the pressure of having to perform and fearing the worst were enough to inhibit his natural sexual response.

Symptom prescription is sometimes used with perfectionists who are deathly afraid of making mistakes. Secretaries are asked to make small mistakes on purpose. Ball players are asked to drop passes, to strike out, or to miss shots. Great care is exercised, however, to insure that such mistakes are not likely to become catastrophes. Purposefully making small, unimportant errors sometimes helps a person to realize that the consequences of failure are not as great as is usually believed. Fear of making mistakes is often incapacitating, and symptom prescription can help to lessen its grip. One's performance may even improve.

Frankl (1960) uses a form of symptom prescription that he calls paradoxical intention. It involves a deliberate attempt to evoke humor in regard to a troublesome behavior. The client is encouraged to deliberately exaggerate a symptom. If the client is afraid of blushing, he is encouraged to turn ever redder and redder until his face is fire-engine red. If he is afraid of sweating profusely in public, he is encouraged to sweat torrents of perspiration that will drench everything in sight. If he is afraid of stumbling through a speech, he is deliberately to stumble as much as he can. He is to imagine the audience booing, grimacing, and laughing raucously. He is to further imagine the newswires and television networks reporting his stumbling performance to a national audience, his performance being taken up on the floor of the General Assembly of the United Nations, and so on *ad absurdium.*

The person being treated with paradoxical intention often cannot resist laughter when imagining himself in such situations. The humor of the exaggerated embarrassment is often enough to defuse a situation of its anxiety-arousing potential.

One can use one of these forms of symptom prescription in an effort to reduce the costly effects of encountered stress. One can also use symptom prescription to gain voluntary control over an involuntary response, to discover that the consequences of mistakes are not as great as feared, or to defuse the anxiety-arousing potential of a situation by making ridiculously funny associations with it.

### Present-Centeredness

A lot of stress results from vain imaginings and fretful worrying about future events. Perls (1970), the father of gestalt therapy, says, "Anxiety is the gap between the now and the then." The antidote for anxiety is present-centeredness, or staying in the present. Very few anxiety-arousing situations are actually as fearful as one's anticipations of them. Consequently, if one can practice taking one thing at a time and staying with the present moment, one can rid oneself of a great deal of unnecessary stress.

One has a natural tendency to ignore painful emotions. Yet, suppressing these emotions sometimes seems to prolong their existence. In such cases it is better to "stay with a feeling," as a gestalt therapist is apt to say. When the full heat of attention is directed at the feeling, it will sometimes melt. This is the approach taken by many Filipinos in dealing with the pain of a headache. The sufferer is urged to direct his attention to the pain signals and ask himself the following questions: Where is it hurting, exactly where? Does it come and go, or is it constant? What can the pain be compared to? It sometimes seems that the pained parts of a body are trying to send signals to an executive in the brain and that these signals persist until the message is decoded. Trying to suppress these signals only prolongs them. It is better to recognize them and perhaps even to amplify them temporarily.

Staying with whatever it is one is experiencing in the present moment implies faith in coping ability. To dodge an issue by deflecting present signals or to try to mentally rehearse future adjustments so completely that the future is placed into the secure past is a truly wasteful approach to life. The authors are not suggesting that persons abandon themselves to immediate impulses. Rather, they suggest that people not "spin their wheels" and create unnecessary problems by fretfully anticipating all possible future consequences connected with a situation.

In this chapter the importance of beliefs in determining stress levels has been stressed. Since persons are responsible for their beliefs and any resulting self-instructions, they are largely responsible for their emotional reactions to stressful situations. The techniques discussed in this chapter all aim in some way to affect these beliefs and self-instructions. Checking the logic (or illogic) one uses in explaining to oneself what is happening often uncovers unnecessary sources of distress. Deliberately instructing oneself to relax, to remain task-relevant, and to endorse oneself for improved emotional control often inoculates one to many forms of self-inflicted stress. Purposefully performing symptomatic behaviors (either overtly or covertly) in some exaggerated form will often render them amenable to conscious control. Purposely making small mistakes may reduce the brittleness of overly perfectionist tendencies and help one to realize that the consequences of making mistakes are often not as great as is anticipated. Ballooning feared consequences until they approach the ridiculous often defuses them of their ability to traumatize. And, last, trusting oneself to live fully in the present rather than to divert one's energies to imaginary future catastrophes greatly reduces stress.

*Scoring Key:* 1. Reasonable self-statement; 2. Self-punishing thinking; 3. Blow-up; 4. Reasonable self-statement; 5. All-or-nothing thinking or self-punishing thinking; 6. Reasonable self-statement; 7. Reasonable self-statement; 8. Projective thinking; 9. Perfectionistic thinking; 10. Blow-up; 11. Perfectionistic thinking; 12. All-or-nothing thinking or self-punishing thinking; 13. Projective thinking; 14. Perfectionistic thinking; 15. Reasonable self-statement.

# Part IV
# Influencing the
# Behavior of Others

Shakespeare's often quoted "All the world's a stage and we are but players on it" is viewed by most people as being irrelevant to their everyday lives. People want to believe that they are sincere and genuine in relationships with others and not merely actors playing roles. Social psychology has shed some light on the "science" of human relationships. It has taught that there are discernable rules by which the game of life is played. Some master these rules; most people bumble along with mixed success, suffering heavily when an interpersonal conflict occurs.

For example, we are usually offended by others' attempts to manipulate us, and scornfully, sometimes violently, we resist such moves. In other words we manipulate others into not manipulating us. In this sense, manipulation and games should be recognized for what they are. They are necessary and normal survival skills that all persons have and use. They are neither good nor bad. The real point of contention is whether the skills are used in the best interest of both communicators or for the advantage of one at the expense of the other.

Since not all persons know the rules, nor are all persons skillful in applying them, this part of the book attempts to demystify the communication and influencing processes. Chapter 10 reviews the basic mechanical process of communication on the premise that people sometimes unknowingly render themselves helpless by the way they talk or listen to others. Chapter 11 contains suggestions of some ways that people are influenced by—and can influence—expectations. Chapter 12 points to principles to be used when influencing the way others behave.

# 10. Opening Channels of Communication

*The music that can deepest reach*
*And cure all ill, is cordial speech.*
Ralph Waldo Emerson

Fulfilling interpersonal relationships is a major component of human happiness. Humans are largely social animals. They depend upon one another for stimulation, for the performance of many of the more important human functions, and for nourishment. The establishment and maintenance of nourishing relations with others depends upon emotional maturity and one's ability to maintain open channels of communication. In this chapter the authors focus on skills involved both in sending clear messages and in facilitating the attempts of others to send clear messages.

## Sending Clear Messages

Often, the essence of our message to others gets lost in the overtones of the language we use. We think we have clearly signalled our intentions or feelings. However, communication involves both *sending* and *receiving* the message. It is quite possible for the content of a message to be entirely missed by the other person as a result of the defensiveness triggered in him by the language and style of expression of a message.

## Avoiding Unnecessary Confrontations

Semanticists, the scientists who study the meaning of words, have suggested that people often pick fights with others by the use of words that imply that they are making statements about reality rather than expressing opinions. Some semanticists suggest that persons invite confrontation and argument when they make heavy use of forms of the verb "to be." English without forms of "to be" is called English Prime.

Forms of the verb "to be," such as "is," "are," "was," "were," "will be," or "shall be," all imply reality, not opinion. Persons can argue among themselves as to the nature of "reality," but they cannot argue about the expression of an opinion. One can express one's opinion about the wisdom of another's opinion, but one cannot tell another that it is *not* his opinion. Consider, for example the differences between the following set of expressions.

*"Reality."* "Bergman's movie, 'Face to Face,' is another example of the worthless, pseudophilosophical trash that he has directed over the past twenty years."

*Opinion.* "I *didn't enjoy* Bergman's movie, 'Face to Face,' at all. In fact, I *haven't* enjoyed a single movie he has produced over the past twenty years."

Can you see the difference between the two expressions? In the first statement, the person is presuming to judge the merits of the film, to tell others how it really is. This kind of arrogance invites others to argue about Bergman's virtuosity as a director. If one happens to like Bergman, one may be pressed to pick up the gauntlet and to do battle. In the second expression, the person presumes to be an expert about one thing only—his or her opinion. All the person is claiming is to know his opinion. Since one cannot know for certain what another person feels or believes, there is really no room to argue about the matter. It is ridiculous to counter with, "No, you don't believe that! You actually enjoy his works." Now consider another example.

*"Reality."* "You are very inconsiderate. Let's face it, John, you never once consider my wishes in such matters. You brush aside my wants and do precisely what you want."

*Opinion.* "You know, John, I never feel like you even consider what I want in such matters. It seems to me that you brush aside my wants and do precisely what you want."

Now, obviously neither expression is likely to make the other person feel well. Indeed, both are likely to put the other person on the defensive. The probability is, however, that the latter expression is likely to raise less defensiveness than is the former. One cannot argue about what one feels. If one feels it, one feels it. One has a right to one's opinion, and this is quite different from telling someone that he is inconsiderate and thoughtless.

It is not easy to talk for long without using some form of the verb "to be." Indeed, the authors are not recommending that anyone seriously try to do so. Perhaps it would be a useful exercise, however, to attempt, for short periods, to modestly stay within one's own opinion rather than to pontificate about the way things really are. One may find that one is interrupted less often with the strong replies of others if one merely expresses one's opinion about reality.

## Adult Communication

Persons often find themselves involved in confrontations that they do not understand at all. There is a certain inevitability about the outcomes of some efforts to communicate with others. It is as though the communication is scripted or programmed to turn out in some hurtful way. Worse yet, one senses the way something is going to turn out from the beginning of the discussion. One senses what is going to happen; it seems inevitable; and yet, we play the script again and again.

There is much insight to be gained from transactional analysis about such impasses. Transactional analysis (TA) is a psychotherapeutic system for analyzing communication. Its founder, Eric Berne (1961), applied his understanding of Freudian and Adlerian psychology to communication analysis. The system is elegant in its simplicity and relevance. It assumes that people communicate from one of three attitudinal postures, which are called ego states. These ego states—*parent, adult* and *child*—tend to elicit differing responses in others. These ego states, or postures, are to be found in each of us, and within the course of a single day, one may shift into each of them many times.

The meaning of these three ego states is quite easily understood since the roles called for are common to one's experiencing. The parent is that part of the personality that represents the attitudes that one perceived in one's parents. The do's and don'ts that they demanded of one as a child are now a part of one's conscience. The parent has two faces: the nourishing parent and the critical parent. Most persons have been fortunate enough to have had parents who were, to some extent, nourishing. They cared, they watched over protectively, and they wanted the best. Normally one internalizes this same nourishing attitude and passes it on to others. But parents are critical as well as nourishing. In the role of the critical parent, they preach, exhort, and scold.

The adult is that aspect of one's functioning that is concerned with solving problems or completing tasks. It is highly objective. It asks who, what, when, where, and why. It does not point fingers, nor does it preach sermons. It is reality-oriented and, consequently, is the best posture to assume when trying to negotiate with others.

The child, like the parent, has two faces. As the natural child, one responds openly, spontaneously, and honestly to others. One is often affectionate and vivacious. As the adaptive child, one often shows the puckish, selfish, rebellious or withdrawing side of one's nature.

One can analyze communication difficulties by identifying the parent, adult, or child postures one assumes while talking with others. Things generally go smoothly as long as one assumes the posture the other person is anticipating. Transactions that conform to anticipated postures are called uncrossed transactions and look like this:

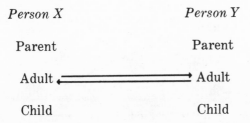

Transactions that do not conform to expected postures are called crossed transactions and look like this:

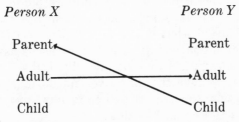

Crossed transactions often cause trouble; they cause one to become defensive. To illustrate this let us assume that B pulls into the driveway at home about 5 P.M. and begins to make preparations to change the oil in the car. He suddenly realizes that his wife may have supper ready, in which case it will soon be necessary to scrub before eating. Consequently, it would not be wise to begin changing the oil. B could crack open the kitchen door and yell, "Mary, is supper about ready?" Assuming one has no ulterior, punishing reason for asking, the transactional posture is that of the adult, and B is directing his question to another adult posture. Let us assume that the abruptness of the question, coupled with the emotional residue of earlier arguments with the children, leads B's wife to feel hassled by the question. Perhaps at this point, she responds, "Will you please leave me alone? Just get off my back! You're always pressuring me to do this or that. I'm doing the best I can." To this point the transaction now looks like this:

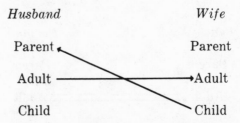

This transaction is crossed. B had meant to come from his adult to his wife's adult, but she came from her child to what she hopes will be his nourishing parent. Since one is likely to be angered by this child response when one had looked for an adult one, her response may indeed hook his parent—but it is likely to be a critical parent rather than a nourishing parent. Now let us assume that one responds critically by saying, "Well, it's because you never seem to take the initiative and do things on your own. And why the hell are you so touchy anyway?" Now the transactions look like this:

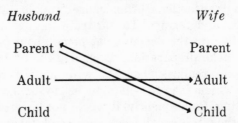

At this point an argument may begin. Both may levy one charge after another, and in the end, both may come out losers.

But let us suppose this situation turned out differently. Aside from the obvious insensitivity of the first ill-timed question, B erred yet a second time when he allowed his parent to be hooked. Let us go back to his wife's response of "Will you please leave me alone? Just get off my back!

You're always pressuring me to do this or that. I'm doing the best I can." Suppose that B senses the hurt she is feeling and remains calm. He remains in the adult and refuses to allow his critical parent to be hooked. He comes back with "Gee, honey, I'm sorry. I didn't mean to hassle you. I was about to change the oil in the car, and I thought I'd better check with you to see if supper was about ready. I guess it did seem quite abrupt, my poking my head in the door and questioning you right off." The likelihood that this honest, straight-forward adult remark will be rewarded is reasonably good. She may catch herself on the heels of his last response and say, "I'm sorry, too, honey, but you wouldn't believe the day I've had!" Now the transactions look like this:

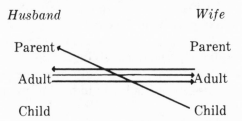

|           |          |
|-----------|----------|
| *Husband* | *Wife*   |

There is now the opportunity for B to shift back and forth between his adult and nourishing parent, and, if all goes well, Mary will feel attended to, and B will get his supper after all.

There are two things that become clear from this illustration: (1) persons have more control over their relations with others than they sometimes believe, and (2) staying in the adult often keeps one out of trouble. Each person plays a significant role in influencing how others are going to respond. Still, this statement must be qualified: persons are not puppeteers who mechanically pull the strings of puppets. They *influence*—not *determine*—the responses of others. As in the hypothetical illustration, the reaction of others is often influenced by factors over which one has no control. When one engages another, one may still be dealing with unresolved anger

from situations in which one perceives that one was be-
littled. Remarks made in such cases may be the precipi-
tating occasion for venting pent-up hostility. One becomes the target for delayed shots that should have been
directed at others. Even in such cases however, one is apt
to make situations better or worse, depending upon one's
communication postures. Suppose C has packed in her
anger all day long since she has been afraid to direct it
toward her supervisor for fear of being fired. Now, suppose she is just looking for battle on the home turf. After
a series of increasingly hostile remarks, she says "Damn
it, seems like everything around here is left for me to
do!" While it is difficult in such situations to predict
with accuracy the effect of any response, would you
agree that the responses triggered by the two following
replies are likely to be different?

*First Reply*: "I swear, all you ever do is complain. You're
always complaining about something. It doesn't make any
difference what it is. If it's not repairing something
around the house, then it's likely to be the finances or the
children."

*Second Reply*: "Honey, you seem really upset about
something, and I don't think it's just the work around the
house. You seem to be trying to deal with something else
that's bothering you. Maybe you'd like to tell me about
it?"

While the second reply may merely trigger further
anger on the part of the spouse, it is at least headed in
the right direction. It comes from the adult. It contains
no venom, no sermons, and it acknowledges the facts. At
least it allows for the possibility that one's spouse will
back off from the "sham" fight and begin to deal with
the underlying cause—her anger with the supervisor.

Perhaps another illustration will help. Let us suppose
that one is trying to help a friend who is angry with his
boss. He says, "I feel like clobbering him." Which of the
following responses would seem most helpful?

PARENT: "John, why don't you grow up. You know you'll be looking for a new job if you punch the boss."

ADULT: "I can see you're really angry with the boss. Why don't you tell me more about it?"

CHILD: "I wish you would hit him. I wish you would blow him out of the water. There's not a supervisor in the whole damn corporation that I would like to see stomped as much as old Smith."

Most therapists would feel that the only viable response in such situations is the adult one. The parent response is likely to be seen for what it clearly is—belittlement. The child response may encourage a friend to take precipitous action and get himself in serious trouble. Even if he does not follow up on a proffered child response, he is likely to think someone who mentions it is even more impulsive and irresponsible than he is. He may thoroughly enjoy getting a child response in receipt for his child response, but he will intuit that there is danger in talking with this person when he is so upset. The adult response gives him license to further express his emotions, to document the basis for his anger. What often happens is that one will think more rationally when one has had an opportunity to talk about one's problems. By talking out the problem, one is usually ready for the first time to deal realistically with a problem.

A person can gain some help in creating more satisfying relations with others if he begins to analyze his responses to others. One interesting exercise that may prove helpful in this regard is the construction of an Egogram. An Egogram is a subjective analysis of the percentage of time one responds to others from each of the TA postures. Ask yourself, "How much of the time do I speak from each of the postures below?"

Obviously, if one comes from one's critical parent most of the time, one is likely to place others on the defensive. They are going to feel the oneupmanship and be irritated by it. They may not uncover the basis for their irritation,

**Figure 10–1.  Egogram of communication postures.**

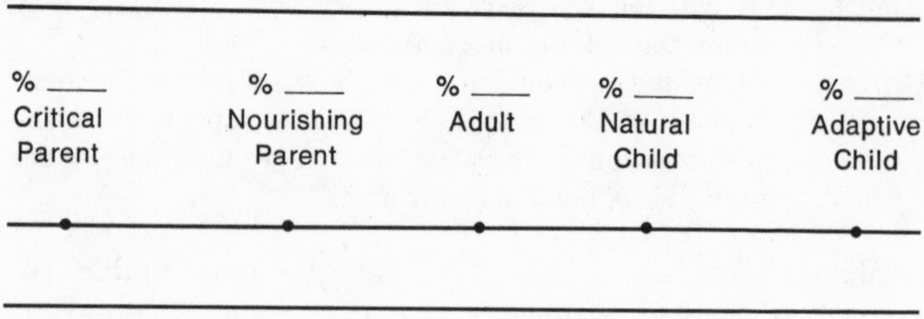

| % ____ | % ____ | % ____ | % ____ | % ____ |
|---|---|---|---|---|
| Critical Parent | Nourishing Parent | Adult | Natural Child | Adaptive Child |

but they will relate to one based on the response. If, on the other hand, one assumes the role of the whining, dependent adaptive child most of the time, one sets others up to care for one, and, at the same time, to more solidly place one in the child's role. Therefore, relations with others are likely to be more satisfying if the higher percentages on the Egogram hover around the center.

Some insight can be gained into problems with a spouse or friends if an Egogram is constructed for them also. As an example, if a spouse tends to come from his or her critical parent much of the time, while the other partner is attempting to communicate from an adult posture, a great deal of difficulty can be expected. Both persons are likely to be unhappy with each other. The adult-oriented spouse will be unhappy with his or her constant complaining and pessimism, and the critical parent-oriented spouse or friend will be put off by his or her partner's seeming blandness or lack of color.

## Assertive Responses

People are often overly tenuous in their responses to each other, even when they have a clear right to be more assertive. The fear of strong responses from others, and the uncertainty over one's rights causes many persons to be tentative and fuzzy in their communication, which, in turn, invites others to define situations in ways that favor their arguments. Lack of assertiveness, then, often sets one up as a patsy, to be taken advantage of by less sensitive persons.

The worst part about being taken advantage of in such situations is the residue of self-contempt with which one is left, plus the knowledge that one is partly to blame for the exploitation, and the loss of further respect for oneself as a result of an unwillingness to stand up for one's rights.

An assertive response is the straightforward but not purposefully unkind expression of how one honestly feels. This clear signalling is the only viable base for satisfying relations with others. It is difficult to sustain and build relationships based upon exploitation. If one is unable to assert oneself, to share one's honest feelings with others, one will tend to withdraw from others. Few demands are made upon others for fear that one will not be able to protect oneself against seemingly unreasonable demands they may make in return. As a result, many live self-encapsulated lives, defensively insulated against the spontaneity that characterizes mutually fulfilling relationships.

Many persons are uncertain as to how assertive they actually are. Bloom, Coburn, and Pearlman (1975) have constructed a checklist that calls for an examination of one's attitudes and likely responses to (1) one's anger, (2) the anger of others, (3) refusing and making requests, and (4) initiating communication with others.

### Assertive Communication Questionnaire*

*Instructions*: The following questionnaire covers five areas that are often blocks to assertive behavior. There are two questions for each area. The first allows you to assess your attitude and irrational beliefs; the second gives you a chance to examine your behavior. Check one or more answers, as they apply to you.

## Dealing with My Own Anger

1. When I am angry with people, I usually:
   a. am afraid to say anything directly, because I don't want to hurt their feelings.
   b. am afraid that if I do say something, it will sound aggressive and they won't like me.
   c. feel O.K. about expressing what is on my mind.
   d. feel anxious and confused about what I want to say.
2. When I am angry with someone, I usually:
   a. drop hints about my feelings, hoping he or she will get the message.
   b. tell the person in a direct way what I want, and feel O.K. about it.
   c. avoid the person for a while until I calm down and the anger wears off.
   d. blow up and tell him/her off.

## Dealing with Others' Anger

3. When someone gets angry with me, I usually:
   a. think he/she doesn't like me.
   b. feel too scared to ask why and to try to work things out.
   c. feel confused and want to cry.
   d. think I have a right to understand why he/she is angry and to respond to it.
   e. immediately feel wronged.
   f. feel angry in return.
   g. feel guilty.
4. When someone gets angry with me, I usually:
   a. end up crying.
   b. back off.
   c. ask him/her to explain his/her anger further, or else I respond to it in some other straightforward manner.
   d. get angry in return.
   e. apologize if I don't understand why he/she is angry.
   f. try to smooth it over.

    g. make a joke out of it and try to get him/her to forget the flare-up.

5. When I need time and information from a busy professional, I usually think he or she will:
    a. resent my taking up valuable time.
    b. consider my request as legitimate and be pleased that I'm interested.
    c. act as though he/she doesn't mind but secretly resent me.
    d. make me feel inferior.

6. When I need time and information from a busy professional, I usually:
    a. put off calling until I absolutely have to.
    b. apologize for taking up his/her time when I call.
    c. state directly what I need and ask for what I want.
    d. let him/her know that I expect immediate attention. After all, I'm important too.

## Refusing Requests

7. If someone asks me to do a favor for him/her and I refuse, I think he/she probably will:
    a. hate me.
    b. be angry with me.
    c. understand and will not mind.
    d. act as though he/she doesn't mind, but secretly resent me.
    e. think I don't like him/her.
    f. hesitate to ask me again.

8. If someone asks me to do them a favor and I don't want to do it, I usually:
    a. do it anyway.
    b. let him/her know that I resent the request, but do it grudgingly.
    d. tell him/her I'd rather not do it.
    e. tell him/her I'd rather not do it, and apologize profusely.

## Making Requests

9. When I need something from someone else, I usually feel:
    a. as though I shouldn't bother her/him by asking.

   b.  as though people don't really want to do things for me.
   c.  as though I don't want to put him/her on the spot by
       asking.
   d.  that it's O.K. to go ahead and ask.
   e.  afraid to ask, because he/she might say no.
   f.  as though he/she should do what I want.
10. When I need something from someone else, I usually:
   a.  don't ask unless I'm absolutely desperate.
   b.  ask and apologetically explain why I need help.
   c.  do nice things for him/her, hoping the favor will be
       returned.
   d.  become demanding and insist on getting my way.
   e.  ask directly for what I want, knowing that he/she can
       refuse my request if he/she wants to.

## *Initiating Communication*

11. When I walk into a party where I don't know anyone, I
    usually think:
   a.  that no one there will talk to me.
   b.  that everyone else is relaxed except me.
   c.  that I'm out of place, and everyone knows it.
   d.  that I won't be able to say the right thing if someone
       does talk to me.
   f.  of ways to get attention.
12. When I walk into a party where I don't know anyone, I
    usually:
   a.  wait for someone to come and talk with me.
   b.  introduce myself to someone who looks interesting.
   c.  stay on the sidelines and keep to myself.
   d.  put a lampshade on my head or otherwise behave in a
       bizarre manner, hoping someone will notice.
   e.  rush for food or drink or a cigarette to make it look
       as if I'm busy and having a good time.

### *Answers*

The following answers on the questionnaire indicate assertive beliefs and behaviors:

| | | | |
|---|---|---|---|
| 1. | c | 7. | c |
| 2. | b | 8. | d |
| 3. | d | 9. | d |
| 4. | c | 10. | e |
| 5. | b | 11. | e |
| 6. | c | 12. | b |

If you didn't do too well don't worry, remember that nobody's perfect. Look over the answers. On questions where yours were the same as those in *Answers,* you probably have no trouble in asserting yourself. Where your answers differ, figure out which of the areas are the most difficult. Then think of specific situations in your life that fit those problem categories. Look at the questionnaire again and try to figure out what irrational beliefs may be blocking your assertiveness.

## Self-Permission

One must become assertive with oneself before one can become assertive with others, that is, one must give oneself permission to become assertive. There are reasons that one fails to be assertive. One may be uncertain about the right to assert oneself, and one may have little confidence in one's ability to express assertiveness in effective, unhurtful ways.

Fuzziness about rights often comes from inappropriately applied cultural training. The culture seems to teach that humility is virtuous. Such thinking can sometimes, however, be highly nonfunctional. Instead of contributing to respectful, loving relationships, such behavior sometimes inhibits them. When a person surrenders rights, he trains others to take advantage of him. Sacrificing rights also results in an overly cautious posture toward others. One does not extend oneself or take risks with others since one anticipates hurt from them. This sense of false humility and altruism destroys existing relationships and prevents new ones from forming. In a sense one might consider whether or not one is being selfish by the refusal to let others know how one feels.

Smith in *When I Say No, I Feel Guilty* (1975) lists certain personal rights that will help to thwart the manipulation of others. Among these are the following:

1. The right to change one's mind.
2. The right to make mistakes.
3. The right to say "I don't know" or "I don't understand."

4. The right to decide whether or not to help others with their problems.

5. The right to offer no excuses or justifications for one's behavior.

6. The right to judge one's own behavior, thoughts, and emotions and to take responsibility for them.

The authors would add that one has the right to make requests of others. This does not mean that one can or will always get one's own way. Still, there is nothing wrong or pushy about expressing preferences. Indeed, it is better than suppressing them and perhaps sulking as a result. There is little chance that even those who care for one will meet one's needs if they do not know what these needs are.

Quite often, one is afraid to express wants for fear that they will be frustrated. Consequently, one withholds wants and then holds others responsible for the failure to figure out what it is one wanted. This attitude is obviously doomed to failure.

One also has the right to refuse the requests of others. One will not always choose to refuse, but one should be able to do so. In the long run one is even a more interesting person and relationships are more rewarding if one exercises the options to comply and to refuse. No one respects a pushover.

When one does choose to accommodate an unpleasant request of another, one should sensitively point out that one is not fond of the option but is responding favorably to the request because of love or respect for another. This clear signal will do two things. It will make others a little less likely to take advantage of one, and it will make them somewhat more likely to respond favorably to future requests that we make of them. They are able to fully appreciate one's caring if one shares one's complete feelings in a situation.

Once one accepts the idea that one has some rights, too, then one must decide on the most effective ways of asserting. The manner of asserting depends on the kind of relationship sought with the other person. There are basically three types of relationships in which assertive responses become appropriate: (1) long-range relationships, where it is important to maintain consideration and respect; (2) short-range exploitative relationships that are totally unimportant; and (3) relationships wherein the other person, for whom we have no deep caring, is constantly critical. Furthermore each of these situations calls for a different kind of assertive response.

## Kelley-Winship Model

Kelley and Winship (1979) have proposed a three-part assertive response that is most appropriate for situations in which one is seeking to find and maintain a high degree of caring and respect. According to this model, the assertive response should include an empathy component, a conflict component, and an action component. The empathic part of the response is recognition of what the other person is feeling. The conflict part is a statement of what one is feeling. And the action part is what one wants to happen. The following example highlights these components. "Jane, I know you're working some overtime at the office these days, and I realize that it would be convenient if I'd pick up your share of the chores around here (empathy). But the way I look at it is that I'm paying my share of the rent and doing my share of the chores (conflict), so I don't plan to do your work, too (action)."

In such situations one has the right to be far more direct if one chooses. One could, of course, merely say, "You do your own damn chores!" One has the right, but one would undoubtedly have to pay for such insensitive bluntness with injury to the relationship. The three-part response softens the statement without obliterating its clarity.

It is important to let the other person know that his position is understood. Persons sometimes persist in their requests because they assume that the other person is not hearing or understanding them. They are more apt to accept refusal gracefully if they know the other person has gotten their message, if the other person acknowledges its importance. Acknowledging the basis of another's request through the empathic component tends to take the drive out of a persistent request, and it also signals respect in that one has bothered to listen and understand.

It is also respectful of us to share the basis for a decision. This often makes it easier for the other person to accept the decision. The following illustration helps to underline the importance of the conflict component. A neighbor bounces into a fellow-student's room and persistently attempts to persuade him to have a couple beers with him at the local bar. Wanting to preserve the friendship, the student replies, "John, I know you're feeling good and just want to be friendly (empathy), but you see, I've got this test in the morning, and I'm really worried about it (conflict), so I want to study quietly for the next couple of hours. Perhaps we could celebrate with a couple beers after that (action)?" Letting the other person know the reason for turning down a request is likely to appear less arbitrary and, consequently, less rejecting.

It is equally important to include an unequivocable action component. If one stops with the conflict component, one merely invites the other person to try to outflank one's logic. When this happens, the likelihood of counterarguments increases the chance of ego damage to one or both persons. It is much better to conclude with a solid action statement. Do not finish the action component with a lilt in the voice. This indicates indecisiveness, and, again, it invites argument.

Broken Record

Smith (1975) suggests the Broken Record technique for situations where one is being exploited by sales representatives, service managers, and the like. The technique involves stating over and over again what it is we want. Calmly repeat, "But the merchandise is faulty, and I want a refund" or "I know you tried, but I want you to adjust the timing so that the engine doesn't ping." The technique, when mastered, allows one, while sticking to the desired point, to feel comfortable in ignoring manipulative verbal side traps, argumentative baiting, and irrelevant logic. In this way one can persist at a point without having to rehearse arguments or suffer angry feelings beforehand in order to be up for an assertive scene.

Sometimes an exploiter is equipped with two or three counterarguments, which can cause an unprepared person to fold. The situation can be turned around, however, by performing like a broken record. Merely restate the demand repeatedly in a calm manner, which usually causes the exploiter to acquiesce after having spent the sum of the arguments he is prepared to offer. Such scenes involve contests of wills, and the person best prepared mentally to persevere often wins. If the technique is used appropriately, the script may look something like this:

YOU: "Hi, I purchased this shirt here last week. When I tried it on, I discovered it was defective. I'm returning it, and I would like a refund."

CLERK: "I'm sorry, sir, but we can't accept returned merchandise without a sales slip."

YOU: "No problem. I've got the slip right here."

CLERK: "Well, what seems to be wrong with the shirt? It's one of the very best we carry, and we just never have anyone unhappy with this brand."

YOU: "The lapel is creased improperly. Since it is permanent press, there is little chance that I could successfully correct the crease by ironing it—so I'd just like to get a refund."

CLERK: "Well, the crease doesn't look improper to me. It's hard to get them to match up perfectly. In fact, it looks pretty good to me. I'm sure no one will notice it."

YOU: "Yeah, well, it looks funny to me, and I'm the one who has to wear it. So I want a refund."

CLERK: "Well, it's awfully inconvenient, this sort of thing.

We'll have to get the manager's approval, and you
might have to wait around awhile."

YOU:       "Well, I want the refund, so you had better see the
manager."

Notice that it was necessary to persistently repeat the
request over each of the clerk's objections. You merely
outlasted him. This is important in such situations. One
should prepare oneself beforehand by giving oneself
permission to make the request. One should remind oneself that one has a perfect right to make the request.
Moreover, one should expect some objections from the
clerk and be prepared to make a request like a broken
record.

Fogging

Many persons suffer enormously from the chronic
criticism of others. Such persons lack the assertive skills
to cope comfortably with nagging. Consequently, they
recoil defensively from the onslaught and often change
their behavior to satisfy the demands. The result is often
bitter disappointment. They fault themselves for their
cowardice, but seem helpless in the face of such criticism.

Smith (1975) recommends fogging as a technique for
handling criticism. One accepts manipulative criticism
by calmly admitting the possibility or probability of some
truth in it without indicating any need to change the behavior. The technique allows one to receive criticism
comfortably without becoming anxious or defensive and
without rewarding the person who criticizes. Criticism
is usually manipulative. The critic is seeking a behavioral change. If one accepts the possibility of the accuracy of the criticism without indicating a disposition
to change the offending behavior, the critic wins an
empty victory.

Through fogging one remains the judge of what one
will do. And destroys the automatic connection between
· the criticism and any change in behavior that is antici-

pated by the critic. The critic believes, as a result of past experience, that one will automatically change if one recognizes the validity of the criticism. The critic is taken back, bewildered by the lack of need to change a behavior in order to erase the criticism. Often the critic will repeat the charge as though one did not understand what was said. Eventually the critic learns that the victory is not worth the battle, that one cannot be manipulated by this cleverly directed criticism. The following is an example of fogging:

CRITIC: "You're late! You're a half hour late! I've stood around here waiting for you while I could have been inside bowling a warm-up line with the team."

YOU: "You're right. I'm a good half hour late. I told you I didn't want to practice before the match. Why didn't you just go on in and join the others?"

CRITIC: "Damn it, you were late last week, too."

YOU: "I believe I got here fifteen or twenty minutes late last week. You're right again."

CRITIC: "Well, I'm not waiting for any half hour next week. You can bet on that!"

YOU: "Good, that's smart. You go on in and warm-up with the team, and I'll get here as early as I conveniently can. As always, I'll be here before the match begins."

CRITIC: "Well, I want you to come early so we can go in together. I don't like going in without you."

YOU: "I like being with you, too, Charlie, but I'm not going to break my neck to get here that early. I'm not asking you to adjust to my schedule, so you just go on in, and I'll be along pretty soon."

It is clear that Charlie wanted something more than a confession of tardiness. He wanted a schedule-change that would conform to his. The critic assumes that he can get his way only if he can verbally outmaneuver others. He attacks their behavior through his "logical" criticism, and he fully expects others to cave in to his demands when his position proves superior to theirs. Fogging is a way of destroying this automatic connection between acknowledged criticism and behavior change. Destroying this connection leaves the critic nonplussed and, perhaps, angrily respectful of one's control over one's behavior.

Fogging is not necessarily the preferred way of handling criticism. Often one wants to be more responsive to criticism if one seeks to build friendships. Living is a matter of getting and giving, which means that one sometimes accommodates the reasonable requests of friends and loved ones. Still, there are times when one must establish sovereignty over one's own behavior. This can be done by making the point that one alone is responsible for what one chooses to do, that one cannot be coerced into disagreeable courses of action by manipulative criticism. And when this is the point that needs to be made, fogging is the preferred response to criticism.

## Non-Verbal Assertiveness

Appearance often contradicts one's statements. In order to make a message effective, one must match nonverbal expressions with verbal ones. Fear often causes one to mute the impact of strong statements with a smile, a lilt in the voice, or a placating posture. More often than not, one is unconscious of these conflicting signals. One senses that words are strong medicine and fears the consequences. Often one fears the guilt that a conscience may inflict for speaking strongly to someone else and the other person's reaction. When one is uncertain of being able to cope with these consequences, one unconsciously destroys the impact with contradictory non-verbal signals.

It is easy to see the weakening influence of these nonverbal signals. Remember seeing someone smile while telling another that his behavior is offensive? What was the effect of the smile on the verbal message? Did the smile weaken the message? The smile allows the other person to conclude that one is not very serious in the expression of irritation. The smile is likely to be taken more seriously than are words. The other person may think that one is merely joking, that the protest is but a good-natured jab that has no real significance.

But if one's irritation is serious enough to be expressed, then the words and the non-verbal signals should be unequivocal. Check facial expression in the mirror while practicing an assertive response. If only the facial signals were read, what was said? Later it will not be necessary to check in this mechanical manner, but it may prove helpful for awhile.

Eye messages are also important communication signals. Poor eye contact is likely to destroy an assertive verbal response. To measure the effect of failing eye contact, have a friend role play the following script in two ways. First have the friend look furtive while repeating the line, "You cut in front of me, and I want you to go to the end of the line." Now have the friend repeat the same words with solid eye contact. Which of the two performances is likely to have the greatest effect? Poor eye contact is generally interpreted as being indicative of fearfulness and lack of self-confidence. If you give yourself poor marks for your eye contact, you can significantly improve your assertiveness by practicing before a mirror. Be careful not to appear to stare in a hostile way at the other person. Proper eye contact is merely meant to connote straightforward, honest communication, not hostility.

Body posture is also a form of communication. Crossed arms and legs suggest defensiveness and resistance. Leaning backward away from the other suggests fearfulness or resistance. Slouching suggests casualness and lack of intensity.

The quality of the voice is one of the more important aspects of communication; it is very sensitive to fear. Fear often affects the natural rhythm, pitch, and intensity of the voice. When fearful the voice may stammer; speed up into a rapid-fire, machine-gun style; or slow down. The pitch usually rises in shrillness, but sometimes it lowers to a whisper. Furthermore, the voice may become very loud. While no one of these voice changes is incontrovertible proof of fearfulness, the combination of two or more of them most often signals fear. To properly diagnose the effects of vocal qualities upon an intended message, tape the voice in simulated assertive situations and listen for its impact.

## I Messages

Gordon (1970) suggests that persons can send clearer messages in regard to delicate themes if they send "I messages" rather than "You messages." Persons create a great deal of antagonism in others when they accuse them, and "you messages" are often accusatory, as in, "You are inconsiderate," "You don't listen," or "You are so loud with that horn that you distract me from my reading." Such charges often cause the other person to become defensive and to argue about the charge.

Sending "I messages" tends to elicit a differing response. For one thing, "I messages" are softer than "You messages." "I feel as though my wishes and my opinions are not considered" may elicit a different response from a spouse or friend than does "You are inconsiderate." Similarly, saying "I don't feel as if you're hearing me" may trigger a somewhat more receptive response than will "You don't listen."

Sending "I messages" is similar in effect to making use of English Prime. When one uses English Prime, one is forced to use more personalized, feeling language. When one sends "I messages," one does not make charges about another's character; one merely tells another how he is feeling. One may suggest that another should not feel in some way, or that a feeling is not a justifiable reaction to one's behavior, but one cannot dispute that the other person actually has the feeling. Each of us is the expert regarding our feelings. Each of us alone can identify feelings and report on them.

The suggestion that one express oneself in terms of "I

messages" rather than with "You messages" is based on the assumption that a response to a message is more likely to be favorable if one does not first offend. If one charges another with thoughtlessness or malice, that person is likely to focus on defending himself rather than on addressing himself to the request or demand. He may resist and refuse a request because he perceives the situation to involve a contest of wills. His integrity demands that he thwart the requester to prove that he is not a doormat to be stepped on. This contest can be avoided if one sticks to one's own feelings rather than lecturing another on his character.

While it is true that parents and others in authority may be able to force their wills upon others with rough and insulting commands, they do so only with the growing resentment of others. Such modes of interacting with others tend to engender a great deal of foot-dragging or, even worse, a form of psychological guerrilla warfare. A change in the way one sends messages is not likely to make others consistently and lovingly oblige one's every request. It will, however, make it possible for others to respond positively to requests with no loss of face. Respectful requests couched in "I messages" are less likely to be perceived as a contest of wills, and the other person can now oblige without losing respect for himself. The interpersonal gain suggested by the use of "I messages" results even in situations where one clearly has the right to demand compliance. The other person knows that a respectful request contains a command, but in this softer form, the command is more readily obeyed. Consider this request: "John, I'm having trouble explaining to the plant manager why it is necessary for you to be late so often, and I'd appreciate it if you would take whatever precautions are necessary to be on time." One is less likely to take serious offense at this request than if one is told "Damn it, John, I want you to be here on time. I've had about enough of your tardiness." Admittedly, there are times in which such bluntness may be appropriate, but when such bluntness is customary, one is likely to pay a considerable price for this indulgence of anger.

Response Cost

Each person needs to recognize a difference between the right to assert and the right to get the response that one wants from others. While one has a right to express oneself, one does not have a right to one's way all the time. Much of the time one must persuade others to consider one's requests favorably. This suggests that the delivery of the request often makes a difference. It is not enough to give oneself permission to assert, to establish that one has a right to fill or refuse the request of another. One must also pay attention to the manner in which a message is sent. One may feel one has a right to speak crudely and bluntly to another because of the enormity of a wrong, but such language belittles the other person. In such events one may win the battle and lose the war. Threatening another person into compliance is done at the expense of making an enemy.

When faced with an array of possible responses, one should choose the least intense response that will get the job done. The goal in all interpersonal situations is harmonious relationships, which are characterized by fairness. Unnecessarily strong expressions are foolishly wasteful of precious human energy.

Self-assertions can be viewed in the context of friendship skills. In this context two observations seem important: first, while it is not always appropriate to do so, one should be able to express irritation, and second, while assertiveness refers to the full range of emotional expression, it is not limited to the expression of negative emotions.

In order to maintain friendships, one must sometimes acquiesce to the requests of others even when one would prefer not to. Assertiveness is not meant to be an excuse for selfishness. Living in society requires consideration of others.

It sometimes happens that persons who feel powerless and exploited encourage more conflict and confrontation in their lives than do persons who feel secure and strong. If one is confident of one's ability to take care of oneself, one often gives off signals that discourage others from manipulative actions. Moreover, if one feels strong and confident, one does not need to engineer arguments in order to provide a laboratory in which to practice the skills of self-defense. And this is sometimes what persons uncertain of their assertive skills seem unconsciously bent on doing. Such persons appear overly sensitive to potential exploitation. More secure persons do not attend to minor clues of potential exploitation because they have confidence in their ability to take care of themselves if an occasion requiring such action arises. When insecure persons encourage conflict, they are often seen as masochistic or desirous of inflicting pain on themselves. These persons seem to pick fights and then lack the skills to defend themselves. While they seem to be seeking punishment, they are more likely to be trying unconsciously to provide the opportunities necessary to learn to defend themselves. Unfortunately, their lack of skill condemns them to additional losing experiences and further confirms their feelings of inadequacy and weakness.

Assertiveness is a matter of being able to express affection as well as irritation. Perhaps people need as much help in expressing warmth, concern, and affection as in expressing anger. Many persons appear awkward and embarrassed with the direct expression of affection. Consequently, they avoid such direct expressions in favor of indirect expressions that are often missed by others. Since many persons hold unhandsome self-images, they are quite sensitive to disapproval but insensitive to expressions of warmth. They miss subtle expressions of affection because they are not set up emotionally to receive them. Therefore, it is often necessary to make explicit expressions of warmth, affection and love. Otherwise, many persons live with others for years without their being certain that they care deeply.

## Facilitating Open Communication by Others

Sometimes a person has trouble receiving a message. The problem may lie either within oneself or within another. The more threatened one is, the fuzzier and more imprecise one is in expressing oneself. Persons may be afraid to be understood. They may remain fuzzy for fear that their opinions will not be well received if they are clearly understood. They fear that others may ridicule them or become angry if they express themselves clearly, so they keep all options open by speaking in vague generalities.

It is in the interest of clearer communication for one to work at reducing the threat that the others experience in expressing themselves. It helps greatly if one is able to assume an open, nonjudgmental stance while listening. It is not necessary to embrace the opinions of the other person; it is enough that one tries to understand them.

It is also possible that trouble in understanding other persons may lie within an individual. One may be resisting the weight of another's position because one senses that the logic of one's own position may suffer. One may conclude that another's opinions do not make sense, when in reality, they may make so much sense that they undermine one's own opinions. The antidote to this resistance is a willingness to readjust one's opinions in the face of new or conflicting information. A person unwilling to change may persistently resist counterarguments by feigning misunderstanding.

### Attending

For someone seriously interested in facilitating the open communication of others, there are a few things that can help. One can respectfully attend to the other person who is expressing an opinion; one can respond in a way that lets him know he is understood; and one can show further interest by initiating considerations that he may not have entertained.

Attending is a matter of positioning ourselves so that we reward the other person for self-disclosure. It involves listening to the full message being expressed. Most persons feel that someone is paying attention only when that person is squarely facing them, shows good eye contact, and assumes a receptive posture. Check this out when talking to someone. Have a person position his body at an oblique angle from you while you are talking with him about a personal matter. Notice that it is more satisfying if the other person twirls around to face you squarely.

Now have the other person avoid eye contact by focusing on the floor or ceiling. Notice the difficulty you experience in continuing a story while another person refuses to look at you. Now ask someone to cross both legs and arms while you are talking. Does he appear resistant in this posture? While such posturing may seem too elementary to be significant, it is just such basics that give others cues for judging whether or not the listener is interested in their expression of opinion. Moreover, it is often helpful if the listener suspends potentially distractive behaviors such as smoking, gum chewing, and finger twiddling. Eliminating these behaviors frees one to concentrate more on the message and causes the speaker to feel more fully attended to than he would otherwise.

Attending is also a matter of reading the other person's nonverbal signals. Look the other person over. What is his energy level? Is he down? How far down? Is he anxious? Fidgeting? Quivering? Ask yourself, "How am I when I look that way?" With practice one can learn to trust oneself in deciphering nonverbal signals.

Attending also involves listening to a spoken message. One must listen for both content and feeling. Most persons are better at ferreting out content than feeling. To understand a feeling properly, one must combine the spoken content with the nonverbal signals. Listen for the central themes. Try to understand the circumstances surrounding the feelings expressed. Silently rehearse what has been said and then ask, "What would be important to me about this message if I had said it?" Learn to listen empathically for the other person's perceptions of things. It is as though one crawls inside the other person's skin and looks at the world as he sees it. By so doing, the truly important aspects of the situation begin to emerge in clearer outline.

## Responding

One can further reward others for their openness by responding to their disclosure in a way that lets them know that they are understood. It is not enough merely to understand; one must convey this understanding through accurate responding. In the same way that one attends to content and feeling in a message, one must acknowledge both in one's response. If one can accurately combine the essence of the feeling and the content in a short response, one can reassure the other person, thereby encouraging him to continue with his story. A simple way of doing this is to make various adaptations of what he has said, possibly in the following format: "You feel_____ because_____ ." Where a feeling can be expressed in a single adjective, be sure to use feeling words rather than thinking words. The sentence, "You feel that you are not going to be able to make it," is a description of thinking, not feeling. If this is what a person is thinking, he or she might be feeling discouragement, depression, or despair. Discouragement, depression, and despair are feeling words. Since people want others to understand what they are feeling, responding with a feeling word is particularly rewarding. Often these succinct responses will clarify matters considerably for the other person, and he may be strongly encouraged to delve further into the matter.

However simple this approach may seem, one thing is certain—it is not practiced often, widely, or well. Let us assume that a close friend says, "I don't know whether I want to try to discuss it with you again. It never seems to help. I honestly think it makes matters worse. We no more than get started until we're shouting at one another. Somehow or other what we start talking about gets lost in the process, and we just end up angry at one another. I know it's important, and I really wish we could work through it. But trying just seems to make things worse. And yet, I don't think I can go on indefinitely this way." If one's purpose is to demonstrate an understanding of the feeling and content of this disclosure and to encourage the person to continue this story in an open, honest manner, which of the following responses is likely to be most effective?

RESPONSE 1 :     "Well, it's obvious that you've given up. You've just written me off, and you don't really care what happens to our friendship."

RESPONSE 2 :     "You seem really worried because we can't seem to resolve issues like this. Nothing we do appears to you to help much, and arguing like this is really punishing."

Response 2 is much more likely to encourage someone to keep talking, to try to work it out, than is Response 1. Response 1 shows a great deal of hurt and defensiveness and would likely rekindle the heat of the argument or increase the extent of a friend's despair. Response 2, on the other hand, indicates that one has listened well, that one senses a friend's discouragement and bewilderment. It admits to a realization that the friend has not written one off, that his discouragement is mentioned only to solicit one's efforts to unravel this gordian knot. Respect and caring are indicated by this nondefensive response. While nothing is ultimately predictable in human relations, this second response seems more likely to encourage the other person to continue his story in an open manner.

Facilitative responses often include both the feeling and content of a person's statement. While either the feeling or the content can sometimes be adequate, a fuller response that includes both is often superior. Consider this one other example: you have had a very difficult time at the office and are licking your wounds and seeking a nourishing response from your spouse. You say, "I don't know why I was stupid enough to allow them to talk me into taking the manager's job. I sometimes wonder if I'm cut out to take all the gaff. I'll bet I had ten customer complaints, and every damn one of them was a lulu." You pause, and your spouse replies:

RESPONSE 1:    "Well, you didn't have to accept the job, you know. I never asked you to take it. I've never complained about the money we've had to live on."

RESPONSE 2:    "Sounds like you've had a bad day and you want a little sympathy."

RESPONSE 3:    "Ten! Boy, that's a lot more complaints than you usually get, isn't it?"

RESPONSE 4:    "If you don't like the job, why don't you just quit? With your skills you can always get another one."

RESPONSE 5:    "You feel tired and worried that maybe this job is going to be more of a hassle than you bargained for."

Which of these responses is most likely to encourage further examination of the situation? While the first response might cause anger, the second would likely cause embarrassment and a slight sense of belittlement. The third seems somewhat irrelevant. The fourth is supportive and may at some point be productive, but it also may be too radical for the moment. The fifth response is the most likely to be facilitative. It identifies both the feelings and content of the disclosure. It does not attempt to solve the problem. It merely indicates that the spouse has listened and deeply understood what was said. Frankly, it is not often that one receives such facilitative responses from others. Persons often must move ahead with a story over the disinterested, oblique, and irrelevant responses of others. Such responses leave one feeling alone and isolated, and one persists only under the most dire of circumstances.

Sometimes one can help further by initiating considerations that the other person may not have yet considered. Timing is of utmost importance in determining whether such initiation will prove helpful or hurtful. When solutions are suggested or contradictory aspects of a disclosure or admonishments are given before a great deal of attending and responding is done, the timing is premature, and the outcome is likely to be unfortunate.

The establishment of a warm and caring relationship is absolutely basic to being able to initiate suggestions. This kind of a relationship can be stretched without breaking, and it has a certain elastic quality to it. Still, if one does not attend and respond sufficiently, the initiation of additional considerations may strain the relationship beyond its ability to remain intact.

In this chapter ways in which one can open channels of communication with others have been suggested. Communication is a two-way process, a matter of sending and receiving clear messages. Persons often cause unnecessary conflict with others by the manner in which they express themselves. Learning to personalize language with statements of opinion rather than using statements of "reality" assists in escaping unnecessary confrontation. Becoming aware of the attitudinal postures that are assumed when conversing with others makes it possible to choose the parent, adult or child posture most likely to obtain an open response from others. Learning to assert oneself with others protects one's rights and leaves one less vulnerable to exploitation by others. Finally, attending and responding empathically to others facilitates increased openness among persons.

# 11. Influencing the Expectations of Others

*People exercise an unconscious selection in being influenced.*

T. S. Eliot

Expectations, which are beliefs about future consequences, powerfully affect behavior. What I expect to happen becomes a guide to my behavior. If I expect to succeed, my resolve receives a significant charge of energy; if I expect to fail, my resolve suffers immensely. Moreover, the expectations that significant others hold of my chances of success or failure also influence my behavior markedly. Tolman (1959) maintained that the single most predictable index of behavior is the set of expectations one holds. In this chapter the ways in which one can affect one's behavior by influencing the expectations of others is covered.

Expectations may be thought of as internal goals that are responsive to many of the same principles that affect external goals. One of these principles, the goal gradient, refers to the fact that the learner's tendency both to approach and to avoid a goal increases significantly as he approaches the goal. Similarly, the learner's tendency to approach or to avoid the goal increases as the strength of his expectations for success or failure increases. The more one believes that one's performance will be rewarded, the stronger is the tendency to perform. Conversely, the more one believes that a performance will be punished, the weaker is the tendency to perform.

Stotland (1969) concluded from his research that the motivation to achieve a goal is in part a function of the perceived probability of attaining the goal. Perceived high probability of attaining an important goal is called hope. Hope is a positive expectation, whereas anxiety is a fearful expectation. Bakker (1975:169) states that "anxiety is the greatest conservative force in human existence, with hope as its most powerful counterbalance." Depression, like anxiety, is related to the perceived unlikelihood of obtaining meaningful reinforcers. If one wants something strongly and believes that one has a good chance of getting it, one is hopeful. On the other hand, if one believes that one is unlikely to get it, one is depressed. Depression and anxiety throttle human energy, while hope unleashes this vital capacity.

Self-expectations and the expectations of significant others strongly influence behavior. Actually, these two forms of expectations are interactional, although they are not exactly reciprocal. The expectations of others influences self-expectations. Cooley (1937) spoke of the "looking glass self." According to him, people see themselves in the eyes of others. They largely adopt the expectations of others as their own, and these introjected expectations comprise a significant part of the self-concept. These expectations guide behavior, and behavior noticeably influences the expectations of others. The events have now run full cycle.

## Self-Expectations

Self-expectations derive in part from an evaluation of the quality of one's performances and from one's perception of the evaluations that significant others hold for one. In time these observations constitute a cumulative filter through which estimates of future success pass. Since this filter accumulates additional layers as one grows older, its influence is much greater for adults than for children.

Self-expectations significantly affect the aggressiveness with which one attacks a task, the persistence that one evidences in the pursuit, and the degree of optimism that one entertains while pursuing the task. In a study of self-expectations among underachieving, academically capable high school boys, Combs (1963) concluded that persons can only function to the degree that they feel adequate to function.

Rotter (1966) suggested that experience leads to a generalized expectancy regarding the relationship between reinforcement and one's actions. He found that some persons believe that rewards and punishments are largely the result of accidents, fate, or luck, while others believe them to follow naturally from their actions. Persons who believe rewards and punishments depend upon chance rather than upon their behavior learn less from their experiences than persons who believe reinforcements are internally controlled.

## Expectations of Others

Much behavior is prescribed by the roles one fills. One also expects certain things from others by virtue of the roles they fill. Parents are expected to earn a living, provide security and protection for children, and to model courage, consideration, and responsibility. Children are expected to show deference to parents and to imitate their mature behavior. Ministers are expected to be circumspect and pious. Professors are expected to be academic and cerebral. Medical doctors are expected to be paternal and totally committed to the welfare of their patients. Each role carries its own set of expected behaviors.

Role-prescribed behaviors serve a purpose—they allow one to predict with some accuracy the behavior of others and thereby to adjust one's own behavior accordingly. In a way, role-prescribed behaviors have survival value. Still, the expectations of others that stem from role-prescribed behavior tend to restrict one's degrees of freedom. Persons are frequently punished in subtle ways when they deviate from the roles into which they have been cast. When they no longer meet the expectations of others, they are said to be "acting out of character," and they are encouraged to drop this behavior and behave "naturally."

Attempts to change are often met with resistance from others because the change will make it necessary for them to relate differently. Any change requires energy and is, consequently, frequently resisted. Moreover, as one changes, one becomes less predictable. One cannot necessarily be counted on as routinely as one was before. Unpredictability occasions unease in others, who may subsequently pressure one to return to a more familiar role.

What others believe and expect of one is important. The idea of the self-fulfilling prophecy is now well documented in the literature (Aronson et al., 1963; Aronson and Carlsmith, 1962; Goldstein, 1962; Rosenthal and Fode, 1963; Shapiro, 1960). According to this concept, just making a prophecy tends to make it come true. Goethe wrote: "If you treat a person as he is, he will tend to remain as he is; but if you treat a person as if he were what he can become, he will tend to become what he could be." In *Pygmalion*, George Bernard Shaw refers to the same concept when he writes, "The difference between a lady and a flower girl is not how she behaves, but how she is treated." In *My Fair Lady*, the musical based on Shaw's work, Eliza Doolittle says to the kindly Colonel Pickering, "Around you I'll always be a lady, but around Professor Higgins I'll never be a lady 'cause he don't treat me like a lady."

Rosenthal and Jacobson (1968) demonstrated the effects of the self-fulfilling prophecy on grade-school children. By manipulating the expectations of teachers for certain children chosen at random, the researchers were able to significantly affect the performance of these children, and as a result, their performance improved significantly over the performance of their peers in the same classes.

Rosenthal and Fode (1963) demonstrated that even laboratory rats do better if the experimenters have been led to believe that these rats constitute a superior breed. Subsequent to Rosenthal's research efforts, 242 additional studies have examined the subject. Approximately one-third of these studies were successful in substantiating the effect of the self-fulfilling prophecy. The effect has been demonstrated with factory workers, United States Air Force Academy students, swimmers, and others (Rosenthal, 1973).

When these expectations of others accord with what one wants for oneself, one is truly fortunate. Negative expectations from others, however, tend to retard growth. Rosenthal (1973) noted that teachers in some of the studies responded negatively toward children when they surpassed the teacher's expectations for them. This was especially true of poor, black children and was equally true for black and white teachers.

The expectations of others tend to encourage stability. If we are trying to change, then such expectations become stultifying. It becomes important to be able to change the expectations others hold in order to strengthen the resolve to change.

## Changing the Expectations of Others

Changing the expectations of others is often difficult. The expectations of others imprison one, but the prison was not constructed without mutual complicity. For years a person may have been building the prison— merely by reacting with consistency in one's behavior toward others. A person may have invited the dominance of others by fawning, placating postures. Or one may have kept them at bay by a torrent of sarcastic comments. One may have invited exploitation by an unwillingness to defend oneself. One may have encouraged parental responses by one's childish manner. If one now wants to change in significant ways, one must work to change the expectations of others.

Self-change requires self-redefinition. One must first begin to think of oneself differently, and then one must begin to behave differently. A change in behavior forces others to respond differently and thereby works to support one's redefinition. Kelly (1955) used fixed-role therapy to help clients to redefine themselves. He advised his clients to construct a sketch of a role that was opposite in key respects to the one that they had been enacting. The sketch was to be written in free-flowing, natural language and to provide as many day-to-day possibilities for behavior as possible. The sketch was also to provide a rationale for the behavior and to suggest specific behaviors for a number of differing social situations. The client was asked to enact the new role for two weeks. The new behavior forces a redefinition, and the intended change is well underway after this length of time.

Religious conversions provide a ready-made format for personal redefinition. The religious body provides a new behavioral sketch, fully reinforced by the sacred literature and the sanctions of the group. Indeed, it was a common practice of early Christianity to give a convert a new name, and Black Muslims in America use the same practice today. The conversion experience involves another significant dimension of change strategy—that is, a public commitment to the new behavioral code. In *Varieties of Religious Experience* (1902), William James pointed out the importance of public commitment to the maintenance of the religious conversion, and recent ingenious experiments by social psychologists (Jones and Gerard, 1967) have provided evidence of its importance in the maintenance of consistency in other forms of behavior.

Putting oneself on record publicly is powerful support

for any intended change. Not only does it cause others to suspend their old expectations, but it gives them an explanation for any odd behavior. This is important, since one's first attempts at changing are imperfect. If, by one's old definition, one was nonassertive and obsequious, the early attempts to demonstrate assertive skills would likely be jerky and somewhat shocking. But if one has announced an intention to become more assertive, others will be more likely to tolerate this embryonic display than they would otherwise. When one first attempts to be assertive, a significant amount of anxiety may accompany the move. The irritation that triggers assertive responses is compounded by this anxiety, and others seldom discriminate between the contribution of these two emotions. As far as others are concerned, the emotion being expressed is entirely anger. This, of course, tends to raise the other person's defensiveness sharply, and he may take action accordingly, whereas if he had known that one was trying to become more assertive, and that one was anxious over the attempt, perhaps his reaction would have been less violent.

In summary, the expectations which we hold for ourselves and the expectations that others hold for us are powerful influences on our behavior. If we plan to change, we must redefine ourselves, both to ourselves and to others. We must hold a different image of ourselves. We must attempt to change others' expectations by publicly announcing our intentions and by our efforts to behave differently. If this strategy is pursued persistently, others are forced to behave differently toward us. Their changed behavior tends to support self-redefinition. In this way one can restructure the social pressures affecting one's behavior in such a way that they help to maintain the intended behavior.

# 12. Social Reinforcement of Behavior in Others

*A community is infinitely more brutalized by the habitual employment of punishment than ... by the occasional occurrence of crime.*

Oscar Wilde

Persons have far more control over their social relationships than they exercise or even understand. Humans are social animals, and they depend on one another for the fulfillment of many of their deepest needs. A significant portion of behavior is devoted to achieving and maintaining satisfying relationships. While most persons need some time alone, they do not normally choose to go for long periods without seeking the company of others. People reward one another with attention and praise. Those who realize the rewarding nature of attention and praise and use them to encourage behaviors they seek in others are considered socially alert. They have impact. Those who fail to recognize the crucial importance of social rewards squander much of the currency with which they could negotiate for the meeting of their needs.

Some persons complain of being lonely even when they are with others. Sometimes they maintain their loneliness by their responses to others. If they have little confidence in their skills to operate comfortably in close proximity to others, they may actually punish any friendly overtures. A relationship may warm satisfactorily only to the point where the other person gets too close for comfort. At this point one may abruptly distance oneself from the other person with caustic remarks or gestures. The other person backs off as though a friendly paw had been bitten. The hurt comes from feeling overextended and cut off. Embarrassment causes him to vow that he will never again attempt to be so friendly. A person may not even be aware of having engineered such a fracture, or he may be ambivalent about the matter. Some persons experience relief when the waning intensity of a relationship no longer requires a response that they fear they are incapable of making, but they are left once again with their loneliness.

What one sees as lack of consideration in others may actually result from a failure to reinforce others' friendly behaviors. If one seems unimpressed with the gracious gestures of others, it is highly unlikely that they will continue to waste them on one. If, on the other hand, one notices these gestures and rewards them with smiles and other expressions of appreciation, one wisely cultivates them. It is dangerous to take the kindnesses of others for granted since one may soon find them being directed at one less often.

## Using Operant Conditioning

The principles of operant conditioning, one school in behavioral psychology, are helpful in shaping the behavior of others.

One principle of operant conditioning is that behavior is strengthened by rewarding consequences. This is the basic tenet of all operant conditioning. One tends to repeat those behaviors that pay off and drop those that do not. This principle probably reflects a biological programming for survival. Usually, behaviors that are pleasurable tend to be those that satisfy basic needs and have survival value. If pleasurable behaviors usually were destructive to cell tissue, or painful behaviors were growth-inducing, an unbelievable amount of will power would be necessary just to survive. Admittedly, some pleasurable experiences—the misuse of drugs and over-eating, for example—are harmful, and some painful experiences such as exercise and surgery are helpful. Generally, though, humans are programmed to seek experiences with survival value because they feel good.

The implication of this principle for social behavior is clear. If one wants others to pay attention to one, then one must reward them for it. If one wants others to telephone more often, one must reward them for it. If one wants them to allow one greater freedom of movement, one must reward them for it.

The frequency of a behavior is lessened, at least temporarily, by punishing consequences. While rewarding consequences tend to increase the frequency of a behavior, punishment tends to decrease it. It does appear that the effects of punishment may be temporary if the intensity of the punishment is fairly mild. For example, barbs that one directs at another may be too moderate to have any lasting effects. The effect may temporarily suppress a response, but the response may appear when the victim perceives that the punishment has been lifted.

Estes (1944) conducted experiments with rats that led him to believe that the effects of punishment are temporary. He taught rats to trip a lever in order to obtain food pellets. After the habit had been established, he divided the rats into two groups and exposed them to one of two conditions set up to break the habit. One of the groups was placed in a cage where they could continue to trip the lever but without obtaining food pellets. The lever for the second group was wired to produce a slight electrical shock each time it was tripped. Estes wanted to know which group would break the lever-tripping habit most efficiently—the group that was not rewarded or the group that was punished. The group that was punished dropped the habit before the nonrewarded group.

The surprising part of Estes' research occurred later when both groups were again exposed to the original condition; they were rewarded for tripping the lever with food pellets. The group that had broken its habit through nonrewarded trials slowly regained the habit, but the punished group reestablished the habit at full strength when it was discovered that the punishment had been removed. Apparently the punished rats had not dropped the habit permanently; they had merely suspended it until assured that they would no longer be punished.

Estes' experiment helps to explain the failure to manage behavior expertly through punishment. Children often resume undesirable habits quite in spite of conscientious efforts to discipline them for doing so. Moreover, it is evident that punishment administered in the form of imprisonment is ineffective in breaking lawless habits; consider the 65–75 percent recidivism rates of criminals.

Persons often unknowingly punish others for the very behavior they are seeking from them. Recently one of the authors and two of his friends were bike riding. Suddenly, a small voice yelled out, "Hi, Dad!" He looked around and saw his youngest son waving excitedly to him. The greeting warmed his heart, and he turned and rode back to him. He greeted his son and asked what he was doing. The son replied that he and a friend were skate-boarding in the street. At first the author showed interest, but he then proceeded to lecture his son about the dangers of skate-boarding on the street. This was enough to kill any enthusiasm the son had earlier shown. After the father resumed the ride, one of his friends chuckled and pointed out how he had effectively punished his son for having warmly greeted him.

The feeling of responsibility that parents feel often

creates such scenes. Concern comes through as scolding, and children soon may learn to keep their distance.

Unfortunately, a favorite way of influencing behavior is through the use of threat. One often ignores the good but notices the bad. Consider the woman who complained to her husband that he was always criticizing her. She asked, "Why don't you ever tell me you like something I've done?" He replied, "You'll know I like it if I don't say anything!" This is standard behavior for some people. They feel awkward with compliments, but are free indeed with their criticism.

Three years ago one of the authors participated in a research study in a school system in Appalachia. The researchers were given a large measure of control over twenty-five classrooms that spanned grades one through nine. The goals of the project were to turn negative classrooms into positive ones, to train teachers to abandon their exclusive use of aversive control measures, and to add a significant use of positive ones as well. Observation revealed that these teachers made thirteen negative references to students for every positive one. The teachers were caught in the criticism trap. They believed that yelling and screaming at children would get the results they desired, and so they made free use of these aversive controls. In the long run, the more the teachers complained about bad behavior, the more of it they got.

The research team made a concerted effort to encourage teachers to become more positive with pupils. After 26 weeks of diligent work by the team, the teachers had reversed the ratio. They were now making thirteen positive references for every negative reference. Classroom monitors also accumulated evidence that the amount of attention the pupils paid in class was directly related to the positiveness of the teacher. At the end of the twenty-sixth week the pupils were observed paying attention 93 percent of the time, almost 20 percent more often than at the beginning of the project. While the project stressed other program features in addition to positive control measures, it was felt by the research team that a significant amount of the project's remarkable success in improving academic performance was due to this emphasis (Matheny and Edwards, 1974).

The chronic use of punishing responses to shape the behavior of others has several unwholesome side affects. It tends to encourage aggressive behavior in others. Animal experimentation has often borne out this fact. Typical of such experiments is the one where two rats are placed in a cage with an electric grid as a floor. The experimenter randomly punches a button that discharges a small electrical current through the grid. At first the animals scurry about, trying to escape. They may subsequently attempt to climb the wall or make noises signalling their pain. When none of these maneuvers works, they ultimately turn on and fiercely attack one another.

Perhaps much of the sadism and brutality witnessed in society reflects chronic punishing conditions to which many public offenders have been subjected. The examples of child abuse currently being given prominent coverage in the media show only the more devastating cases. These blatant cases of child abuse are sensational and readily catch the public's eye, while the chronic negative conditions under which thousands of children are reared annually receive little attention.

For the most part, the twisting and warping of personalities comes not so much from acute traumas to which one is subjected but rather from low-level, chronic negativism within homes. For many years parents are the most important persons in a child's life. Since a child has such a meager basis for judging his or her own personal worth so early in one's life, one looks to parents for self-validation. If they are continually nagging, complaining, and harassing, one assumes that they hold a low opinion of one's worth, and one is likely to incorporate such discouraging views into one's own self-concepts. However well intentioned the use of chronic punishment may be, its use is likely to lower seriously the self-esteem of the victim.

Chronic punishment only teaches one to escape the punisher. If someone is constantly pointing out one's foibles and complaining about one's conduct, one will avoid them if one possibly can. How sad that parents, spouses, and friends who really care may drive others away by their constant criticisms.

Absenteeism in the classroom, for example, may reflect a student's effort to escape a punisher. Thousands of students experience failure daily as a result of classroom assignments that grossly overestimate their levels of academic readiness. Many of these students remain physically in the classroom but have turned off their minds as a way of escape.

On the other hand, in efforts to help one another, zealousness has the potential of crippling a relationship. One may find such help so punishing that one responds defensively and seeks distance. Certainly one is well advised in such cases to desist from such badgering and look for evidence of positive change that one can reinforce in others. Operant psychology teaches that reinforcing good behavior is far more successful than punishing bad.

Many persons are deterred from using rewards to reinforce good behavior because they believe that this practice constitutes bribery. But rewarding persons for doing what is ethically right is hardly bribery—it is just good common sense. Parents who believe that the use of rewards is bribery often set up a no-win condition for managing the behavior of their children. If the child does the wrong thing, he is punished. If he does the right thing, he is ignored. Under such conditions the child cannot win—at best he breaks even; at worst he is punished. Under this regimen the child learns to avoid risks, to refrain from extending himself, to play it safe. The resulting personality type is bland, nonspontaneous and non-initiatory.

Attention and appreciation are powerful rewards for most persons. One tends to think of material things such as money and gifts when one is asked to define rewards, but the most powerful rewards are likely to be social— attention and appreciation. One never outgrows the need for appreciation from others. Adults remain children in this sense for their entire lives.

Results of morale studies among industrial workers often show that social rewards rank high among rewards that are eagerly sought. In one study conducted in 24 industrial plants, each with a large number of workers, supervisors were asked to rate morale features in the order in which they thought they would be rated by the workers. The morale features they selected with greatest frequency are listed below in descending order of importance:

1. Good wages
2. Job security
3. Promotion and growth in the company
4. Good working conditions
5. Work that keeps one interested
6. Personal loyalty to workers
7. Tactful disciplining
8. Full appreciation of work done
9. Sympathetic help on personal problems
10. Feeling "in" on things

Employees in these same plants were then asked to speak for themselves, indicating the morale factors that were most important to them. They arranged the factors as follows:

1. Full appreciation of work done
2. Feeling in on things
3. Sympathetic help on personal problems
4. Job security
5. Good wages
6. Work that keeps one interested
7. Promotion and growth in the company
8. Personal loyalty to workers

9. Good working conditions
10. Tactful disciplining

Notice the stark contrast between these two lists. The last three factors on the supervisors' list were elevated to the top of the workers' list. And what do these top three factors have in common? They all relate to social rewards—to attention and appreciation. Workers passed up such basics as good wages, job security, and promotion and growth in the company in favor of these social rewards.

Some persons are skeptical of the importance of these social rewards. Yet the very persons who most doubt the importance of social rewards often turn out to be the ones who least make use of them. Persons often find that the force of old habits makes it difficult to notice good performance and to express appreciation for it. Becoming a positive person takes time and effort, as it is necessary to overcome the negative conditioning of the past.

There are a few rules for the use of praise that render it more effective in influencing the behavior of others. First, and perhaps most important of all, praise must be genuine. If praise or appreciation does not come from the heart, it is perceived as manipulative by others.

Second, praise, or for that matter, criticism, should be directed to a specific performance. "I appreciate the fact that you put the dishes in the dishwasher and straightened up the kitchen before you left for work this morning. I know you were in a hurry, and I think it was very considerate of you" is likely to prove more effective than is, "You know, Sam, you're a considerate person." There is no demonstrated basis for the last compliment, and consequently, Sam may brace himself for some request to follow.

Third, praise should follow the behavior it is intended to reinforce as soon after it occurs as possible. Both positive and negative consequences of a behavior influence behavior more strongly if they immediately follow the behavior. The longer the interval between behavior and consequence, the weaker the effect. One of the greater shortcomings in the criminal justice system is the unconscionably long delays between arrest and sentencing.

The relation of consequences to the time of a behavior accounts for the maintenance of a great deal of self-defeating behavior. Alcoholism is a good example. Shortly after an alcoholic takes a drink, he receives a small reward. The alcohol is quickly absorbed into the blood system and travels throughout the body. When the alcohol in its converted form reaches the prefrontal lobes of the brain, it anesthetizes the neural pathways responsible for anxiety. This reduction in anxiety is rewarding. Later, one begins to pay for the experience with a hangover, complaints from a spouse, excuses to be made for one's absence from work, and so on.

An outsider may judge that the punishment far outweighs the reward to be gained from the indulgence and wonder why the alcoholic persists in such self-defeating behavior. The answer to the question rests in the time that has elapsed between the drinking and the consequences. A small reward occurs almost immediately after the drinking, whereas the punishment occurs many hours later. The immediate reward has more effect upon the frequency of drinking than the punishing consequences that occur much later. One way of discouraging a drinking habit would be to bring punishing consequences closer in time to the behavior. One common medical treatment for alcoholism does just that. The patient is asked to voluntarily take a drug called antabuse on a daily basis. This drug, when combined with the smallest amount of alcoholic beverage, has an immediate, catastrophic effect upon the body in the form of wrenching nausea. The response is so painful that the alcoholic will refrain from drinking as long as he continues to take the antabuse.

In summary, if one sets out to influence the behavior of another, it is important to offer praise, recognition, and attention as soon after the behavior as is possible. These social reinforcers are indeed powerful, and people tend to greatly underestimate their effectiveness. They dislike acknowledging that they are subject to such influences. Madsen and Madsen (1970) conducted a summer program for hard-core, public school dropouts. In recruiting them from the street, they explained that the program would be designed to motivate them to superior performance through the use of three types of rewards. They were first to be rewarded by attention and praise, then by favorite activities, such as free time in the gymnasium, and last by tangibles, such as popular record albums offered on a rotating weekly basis. When asked which of these rewards they felt they would respond to most favorably, they replied "the albums." In actuality, though, they performed best when reinforced with attention and praise. At the end of the program, they were asked under which of these conditions they had produced the most work, and they replied once again "the albums." While it is embarrassing to think that people are so easily influenced by such social reinforcers as attention, praise, and recognition, nevertheless, this is clearly the case.

Social reinforcers can be overworked. If they are used loosely without adequate reason, they will be seen as manipulative. Moreover, if one uses them continuously for the flimsiest of reasons, they will eventually lose their motivating effect. Simply expressing appreciation is a powerful inducement, but it can be overdone.

A reasonable formula for influencing the behavior of others through social reinforcement includes the following steps:

1. Clearly signal what you would like. Express your wishes in terms of preferences rather than in demands backed by veiled threats.
2. Do not expect perfect compliance with your wishes. Accept approximations of the behavior you want.
3. Recognize and reward this accommodating behavior with attention and appreciation.

4.  Be willing to reciprocate others' behavior with your
    own accommodations and thoughtfulness.

The skillful use of this formula can significantly improve relationships with others. One is likely to be sur-
prised by one's increased effectiveness in influencing the
behavior of others.

In this chapter the importance of positive attention in
affecting the behavior of others has been emphasized.
Operant principles and common sense seem to be the best
references one can offer for the eminence such a position
should have. While it may have many champions, negative attention—punishment—seems to have limited
value. Indeed, punishment frequently results in the opposite of what is intended.

# Epilogue

Will Rogers once said, "We're all ignorant...only on different subjects." Such a simple fact of life fairly represents the spirit with which the authors offer this volume. We are truly ignorant regarding many areas of our lives, and this book will not obliterate that fact. Sometimes this ignorance is bliss; sometimes it is even helpful. Oftentimes, however, it is inconvenient, counterproductive, or downright painful.

Self-change, self-improvement, and self-actualization are far too complicated for anyone to inspire in someone else if the inclination is not already there. In this respect the authors feel ignorant. Perhaps there is an art to inspiring change. Perhaps there is some obtainable wisdom that can accurately determine when and if change is desirable. We have searched for all of those and, at times, have felt that we may have found them. In our teaching and counseling, we have sometimes been convinced of our own power to cause beneficial change in others, only to find that the ultimate choice was that of the student or client. Ultimately we rejoice in that fact. The power is where it belongs—with the individual.

We are convinced, however, that there is a technology of help. We believe that help is not where you find it, but where you look for it. In this handbook of self-change, we have attempted to impress the reader with the vast reservoir of personal power that is his or hers for the taking. We hope that the reader will recognize untapped resources that can be used to design the person he or she would like to be.

We have tried to raise the readers' expectations for better things, while duly respecting the realities in their lives. We have simplified cryptic psychological techniques while pointing out certain pitfalls that are frequently encountered along the path to self-directed change. We have highlighted the salient factors involved in change and have suggested a game plan for accomplishing it. We have cautioned repeatedly against crash programs and fits of desperation and have emphasized the importance of time and practice. Above all, we have stressed the essential role of sustained motivation in self-help strategies.

We have acquainted the reader with the technology for increasing the motivation to change. And yet, we have recognized that it is sometimes wiser to accept certain things about oneself than it is to attempt to change them. Some things simply cannot be changed. And other things are so refractory that the cost involved in changing them is too great. If one fails to recognize that some situations are unsolvable or too costly to solve, one tends to make things worse by repeated and futile efforts to change them. If one accepts such realities, one can bend with the pressure. If one fights them, one may only break oneself in the effort.

The authors have challenged the reader to give up favorite villains that may only serve as excuses for not investing the energy required to change. False beliefs in the unyielding hold by internal forces, by past influences, and by one's current environment on one's behavior were attacked for keeping one from taking full responsibility for behavior and feelings. The reader is encouraged to use his or her imagination to strengthen motivation, to engineer personal change through careful planning, and to make use of good books and good companions as auxiliaries to one's resolve to change.

Various aids have been provided to help in checking one's current state of physical fitness, and a format has been suggested for the construction of a plan for improving functioning. The bitter price people pay for unnecessary stress in their lives, and many specific techniques for coping with it, have been described.

Moreover, techniques have been provided for improving one's relationships with others. Some of these techniques can be used to open clear channels of communication with others; some to influence what others expect; and yet others, to honestly reward persons for doing what one wants them to do.

Each person must choose his own means of change, should change seem warranted. The authors have deliberately not emphasized formal psychotherapies, while fully recognizing that they may sometimes be the exact help one needs. Indeed we have portrayed the goal of any helpful therapy as one of helping an individual ultimately to provide for his own therapy.

Success in self-change is sweet. To engineer one's own change is exhilarating. Once one comes to believe that one is capable of changing, the process itself is its own reward. Still, it is unquestionably the fate of humans to live and die with imperfection. Try as one may, there will always be things about oneself that invite change. Indeed, the authors frequently cringed as they pondered their own imperfections while exhorting the reader to move efficiently in correcting his. They feared that the reader surely would expect writers who profess some expertise in lighting the pathways to self-change to themselves be close to perfection. But life, perhaps, has no higher purpose than the unrelenting pilgrimage to become what one is capable of becoming. In this endeavor, fellow traveler, we wish you Godspeed.

# Bibliography

## Chapter 1

Bach, R. *Jonathan Livingston Seagull*. New York: Macmillan, 1970.

Beecher, W., and Beecher, M. *Beyond success and failure*. New York: Simon and Schuster, 1971.

Eysenck, H. The effects of psychotherapy. *International Journal of Psychiatry* (1965): 90-144.

Illich, I. *Deschooling society*. New York: Harper and Row, 1971.

Kavanaugh, J., *Celebrate the sun*. Plainview, N.Y.: Nash, 1973.

Krishnamurti, J. *Think on these things*. New York: Harper and Row, 1964.

Lair, J. *I ain't much, baby, but I'm all I've got!* Garden City, N.Y.: Doubleday, 1972.

Levi-Strauss, C. *Elementary structures of kinship*. Boston: Beacon Press, 1969.

Lewis, H., and Streitfeld, H. *Growth games*. New York: Harcourt Brace Jovanovich, 1970.

MacLeish, A. The great American frustration. *Saturday Review*, July 13, 1968, pp. 13-16.

Prather, H. *Notes to myself*. Moab, Utah: Real People Press, 1970.

## Chapter 2

Bakker, C. Why people don't change. *Psychotherapy: Theory, Research and Practice*, 12(2) (1975).

Bem, D. Self-perception theory. In L. Berkowitz (ed.), *Ad-*

*vances in experimental social psychology,* vol. 6. New York: Academic Press, 1972.

Frankl, V. *Man's search for meaning.* New York: Beacon Press, 1959.

Seligman, M., and Maier, S. Failure to escape traumatic shock. *Journal of Experimental Psychology,* 74 (1967) : 1–9.

Stotland, E. *The psychology of hope.* San Francisco: Jossey-Bass, 1969.

## Chapter 3

Barber, T.; Spanos, N.; and DeMoor, W. Hypnosis and behavior therapy: Common denominators. *American Journal of Clinical Hypnosis,* 16 (1973) : 45–62.

Coué, F. *How to practice suggestion and autosuggestion.* New York: American Library Service, 1923.

Frank, J. *Persuasion and healing.* New York: Schocken, 1975.

Kelly, G. *The psychology of personal constructs.* New York: Norton, 1955.

Maltz, M. *Psycho-cybernetics.* Hollywood, Calif.: Wilshire, 1960.

Platonov, K. Method of verbal suggestion. In H. Greenwald (ed.), *Active psychotherapy.* Atherton Press, 1967.

Rogers, C. *Client-centered therapy.* Boston: Houghton Mifflin, 1951.

Sontged, A. *Self-hypnosis,* Audio-tape by Automated Learning, Inc., 1972.

Suinn, R. Body thinking: Psychology for Olympic champs. *Psychology Today,* July 1976, pp. 38–43.

## Chapter 4

Bridgeman, P. *The way things are.* Cambridge, Mass.: Harvard University Press, 1959.

Ferguson, M. *The brain revolution.* New York: Taplinger, 1973.

Fromm, E. Values, psychology, and human existence. In A. Maslow (ed.), *New knowledge in human values.* New York: Harper, 1959.

Greenburg, D. *How to be a Jewish mother.* Los Angeles: Price Stern, Sloan, 1964.

Koestler, A. *The sleepwalkers.* New York: Grosset and Dunlap, 1963.

Kopp, S. *The hanged man: Psychotherapy of the forces of darkness.* Palo Alto: Science and Behavior Books, 1974.

Lilly, J. *The center of the cyclone.* New York: Julian Press, 1972.

Mahoney, M., and Thoresen, C. *Self-control: Power to the person.* Monterey, Calif.: Brooks/Cole, 1974.

McClelland, D. Toward a theory of motive acquisition. *American Psychologist 20* (1965): 321–33.

Narciso, J., and Burkett, D. *Declare yourself: Discovering the me in relationships.* Englewood Cliffs, N.J.: Prentice-Hall, 1975.

Rank, O. *Will therapy.* New York: Knopf, 1936.

Selye, H. *Stress without distress.* New York: New American Library, 1974.

Thoresen, C., and Mahoney, M. *Behavioral self-control.* New York: Holt, Rinehart and Winston, 1974.

Watzlawick, P.; Weakland, J.; and Fisch, R. *Change: Principles of problem formation and problem resolution.* New York: W. W. Norton, 1974.

Wheelis, A. *How people change.* New York: Harper and Row, 1973.

## Chapter 5

Adams, S., and Orgel, M. *Through the mental health maze: A consumer's guide to finding a psychotherapist.* Washington, D.C.: Health Research Group, 1975.

Bandura, A. *Principles of behavior modification.* New York: Holt, Rinehart, and Winston, 1969.

Davidson, B. They shared a victory over heroin. *Good Housekeeping,* October 1975, 102–3.

Dollard, J.; Doob, L.; Miller, N.; and Sears, R. *Frustration and aggression.* New Haven: Yale University Press, 1939.

Dreikurs, R. *Children: The challenge.* New York: Duell, Sloan and Pearce, 1967.

Fiedler, F. The concept of an ideal therapeutic relationship. *Journal of Consulting Psychology, 14* (1950): 239–45.

Freed, H.; Borus, J.; Gonzales, J.; Grant, J.; Lightfoot, O.; and Uribe, V. Community mental health—Second-class citizen? *Mental Health, 56* (Summer 1972).

Glasser, W. *Reality therapy.* New York: Julian Press, 1967.

Grosz, H. *Recovery Inc., survey, second report.* Chicago: Recovery, Inc., 1973.

Hauser, G. *New guide to intelligent reducing.* Greenwich, Conn.: Fawcett, 1967.

Lieberman, M.; Yolom, I.; and Miles, M. Encounter: The leader makes the difference. *Psychology Today,* March 1973, pp. 70–76.

Low, A. *Mental health through will training.* Boston: Christopher Publishing House, 1950.

Nidetch, J. *The story of weight watchers.* New York: New American Library, 1972.

Norris, J. World dialogue on alcohol and drug dependence. In E. D. Whitney (ed.), *Alcoholics anonymous.* Boston: Beacon Press, 1970.

Park, C., and Shapiro, L. *You are not alone.* Boston: Little Brown, 1976.

Recovery, Inc.: *What it is and how it developed.* Chicago: Recovery, Inc., 1973.

Smoke Watchers International Inc. *The smoke watchers' how-to-quit book.* New York: Bernard Geis, 1970.

*Some Principles of Neurotics Anonymous.* 1965.

*St. Elizabeth's Reporter.* Summer 1972.

Toffler, A. *Future shock.* New York: Random House, 1970.

Truax, D., and Carkhuff, R. *Towards effective counseling and psychotherapy.* Chicago: Aldine, 1967.

## Chapter 6

Alberti, R., and Emmons, M. *Your perfect right: A guide to assertive behavior.* San Luis Obispo, Calif.: Impact Publications, 1974.

Bach, G., and Wyden, P. *The intimate enemy: How to fight fair in love and marriage.* New York: Avon, 1968.

Belliveau, F., and Richter, L. *Understanding human sexual inadequacy.* Boston: Little Brown, 1970.

Benson, H. *The relaxation response.* New York: Morrow, 1975.

Bolles, R. *What color is your parachute: A practical manual for job hunters and career changers.* Berkeley, Calif.: Ten Speed Press, 1976.

Boston Women's Health Book Collective. *Our bodies, ourselves.* New York: Simon & Schuster, 1973.

Carr, A. *Business as a game.* New York: New American Library, 1969.

Ellis, A., and Harper, R. *A new guide to rational living.* North Hollywood, Calif.: Wilshire, 1976.

Frankl, V. *Man's search for meaning.* New York: Washington Square Press, 1970.

Gordon, S. *The sexual adolescent.* North Scituate, Mass.: Duxbury Press, 1973.

Harris, T. *I'm OK, you're OK: A practical guide to transactional analysis.* New York: Harper and Row, 1969.

Holland, J. *Making vocational choices: A theory of careers.* Englewood Cliffs, N.J.: Prentice-Hall, 1973.

Kelley, J.; and Winship, B. *I am worth it.* Chicago: Nelson-Hall, 1977.

Krantzler, M. *Creative divorce.* New York: New American Library, 1974.

Lazarus, A., and Fay, A. *I can if I want to.* New York: Morrow, 1975.

Lederer, W., and Jackson, P. *The mirages of marriage.* New York: W. W. Norton, 1968.

McCary, F. *A complete sex education for parents, teenagers, and young adults.* New York: Van Nostrand Rheinhold, 1973.

Narciso, J., and Burkett, D. *Declare yourself: Discovering the me in relationships.* Englewood Cliffs, N.J.: Prentice-Hall, 1975.

Patterson, G., and Gullion, M. *Living with children.* Champaign, Ill.: Research Press, 1968.

Puzo, M. *The godfather.* New York: Putnam, 1969.

Salter, A. *Conditioned reflex therapy.* New York: Creative Age Press, 1949.

Selye, H. *Stress without distress.* New York: New American Library, 1974.

Selye, H. *The stress of life.* New York: McGraw Hill, 1956.

Smith, H. *The religions of man.* New York: Harper and Row, 1958.

Smith, M. *When I say no, I feel guilty.* New York: Dial Press, 1975.

## Chapter 7

Atkins, R. *Dr. Atkins' diet revolution.* New York: Bantam Books, 1972.

Cooley, D., (ed.). *Better homes and gardens family medical guide.* New York: Better Homes and Gardens Books, 1973.

Cooper, K. *The new aerobics.* New York: Evans, 1970.

Feinbloom, R. *Child health encyclopedia.* Boston: Delacorte, 1975.

Hittleman, R. *Be young with yoga.* Englewood Cliffs, N.J.: Prentice-Hall, 1962.

Hittleman, R. *Yoga for physical fitness.* New York: Warner, 1964.

Kraus, B. *The dictionary of calories and carbohydrates.* New York.: Grosset and Dunlap, 1974.

Morehouse, L., and Gross, L. *Total fitness in 30 minutes a week.* New York: Simon and Schuster, 1975.

Myers, C. *The official YMCA physical fitness handbook.* New York: Popular Library, 1975.

Stillman, I., and Baker, S. *The doctor's quick weight-loss diet.* New York: Dell, 1967.

Thompson, W. (ed.). *Black's medical dictionary.* New York: Barnes and Noble, 1974.

## Chapter 8

Benson, H. *The relaxation response.* New York: Morrow, 1975.

Brown, B. *New mind, new body—bio-feedback: New directions for the mind.* New York: Harper and Row, 1974.

Goleman, D. Meditation as metatherapy. *Journal of Transpersonal Psychology 1* (1971): 1–25.

Gutwirth, S. The prevention and elimination of 'nervous breakdowns' through cultivated tension control methods. In *Tension control: Proceedings of the first meeting of the American association for the advancement of tension control.* Blacksburg, Va.: University Publications, 1975.

Holmes, T., and Rahe, R. The social readjustment rating scale. *Journal of Psychosomatic Research 11* (1967): 213.

Jacobson, E. *Progressive relaxation.* Chicago: University of Chicago Press, 1938.

Kamiya, J. Operant control of the EEG alpha rhythm and some of its reported effects on consciousness. In C. Tart (ed.), *Altered states of consciousness: Book of readings.* New York: Wiley, 1969.

Kamiya, J. Taken from his lectures at UCLA in 1971 as reported in M. Ferguson, *The brain revolution*. New York: Taplinger, 1973.

Miller, N. Learning of visceral and glandular responses. *Science, 163* (1969): 434–45.

Naranjo, C., and Ornstein, R. *On the psychology of meditation*. New York: Viking, 1971.

Perls, F. Four lectures. In J. Fagan and I. Shepherd (eds.), *Gestalt therapy now*. New York: Harper Colophon Books, 1970.

Piaget, J. The stages of the intellectual development of the child. *Bulletin of the Menninger School of Psychiatry*, March 6, 1961.

Pirsig, R. *Zen and the art of motorcycle maintenance*. New York: Bantam Books, 1974.

Selye, H. *The stress of life*. New York: McGraw-Hill, 1956.

Selye, H. *Stress without distress*. New York: Signet, New American Library, 1974.

Smith, A. *Powers of mind*. New York: Random House, 1975.

Wallace, R., and Benson, H. The physiology of meditation. *Scientific American 226* (1972): 85–90.

## Chapter 9

Castaneda, C. *A separate reality: Further considerations with Don Juan*. New York: Pocket Books, 1972.

Dunlap, K. *Habits, their making and unmaking*. New York: Liveright, 1932.

Ellis, A. *Reason and emotion is psychotherapy*. New York: Stuart, 1962.

Ellis, A. The no cop-out therapy. *Psychology Today*, July 1973, pp. 56–62.

Farber, I. E. The things people say to themselves. *American Psychology, 18* (1963): 185–97.

Frankl, V. E. Paradoxical intention: A logotherapeutic technique. *American Journal of Psychotherapy, 14* (1960): 520–35.

Luria, A. *The role of speech in the regulation of normal and abnormal behavior*. New York: Liveright, 1961.

Meichenbaum, D., and Cameron, R. The clinical potential of modifying what clients say to themselves. In M. J. Mahoney, and C. E. Thoresen, *Self-control: Power to the person.* Monterey, Calif.: Brooks/Cole, 1974.

Nisbett, R., and Schachter, S. Cognitive manipulations of pain. *Journal of Experimental Social Psychology, 2* (1966): 227–36.

Perls, F. Four lectures. In J. Fagan and I. Shepard, *Gestalt therapy now.* New York: Harper and Row, 1970.

Rimm, D. C., and Litvak, S. B. Self-verbalization and emotional arousal. *Journal of Abnormal Psychology, 74* (1969): 181–87.

Rosenthal, R. *Experimenter effects in behavioral research.* New York: Appleton-Century-Crofts, 1966.

Schachter, S., and Singer, J. E. Cognitive, social, and physiological determinants of emotional state. *Psychological Review, 69* (1962): 379–99.

Velton, E. A laboratory task for induction of mood states. *Behavior Research and Therapy, 6* (1968): 473–82.

Vygotsky, L. *Thought and language.* New York: Wiley, 1962.

## Chapter 10

Berne, E. *Transactional analysis in psychotherapy.* New York: Grove Press, 1961.

Bloom, L. Z.; Coburn, K. L.; and Pearlman, F. C. *The new assertive woman.* New York: Delacorte, 1975.

Gordon, T. *Parent effectiveness training.* New York: Wyden, 1970.

Kelley, J., and Winship, B. *I am worth it.* Chicago: Nelson-Hall, 1979.

Smith, M. F. *When I say no, I feel guilty.* New York: Dial Press, 1975.

## Chapter 11

Aronson, E.; Carlsmith, J. M.; and Darley, J. M. The effects of expectancy on volunteering for an unpleasant experience. *Journal of Abnormal Psychology, 66,* (1963): 220–24.

Aronson, E., and Carlsmith, J. M. Performance expectancy as a determinant of actual performance. *Journal of Abnormal and Social Psychology, 70* (1962): 210–12.

Bakker, C. B. Why people don't change. *Psychotherapy: Theory, Research and Practice, 12* (Summer 1975).

Combs, C. F. A study of the relationship between certain perceptions of self and scholastic underachievement in academically capable high-school boys. *Dissertation Abstracts, 24* (1963) : 620.

Cooley, C. *Social organization.* New York: Charles Scribner's Sons, 1937.

Goldstein, A. P. *Therapist-patient expectancies in psychotherapy.* New York: Macmillan, 1962.

James, W. *Varieties of religious experience.* New York: Random House, Modern Library, 1902.

Jones, E. E., and Gerard, H. B. *Foundations of social psychology.* New York: Wiley, 1967.

Kelly, G. *The psychology of personal constructs.* Vol. 1. New York: Norton, 1955.

Rosenthal, R. *Experimenter effects in behavioral research.* New York: Holt, Rinehart and Winston, 1968.

Rosenthal, R. The pygmalion effect lives. *Psychology Today,* September 1973.

Rosenthal, R., and Fode, K. L. The effect of experimenter bias on the performance of the albino rat. *Behavioral Science, 8* (1963) : 183–89.

Rosenthal, R., and Jacobson, L. *Pygmalion in the classroom.* New York: Holt, Rinehart and Winston, 1968.

Rotter, J. B. Generalized expectancies for internal versus external control of reinforcement. *Psychological Monographs: General and Applied 80* (1966) : 1–28.

Shapiro, A. K. A contribution to a history of the placebo effect. *Behavioral Science, 5* (1960) : 109–35.

Stotland, E. *The psychology of hope.* San Francisco: Jossey-Bass, 1969.

Tolman, E. C. Principles of purposive behavior. In S. Koch (ed.), *Psychology: A study of science,* vol. 2. New York: McGraw-Hill, 1959.

## Chapter 12

Estes, W. K. An experimental study of punishment. *Psychological Monographs 57* (1944) : 3; Whole No. 263.

Madsen, C., and Madsen, C. *Teaching/discipline: Behavioral principles toward a positive approach.* Boston: Allyn and Bacon, 1970.

Matheny, K., and Edwards, C. Academic improvement through an experimental classroom management system. *Journal of School Psychology, 12* (1974) : 222–32.

# Index

279